Back in Time

Back in Time

My Life, My Fate, My Epoch

The Memoirs of Nadezhda A. Joffe

Translated from the Russian
by Frederick S. Choate

Labor Publications, Inc.
Oak Park, Michigan

Published by Labor Publications, Inc.
25900 Greenfield Road, Suite 258
Oak Park, Michigan 48237

Printed in the United States of America

Library of Congress Cataloging-in-Publication Data

Joffe, Nadezhda A., 1906–
    Back in time: my life, my fate, my epoch: the memoirs of Nadezhda A. Joffe/
translated from the Russian by Frederick S. Choate.
    p.   cm.
    Includes bibliographical references and index.
    ISBN 0-929087-70-4
    1. Joffe, Nadezhda A., 1906–   . 2. Women political prisoners — Soviet
Union — Biography.   3. Political persecution — Soviet Union.   4. Soviet Union —
History — 1925–1953.   I. Title.
    DK26B.J63A3 1995
    947.084'092 — dc20
    [B]
                                                                94-32353
                                                                CIP

Cover photographs: Nadezhda Joffe in 1990; her father Adolf Abramovich Joffe in 1918

♾ This book is printed on acid-free paper.

FOREWORD

From out of the nightmare years of Stalinist repression, there has emerged a significant literary genre, which includes such works as the memoirs of Nadezhda Mandelshtam, Evgenia Ginsburg, Margarete Buber-Neumann and Anna Larina. But even within this illustrious group, the present work is of exceptional importance. It is not that the others suffered less than Nadezhda Joffe or that their depictions of the terror through which they lived are less compelling. Rather, what imparts to this memoir its unique and historically significant character is the political perspective of the author. Nadezhda Joffe was, even before her first arrest, a conscious and politically active opponent of Stalinism. This is the only memoir to be written in the post-Stalin Soviet Union by a member of the Left Opposition that had been formed under the leadership of Leon Trotsky in 1923.

There might have been many more such works had Stalin and his henchmen not been so demonically efficient in organizing the physical annihilation of all Marxist opponents of the Soviet bureaucracy. To be accused of "KRTD"—the Russian acronym for "Counterrevolutionary Trotskyist Activity"—signified all but certain doom. Those charged only with "KRD"—"Counterrevolutionary Activity"—could still hope to escape with "merely" five years in a labor camp, which, in the context of the enormities of the Stalinist terror, might be considered the equivalent of a slap on the wrist. But the insertion of the "T," associating the accused with the ideas of Stalin's most implacable opponent, placed the victim in a realm from which no return could be expected.

Countless thousands of those condemned as KRTDs never, in fact, had the slightest association with Leon Trotsky or the Left Opposition. But Nadezhda certainly did. She was the daughter of Adolf Abramovich Joffe, who was one of Trotsky's closest personal friends and political allies. In November 1927 Joffe committed suicide to protest the expulsion of Trotsky from the Russian Communist Party. By this time Nadezhda was 21 years old and already had acquired considerable political experience in the struggle then being waged by the Left Opposition against the Soviet bureaucracy. Unlike so many others who were to be swept up by the terror, Nadezhda did not consider herself to be the victim of an arbitrary and incomprehensible fate. She knew herself to be a political opponent of the regime and, moreover, understood the political motivations behind Stalin's crimes. Most of those who were thrown into the labor camps simply did not know why they were there. As another memoir of one such victim later recalled, the Trotskyists "had an enormous advantage over us of having a coherent political system capable of replacing Stalinism. They had something to cling to in the midst of their profound distress at seeing the revolution betrayed."[1]

An introduction to this volume requires a brief synopsis of the political career of the author's father. Adolf Joffe was born in 1883. Despite his family's great wealth and his own frail health, he entered the Russian revolutionary movement at the turn of the century. Like so many others of his generation, Joffe was compelled to leave Russia after the 1905 revolution. In 1908, while living in Vienna, he became closely associated with Leon Trotsky, whom he assisted in the publication of a new Russian-language newspaper, *Pravda*. At that time Trotsky did not belong to either the Bolshevik or Menshevik factions of the Russian Social Democratic Labor Party. His theoretical analysis of the events of 1905, which had led him to the conclusion that Russia, despite its economic backwardness, stood on the verge of a socialist revolution, left him politically isolated. Even Lenin dismissed Trotsky's theory of "permanent revolution" as "absurdly left." Joffe was one of the very few who appreciated the prescience of Trotsky's perspective. But the two men were drawn to each other not only by their common political views. They shared a wide range of cultural and scientific interests. It was through Joffe, who had himself undergone psychoanalysis by the renowned Alfred Adler, that Trotsky was introduced to the writings of Freud.

Joffe returned to Russia to develop the work of *Pravda*. He was arrested in Odessa, imprisoned and finally transported to Siberia, where he remained until he was liberated by the collapse of the czarist regime in February-March 1917. He returned to Petrograd as a leading member of Trotsky's influential Mezhraiontsy (Inter-District) group. As the experience of the World War and the new eruption of revolution in Russia had dissolved the old differences between Lenin and Trotsky, Joffe supported the fusion of the Mezhraiontsy into the Bolshevik Party, within which he soon became a major figure. He was one of five members of the Military-Revolutionary Committee, which under Trotsky's leadership organized the overthrow of the bourgeois Provisional Government and the establishment of the Soviet government in October 1917.

Lenin was a shrewd judge of men and he recognized in Joffe the qualities that were to distinguish him as the most outstanding Soviet diplomat during the early years of the revolution. Joffe's first foray into the dangerous waters of international power politics was as part of the Soviet delegation to the peace negotiations at Brest Litovsk. Later he represented Soviet Russia in crucial missions to Germany, China and Japan. Joffe's impeccable bearing and vast erudition unnerved bourgeois diplomats, who had hardly imagined that they would encounter such intellectual refinement in a plenipotentiary of a revolutionary workers state. But Joffe, notwithstanding his relaxed mastery of the subtle etiquette of diplomacy, was a revolutionist first and foremost. An American reporter later recalled that Joffe's Berlin embassy "served as staff headquarters for a German revolution. He bought secret information from German officials and passed it on to radical leaders for use in public speeches and in articles against the government. He bought arms for the revolutionaries and paid out 100,000 marks for them. Tons of anti-Kaiser literature were printed and distributed at the Soviet Embassy's expense. 'We wanted to pull down the monarchist state and end the war,' Joffe said to me. 'President Wilson tried to do the same in his own way.' Almost every evening after dark, Left-wing independent socialist leaders slipped into the embassy building in Unter den Linden to consult Joffe on questions of tactics. He was an experienced conspirator. They wanted his advice, guidance and money."[2]

When the German government denounced Joffe for spending 105,000 marks to overthrow the state, he remarked ruefully to a socialist leader that the Kaiser's accounting was wrong; he had actually spent hundreds of thousands of marks.

Adolf Joffe also played an important role in the early spread of Soviet influence in Asia, particularly during his sojourn in China in 1922-23. He possessed the tactical finesse required to conduct delicate negotiations with Sun Yat-sen, while at the same time promoting Marxist ideas among Chinese intellectuals and students active in the young Chinese Communist Party, whose rapid growth alarmed the conservative bourgeois nationalists in the leadership of the Kuomintang.

Joffe's diplomatic assignments kept him somewhat distant from the daily struggles of the Left Opposition. Indeed, Stalin often used his position as general secretary, which gave him the power of appointment, to send supporters of Trotsky on missions outside the Soviet Union. Still there was no question of Joffe's wholehearted agreement with Trotsky's critique of the bureaucratization of the Soviet regime and the dangers it posed to the survival of the workers state and the cause of international socialism. There are indications that Joffe had concluded, earlier even than Trotsky, that the rise of Stalin marked the onset of a protracted period of political reaction in the Soviet Union.

Joffe's sober evaluation of the deteriorating political situation played an important role in the decision he made in late 1927, at the climax of the inner-party struggle, to end his life. It was not demoralization, however, that led him to choose suicide as the most appropriate response to the anathematization of Trotsky. Rather, Joffe concluded that the desperate character of his illness, for which he was denied proper treatment by the Stalinist faction that was in complete control of the party, removed the possibility of participating effectively in the political struggle. The reasons for his actions were presented in a letter to Trotsky that he wrote only hours before taking his life. Sections of this extraordinary document have been quoted often. The full text is published in English for the first time in this volume. The political sections of this document are, it goes without saying, of extraordinary interest. But perhaps the most important passage is that in which Joffe expressed with eloquent simplicity his moral credo: "I think I have the right to say that for all of my conscious life, I have remained faithful to my philosophy, that is, I have passed through my life in a meaningful way, working for the good of mankind."

Nearly 70 years after the tragic death of her father, the memoir of Nadezhda Joffe recalls a period of history when Marxism provided the intellectual and moral impulse for a powerful worldwide movement for social liberation. Nadezhda's generation came of age in the 1920s, before Stalinism had suppressed the ideals and dreams that inspired October's youth. Her memoir evokes the spirit of that doomed generation: "We wanted nothing for ourselves, we all wanted just one thing: the world revolution and happiness for all. And if it were necessary to give our lives to achieve this, then we would have done so without hesitating."

The culture that encouraged and nourished these aspirations was destroyed by Stalinism. The stabilization of the bureaucratic regime required the annihilation of all those who in one way or another represented the principles and traditions of October 1917. Herein lay the essential motive of the antisocialist political genocide unleashed by Stalin. Had Nadezhda's father not taken his own life, he would have certainly been among those shot between 1936 and 1938. But not even the early death of Adolf Joffe could save his family from the Stalinist terror. Nadezhda was consigned to the labor camps and her husband, Pavel, was murdered.

Nadezhda Joffe survived and her memoir provides us with the testimony of one who experienced, with a high degree of political consciousness, the most tragic events of this century. Its publication in English and its presentation to a world audience could not be more timely.

The Soviet Union no longer exists, and it has become fashionable, not to mention lucrative, for those who only a short time ago enjoyed positions of considerable influence within its bureaucratic apparatus to write histories and memoirs that attribute to Lenin, Bolshevism and Marxism full responsibility for the crimes of the Stalinist regime. In this way they absolve themselves of all responsibility for what they did during the many years when they contributed to the perpetuation of the Stalinist system.

Nadezhda Joffe's memoir represents a moral, no less than factual, refutation of this new post-Soviet school of Stalinist falsification; for she reminds those who have perhaps forgotten and informs those who probably have never been told that countless thousands sacrificed their lives in the struggle against Stalinism because they understood "that the socialism which had been built in the Soviet Union was not the same socialism about which the best minds of mankind had dreamed."

DAVID NORTH
SEPTEMBER 13, 1994

INTRODUCTION

I began writing these memoirs, or rather the history of my life, during the time of "stagnation" under Brezhnev. I wrote them with little hope of ever seeing them printed. But, nevertheless, I kept writing.

I wanted to leave them for my children, grandchildren and great-grandchildren. And I hoped that others would also read my memoirs, if only in the form of samizdat, which existed at that time.

I considered it my duty to write them.

My duty to those who were with me in prison cells and on the double bunks of the Kolyma camps; to those who traveled behind the bars of the Stolypin wagons; to those who walked next to me on our way to the camps, accompanied by the barking dogs and the famous prison-convoy formula: "step to the right, step to the left—we'll shoot without warning."

My duty to those who didn't survive. They were a wide range of people: members of the party (many with pre-October party membership) and nonparty Soviet citizens—workers, engineers, physicians, collective farm workers, actors and students.

Some of them were in prison for belonging to various political groupings, but they were few in number. The majority were there because of a husband, a brother, a friend; because of conversations, jokes; because they read the wrong book or praised the wrong play. In other words, for nothing at all.

I belonged to the minority; I was there "for something."

If there had been more of us, if we had had more of a chance, much could have been different. But the sides were uneven.

On Stalin's side there was the entire bureaucratic and police apparatus, whereas we....

We were young and inexperienced, and our older comrades, people who had worked alongside Lenin, did not heed soon enough his warnings about Stalin's personality—they underestimated this master at "preparing spicy dishes." They fought as cultured people, as educated Marxists, with the methods of inner-party discussions. In other words, they fought with parliamentary methods.

But the person they fought against was a man lacking the most elementary human feelings: decency, respect for old age, pity for children. At the same time, he was fully possessed by pathological suspicion, vengefulness and craftiness.

In addition, during certain periods Stalin was supported by people who rightfully enjoyed great authority in the party.

In the beginning there were Zinoviev and Kamenev. And with their help he dealt with Trotsky.

For a certain period, Bukharin was Stalin's "ideologist." And with his help he dealt with Zinoviev and Kamenev. And not long afterwards, it was Bukharin's turn.

However, it is not my job to dwell in detail on Stalin's personality or his methods. Much has been written about that already. And much more will probably be written.

I simply wanted to tell the story of my life. But my life turned out to be so closely linked with the history of my country, that to a certain degree it proved to be a piece of history in general.

PART 1

1

In order to tell the story of my life, I probably should first of all talk about my father. He played an enormous role in my upbringing, both as a father and as a personality.

Adolf Abramovich Joffe was the second son of a wealthy merchant in Simferopol. His father, and my grandfather, came to Simferopol as a young man, in worn-out boots and a borrowed jacket. Within twenty years my grandfather had become the owner of all the postal and transport services in the Crimea, owned a house in Moscow, bore the title of hereditary honorary citizen and was considered the "favorite Jew" of Prime Minister Witte.

In the Crimean museum of local history, in Alushta, there is not a single word about the revolutionary Joffe (his pseudonym had even been Krymsky, "the Crimean"), but there is a whole display devoted to the merchant Joffe. One can see photographs there of carriages, wagons and coaches; there are photographs of the first automobiles which we now see in the old silent films.

Of his many offspring, only my father became a revolutionary.

I once asked him how it was that in such circumstances, in such a family, he was already reading illegal literature in the upper classes of the gymnasium and at age nineteen had become a member of the Rus-

3

sian Social Democratic Labor Party. He thought for a bit, then laughed and said, "Probably it's because when I was young, I was very fat." Being ashamed of his weight, he didn't run around, didn't take part in outdoor games, didn't go to dances. He sat and read books. And that's how he became widely read.

When he finished the gymnasium, he went with his wife to continue his education in Germany. There he enrolled in the medical school. He had married very early, but his father didn't object. From this son of his he could expect almost anything—he might marry a chambermaid or a prostitute. But in fact he married a beautiful and respectable girl from a family of intellectuals. It is true, she had no dowry, but my grandfather could allow himself the luxury of having a propertyless daughter-in-law.

In 1906, my father carried out the party assignment of maintaining a conspiratorial apartment in Berlin. After the defeat of the revolution in 1905 in Russia, many of its participants had to emigrate. Among them were people who found themselves abroad for the first time. They didn't know the language, they had no financial means. They had to be met, taken in, taken care of and sent somewhere. Adolf Abramovich devoted a lot of time to this, as well as the greater portion of the money sent to him by his father.

While he himself had no formal education, grandfather always dreamt that his children would become educated people. He was very pleased that his son was studying to be a "doctor," but at the same time he was greatly saddened by his revolutionary activity. "Son," he would say, "what do you need this revolution for? Finish your medicine, and I'll buy you an office. If you want, in Moscow on Tverskaya or in Petersburg on Nevsky Prospect. Why do you need a revolution?"

Because of this revolutionary activity, the German government decided to expel my father as "an undesirable alien." This was in May 1906, but he couldn't leave because his wife was expecting a child any day. He had to remain in Berlin and live there illegally.

He first saw his newborn child, me, after he had shaved off his beard and put on dark glasses.

At that time, an article appeared in the press written by August Bebel, who accused the German government of being harsh toward

Russian emigrants. As an example he gave my father, who had received a notice of deportation on the eve of his wife giving birth.

Upon returning to Russia, my father immediately organized the
escape of Feldman, one of the participants in the uprising on the
Potemkin, from the Sevastopol military prison. It was urgent that he be
taken from Sevastopol to Yalta and put on board a steamer which was
going abroad. This was not so simple, if you consider that Yalta was
the summer residence of the imperial family, and all along the sea-
shore stood city policemen wearing spotless white gloves. One might
assume that the escapee had to be driven unnoticed, either late at night
or early in the morning. Adolf Abramovich did this openly, in broad
daylight, right in front of dozens of people. He took one of the large
carriages belonging to his father (they of course didn't refuse to let
him take it, since he was the son of their omnipotent master), sat
Feldman in it in a fine suit, and put my mother next to him. And so, in
a beautiful carriage, sitting next to a beautiful and well-dressed woman,
the escapee drove along the entire waterfront and successfully boarded
the steamer.

My father was unable to continue his education in Germany. In
1908 he settled down in Vienna. There he finished medical school and
received his physician's diploma. He always remained interested in
medicine, particularly psychiatry, and was one of the students and
followers of Alfred Adler.* However, the true meaning of his life was
always revolutionary activity.

In Vienna, my father took direct part in founding the Social Demo-
cratic newspaper *Pravda.* The main publishers and editors of the
Viennese *Pravda* were a group of four: Parvus, M.I. Skobelev, L.D.
Trotsky and A.A. Joffe.

A talented journalist, Parvus (whose real name was Helphand)
was always absorbed by what he was doing at any given moment. My
father used to say that he even played chess as if his whole life depended on the outcome of the game. The newspaper needed money,
and Parvus began to get involved in business. Gradually this activity

---

* A student of Sigmund Freud, the founder of individual psychology, who exerted a major influence on neo-Freudianism.

became the center of his attention; he accumulated great wealth and left the revolutionary movement.

Running ahead, I will say that in 1918 in Berlin, where my father was Soviet ambassador, Parvus tried to meet with him. However, the ambassador didn't want to meet with him. At that time, Parvus was a wealthy man, an extremely successful merchant, and, as they said, had a far from irreproachable reputation. The ambassador of Soviet Russia simply couldn't allow himself such an encounter.

Matvei Ivanovich Skobelev, who later became minister of labor in the Kerensky government, emigrated after the October Revolution and lived in Paris. In 1920, on the advice of L.B. Krasin, who was our ambassador in France at that time, he returned to Russia. There he quietly worked in some modest position until 1937, when he was arrested and shot.

Leon Trotsky and Joffe, however, remained friends and cothinkers until the day my father died.

Having returned to Russia to continue his underground work, my father was arrested in 1912 in Odessa, together with the entire Odessa party organization. There was no specific evidence against him, and, after some time in solitary confinement, he was sent into administrative exile for four years to the Tobolsk province. He spent his time in exile in the village of Demianovsk. I will allow myself to use a quotation from a book written by a peasant in the village, Ilya Doronin. Under the influence of the exiles living in Demianovsk, Doronin became a revolutionary. His book came out in 1964 in Sverdlovsk. Here is what he wrote: "The most well-to-do, and of course, the most generous exile was the physician A.A. Joffe, who had been uncovered in Odessa as belonging to the RSDLP and sent into exile in the northern regions of the Tobolsk province. Adolf Abramovich was a very pleasant and joyful person, but he caused no few problems for the Demianovsk higher-ups. They even arrested him because he 'exerted a bad influence on the students at the school, after he moved in to stay with their school teacher.'"

In 1913, while he was in exile, my father was indeed arrested, but not for having a "bad influence on the students." At that time, a major trial was under way in Odessa concerning the Black Sea sailors. During the investigation it became clear that my father had participated in this organization. Since he was in exile, he was arrested, returned to Odessa and put on trial. As a result, he was deprived of all civil rights and sentenced to eternal exile, but this time in Siberia.

While he was in exile in the village of Aban in the Krasnoyarsk region, he practiced medicine for the first and last time in his life. He rented an apartment, or to be more precise, a hut, from a family whose child fell ill. They dressed the child in a clean shirt and lay him down "beneath the icon." "What God wills." "God wills" means he will get better; if not, then it means that "God has taken him." That's how it was when my father practiced medicine. He wrote a prescription for the necessary medicines from the nearest city of Kansk and began to cure the child. When they noticed this, the local authorities sent him on a compulsory assignment as physician to the mica mines.

He was freed from there by the February Revolution. In April 1917 he was already in Petrograd, and in the summer, along with an entire group of the so-called Mezhraiontsy (Inter-District) group, my father became a member of the Bolshevik Party. He then actively participated in the October Revolution.

It's an amazing thing.

For practically five years I didn't see my father, not counting short meetings in the Odessa prison. In Petrograd, too, he wasn't able to devote much attention to me. But being with him even briefly was of such significance for me. I remember how, when I was at a dacha in Terioky (now Komarovo), I came running up from somewhere, completely out of breath. I wanted a drink very much and asked the maid to bring me some water. My father stopped the maid and said to me very softly, "Nadiusha, please, get the water yourself. And in general, I would very much want you to do everything you can for yourself." It seems to be such a simple comment, but for me it became one of my basic principles of life: everything that you can do, you should do yourself, without shifting anything onto anyone else.

In the summer of 1917, when we lived at the dacha, mama and I often went into Petrograd. Everything there was so interesting: crowds of people walked along the streets, some with flags and some without, on every corner meetings spontaneously arose and someone was always making a speech. In the evenings mama and I went to the movies. And what pictures they were! For some reason they all had the titles of popular romances of the time: *Be Silent, Sorrow, Be Silent*; *A Tale of Dear Love* and so forth. And what actors! Vera Kholodnaya, Maksimov, Runich, Mozzhukhin and Lysenko. They were all so handsome, and their love was so beautiful. They were simply bursting with passion! The enchanting Vera Kholodnaya would throw herself from the window of a five-story house and lie there down below, looking as neat and unruffled as if she had just returned from a beauty salon. But she was a wonderful actress.

After the July demonstration which was broken up by the Provisional Government, Lenin and Zinoviev went into hiding in the Gulf of Finland. Trotsky was in prison, in Kresty, and Natalia Ivanovna brought his two young sons to stay with us. I remember once that we were walking near our dacha, and we were met by a group of sailors from Kronstadt. I don't know why they talked with us, young children, but I remember that when they found out whose boys these were, they patted them on the shoulder and said, "Don't be sad, kids, soon we'll go and set free your papa, with bayonets and music!" We were terribly impressed: "with bayonets and music."

At the Sixth Congress of the party in August 1917, three of the Mezhraiontsy joined the Central Committee: Trotsky and Uritsky were made full members, and Joffe was made a candidate member. Out of the twenty-four members of this Central Committee, which made the October Revolution, eleven were shot, a twelfth died in prison, Trotsky was murdered on Stalin's orders, and Joffe committed suicide.

Once my father came home towards morning, tired but happy. He said, "Congratulations, we have taken power." We set off for Smolny. I saw Trotsky, who was so exhausted he was barely able to stand. I remember how my father smiled and said to him, "Congratulations, Lev Davidovich." The latter, obviously thinking that my father was referring to the recent events, replied, "Congratulations to you, too." My father kept on smiling and said, "No, I'm congratulating you personally, Lev Davidovich, on your birthday." Trotsky looked at him with surprise, then slapped his palm against his forehead, began to laugh and said, "I completely forgot! And, I might add, it's not a bad way to celebrate a birthday." Then I saw V.I. Lenin for the first time and listened to his speech at the congress of the Soviets.

Father became a member of the military-revolutionary committee and spent very little time at home. Meanwhile, life became much more difficult. My mother, who had not become accustomed to the difficulties, left with me against my father's wishes to join her mother in Baku. She intended to go for a month or so, but the Mussatavist uprising took place in Baku, cutting off Azerbaijan from Russia, and we lived there until the spring of 1918, when the Bolsheviks came to power. The main figure in the city was Stepan Shaumyan, one of the twenty-six Baku commissars subsequently shot by the English. From him we learned that father was neither in Petrograd nor Moscow, but in Berlin. Shaumyan told us that father had sent for us. We set off for Moscow and from there to Berlin.

2

And so we arrived at the embassy. I had never seen such a place. In the bedroom there was a square bed which was so wide that ten people could stretch out on it. In the conference hall you could go from one end to the other on a bicycle, and the banquet hall was even larger.

In the embassy all the staff were Russians, but all the servants were Germans who had been left behind by their former masters. The main house director was Frau Marta. She greeted me with a special "speech," the gist of which was that "in a household, a child is like the sun." She then told me that they had called the former ambassador "Excellenz" ("Your Excellency"), but that the present ambassador, i.e., my father, had forbidden them to address him this way, so they called him "Herr Botschafter"—"Mr. Ambassador." Life was hard for my father. The most difficult and responsible work fell upon him, and to a certain extent the fate of the government depended on its successful outcome. He was thirty-five years old, a physician by training and a revolutionary by profession. He had no experience in diplomatic work (if the Brest-Litovsk negotiations are not counted), and he had to deal with the most experienced European diplomats.

Moreover, he had to learn the rules of diplomatic protocol "on the fly." This led to occasional curious incidents. Once, when he was going to a reception at the ministry of foreign affairs, my father told the chauffeur to dress more appropriately; the latter showed up in striped silk pajamas.

Since there was no Russian school in Berlin, I had a tutor at home. I didn't like my teacher and studied poorly. Fortunately, the embassy had a wonderful library. No one controlled my reading, so I went through one book after another. I read Dostoevsky's novels and popular romances with bright covers. In the embassy, where I was the only child, everyone was very kind to me, but most of all I loved Leonid Borisovich Krasin. What an amazing man he was—intelligent, quick-witted and sincere.

He had left Russia after the defeat of the 1905 revolution, in which he played a major role both as the party's "financier" and as the head of its fighting detachments. In later years he worked as an engineer for the electronics firm Siemens-Schukkert. Apparently he was a gifted engineer, for he occupied the post of general director of this firm.

Immediately after the 1917 revolution, he returned to Russia and actively engaged in the work being done. He was sent to Berlin by Lenin, who placed hopes in his personal authority in Western European business circles. At first he felt himself to be a bit out of place. I remember his conversations with my father. If he was dissatisfied with something, he would say: "Why do you people do it this way?" Father would smile and correct him: "Why do *we*, Leonid Borisovich, why do we...." "Well, all right, why do we do it this way?" He was bound to my father not only by common work, but by a warm friendship. Once when he was going on vacation, Leonid Borisovich took me with him. His family, a wife and three daughters who were approximately my age, lived at that time in Sweden, at a resort which was called Bostad. I stayed with them during his entire vacation. Later he would laugh, calling me the "corrupter of his poor daughters." I taught them not to believe in God and not to obey their mother; at this time such was my life's credo.

Twelve years of experience had taught me not to obey my mother, but I had stopped believing in God when He betrayed my expectations. When my father was in prison in Odessa, and then in exile, I lived with my relatives in Simferopol. I was very fond of the skin which forms on the surface of the kissel, a dessert, and once, when I had gotten into the pantry, I ate the skin from a whole dish of kissel. I then prayed, "Oh, Lord, make another skin appear on the kissel." But He didn't do this, and I got into trouble. After that, I stopped believing in God.

Days at the embassy were very tense after the German ambassador Mirbach was killed in Moscow.

My father was informed of his murder by direct wire. He was told that the assassin was a Left Social Revolutionary and a member of the Cheka. At that time the Left SRs had joined the government. My father was warned not to receive any unfamiliar people alone and not to go out onto the street unaccompanied. Probably there was good reason for such warnings, because anonymous letters began to arrive at the embassy: "Since you killed ours, we will kill yours." Father never paid any attention to these threats, but the entire affair complicated his relations with the Germans.

His work was also made much more complicated (not only then, but in general) by the absence of business-like contact with Chicherin, who at that time was narkomindel (people's commissar of foreign affairs). It now seems to me that the reason for this, first of all, was the difference in their characters, their differing styles of work. Father was a very organized, perhaps even pedantic, person. He never was late for anything. He loved to say that when he arrived at a meeting scheduled for six o'clock, the clock would be striking six. Chicherin, on the other hand, worked for the most part at night, and because of this his entire staff was forced to work at night as well. He might call by direct wire at five in the morning in order to receive some information which might just as well have been sent a few hours later. This greatly irritated my father. In addition, they very often differed on principled questions.

Father was a man of very independent views, and he pursued the line which he considered to be correct. As they used to say, "The Narkomindel has moved to Berlin."

In a collection of Lenin's letters, there is a letter from Lenin to Joffe which was written during this period. Lenin reproaches my father for not wanting to establish contact with Chicherin. He speaks very favorably about Chicherin, and writes: "his [Chicherin's] weakness is the absence of 'bossiness,' but this is not bad; there are plenty of people with the opposite weakness!"

At the same time, Lenin sent a telegram marked "secret" to Leonid Borisovich Krasin. Evidently Krasin had asked him to support my father in his conflicts with Chicherin.

Here is the telegram:

"I fully value Joffe's work and unconditionally endorse it, but I insist that Joffe behave like an ambassador, above whom stands the narkom of foreign affairs, that he observe proprieties, without scolding or slighting others, that he consult the narkom of foreign affairs about everything that is important. Only then can I and will I support ambassador Joffe. I am counting on your tact in impressing this upon ambassador Joffe and I await your reply. Lenin."[1]

In October 1918 Karl Liebknecht showed up at the embassy. He probably came to us directly from prison, because his arrival was accompanied by a large and friendly demonstration in front of the embassy.

A banquet was held at the embassy and I was seated next to Franz Mehring. He was the oldest at the banquet and I was the youngest. (Mehring was one of the oldest German Social Democrats and a Spartacist. At that time he must have been over seventy.) After this official reception Liebknecht often came to visit us with his family. His wife was a Russian, Sofia Borisovna, and they had three children. In conversation he was very cordial and kind-hearted. But he had only a few weeks left to live.

New and very interesting people showed up at the embassy — Christian Georgievich Rakovsky and Nikolai Ivanovich Bukharin.

Rakovsky was born in Bulgaria, grew up in Romania, received his education in France and ... became a Russian revolutionary. He spoke with equal fluency in Romanian, Bulgarian, Russian and a few other European languages. We didn't know which language was his native language. I remember how I once asked him which language he thought in. Rakovsky reflected for a bit and said, "Probably in the language which I am speaking at any given moment."

Everyone immediately took a liking to Bukharin and affectionately called him "Bukharchik." Lenin had good reason to call him the favorite of the party.

He excited my twelve-year-old imagination when, while accepting congratulations on his birthday, he jumped up onto the long banquet table, ran to the middle and stood on his head. Later on I had occasion to meet with both Bukharin and Rakovsky.

In 1919 I joined the Komsomol. I was thirteen years old, and the rules of the Russian Communist Union of Youth, RKSM, stated that you had to be fourteen. But there were not many who wanted to join at that time, and the rules, in this case, were not followed very strictly.

Perhaps I would not have asked for a recommendation from Nikolai Ivanovich, but we talked about the Komsomol in his presence, and with his inherent kind-heartedness, he offered to recommend me himself.

In later years, Rakovsky played a major role in my life. But that is a different subject and I will return to it further on.

Soon after Kaplan's attack on Lenin, which upset us all very much, a new person appeared at the embassy. He was tall, thin, had a pointed beard and went by the name Damansky. I remember how surprised I was when I heard my father say to him, "How could this have happened? How did you allow it?" I simply couldn't understand why someone called Damansky should be responsible for the attempt on Lenin's life. It was Dzerzhinsky. He had come to Berlin on some special assignment and under another name. He didn't spend a long time at our place, but I remember that he talked a great deal with our general consul Menzhinsky.

When he returned to Moscow, Vyacheslav Rudolfovich Menzhinsky worked at the VChK, at first as a member of the collegium, then from 1923 as Dzerzhinsky's deputy, and after the latter's death and until his own death in 1934, as head of the OGPU. That means that during the period of the most terrible repression, he was no longer among the living. However the mass exiles of old (and young) members of the party and Komsomol in 1928-29 and the political isolators[*] into which the Oppositionists were placed—all

---

[*] Special closed prisons for "particularly dangerous political prisoners."

this was his own special monument, "crafted not by human hands."*

To the extent that I remember him, he was a man of few words, a bit gloomy and unusually polite — even with me he used the polite form of address, which was seldom done with children.

At this time I began to become interested in politics. I read both German and Russian newspapers and turned to my father with every conceivable question. I must say that he never told me, "This is not for you to understand," "You'll know when you grow older," or other similar phrases which adults often use to get rid of overly inquisitive children or adolescents. No, father always answered all my questions, and it seemed to me that I understood everything. It seemed to me in general that I understood everything, both in politics and in life.

However I didn't understand at that time what was for me the most important thing: I didn't understand that there, in the house on Unter den Linden,† my childhood came to an end.

That was the last time I lived with my papa and mama. I was on my own, like Kipling's cat.

---

* From Pushkin's poem of 1836, "Unto myself I raised a monument, crafted not by human hands." The reference to the lofty creation of Pushkin's poem is ironic here.

† Unter den Linden ("under the lime trees) — the street in Berlin where the Russian and then the Soviet embassy stood.

3

In November 1918, not long before the revolution in Germany, the staff of the Soviet embassy was expelled from Germany. As a result of the German uprising, our train was delayed in Borisova. Father talked by direct wire both to Berlin and Moscow, but we didn't return to Germany.

At this time, my parents separated for good; my mother and I stayed in Moscow, and my father left with his second wife to live and work in Petrograd. In the summer of 1919 they had a son, Vladimir.

I will write about my brother later on.

Mother and I lived in the First House of the Soviets (now the Hotel National). Our room was a typical hotel room, with the standard furniture, an alcove with two beds and a bathtub without running water.

There was an enormous communal kitchen below, but nobody used it. There was nothing to cook in any case, and everyone was given coupons for food in the dining room.

The winter of 1918-19 was very harsh in Moscow; food was very scarce. We lived a bit better than the average Muscovite. Black bread sprinkled with a few grains of sugar was a rare delicacy, much like pastry. I remember how mama once managed to obtain a piece of meat, and she went to the communal kitchen to cook it. When she was going up the stairs, she tripped and dropped the pan. She was gone for a long time and I went looking for her. She was sitting on the stairs, holding the pan in her hands and crying. And mama was hardly a crybaby.

But this didn't concern me very much—my life in general was spent outside the home. I studied in school, or to be more precise, I didn't study, but I visited school, since we didn't particularly burden ourselves with schoolwork, spending most of our time engaged in politics. The school in which I was enrolled, the former private gymnasium of Popova and Kirpichnikov, was known in Moscow as one of the most liberal and progressive. There, even before the revolution, there had been joint classes for boys and girls. Many teachers were Social Democrats, and our mathematics teacher was even a member of the Moscow Committee of the RSDLP(m). It thus turned out that, whereas in other former gymnasia which were not progressive and not liberal, the teachers quietly continued to teach their own subjects as well as they could, our teachers, like ourselves, were engaged in politics and came into conflict with us. Those who directed things, such as the Commissariat of Education and the Russian Communist Party, etc., naturally supported our side, because we were actively for the Soviet regime, and our Menshevik teachers were against.

In the beginning of 1919, I joined an organization called the Union of Student Communists. In the summer of 1919, this organization ceased to exist and joined the RKSM. This period also marked the beginning of my Komsomol membership. I worked in the school section, which organized Komsomol cells in the second degree schools. At that time, secondary school lasted seven years. The first three groups (not classes, but groups) were called the first degree and the remaining four, the second degree. We went to the schools (which had only recently been gymnasia), held general conferences and called on the students (yesterday's gymnasium students) to join the Russian Communist Union of Youth.

In our school section, I was the only girl and they literally worked me to death. The reason was that if a young fellow came to the former all-male gymnasium as an agitator, they put him "in the dark," that is, they covered him with coats and beat him. According to gymnasium traditions, it was not acceptable to beat girls. Therefore I often left these meetings to the accompaniment of boos and whistling, but nevertheless I was not beaten.

While working in Petrograd, father often came to Moscow. Once he took me to the theater. I must say that my father's tastes were strictly classical: in prose — Tolstoy, in poetry — Pushkin. His attitude toward Severianin, who was immensely popular at that time, was one of irony; in exile he wrote wonderful parodies of the poet, which he signed "Adolfo Sibirianin." Nor did he like Mayakovsky. Of all the Moscow theaters he preferred the Maly. And so, he and I went, as I now remember, to the Maly Theater to see *Wolves and Sheep*.

We went into the box called the sovnarkom, which faced the stage. The box was very large and could probably hold thirty people. When we entered, it was overflowing. Most of those present were young people, but in the back row sat a man of approximately my father's height with a black mustache. My father greeted him and shook his hand. The administrator in charge guided us to the front row. Father sat down, looked around and said in a very irritated voice: "Who the hell knows what is going on! This is called the government box. They sat here some young girls who are typists or what not, but for a member of the Central Committee they can't find a decent place to sit." This member of the CC with a black mustache was Stalin.

My Komsomol activity of this period ended rather sadly.

In the fall of 1919 "front week" was declared and Komsomol members were mobilized for work in Red Army hospitals. They sent only volunteers to the typhus hospitals, and I, of course, was among them. We were supposed to help the orderlies, and in general, do everything that had to be done: write letters for the patients, organize activities and give out bedpans.

It is hard to imagine what such a hospital was like even in Moscow. People lay in the corridors, two to a cot, and sometimes simply on the floor. Lice could be seen by the naked eye. My useful activity ended when I came down with a very serious form of typhus. For two weeks I was in a coma, and the physicians said that only my age saved me from certain death; it seems that children rarely die from typhus. During an unbroken two weeks of delirium, I thought that Moscow had been taken by the Whites, and that they had covered it with some kind of bell jar. They killed Lenin and in his place put two dummies with cardboard bald spots.

When I recovered a bit, one of our acquaintances, Vorovsky, it seems, told Lenin that Joffe's thirteen-year-old daughter had contracted typhus and that she had imagined the following in her delirium. He laughed a lot, and when he saw me, asked: "How's the girl who had such a clearly expressed political delirium?"

When I began to walk, mama and I were sent to Kislovodsk. Rest homes and sanitoria had already begun to operate there.

The mineral waters had only recently been liberated from the Whites, and in the areas surrounding Kislovodsk, remnants of various bands still roamed.

The local committee of the Komsomol organized a round-the-clock patrol. On the day after we arrived, I appeared before the committee and said that I was a member of the RKSM and that I was ready to be on duty. But evidently I looked simply horrible — I was greenish, skinny, my hair was closely cropped. They didn't accept me for patrol duty.

Perhaps none of this is of great interest, but I would like to give a sense of the atmosphere of those years.

When he came to Moscow, father lived in one of the Soviet houses. And once when I was at his apartment, I met an unusual man — Chaliapin. He had been to see my father in Petrograd and came to visit in Moscow as well. He was accompanied by his second wife, Maria Valentinovna, a lady who had grown a bit stout, and his older daughter from his first marriage, Irina, a thin, dark-haired girl of eighteen.

While introducing us, Chaliapin said, "My daughter — Arina." He then thought a bit and added, "Fedorovna." "My wife," again he thought a while, "Mashka."

I heard him in nearly all his operas and concert programs. How he sang — everyone knows. But probably not everyone knows what a great storyteller he was. Many times I have tried to transmit the content of his stories. But it seemed that there was nothing interesting. The secret was not what he said, but how he told it. After all, he was a brilliant dramatic actor, a stunning director, an unusual artist and sculptor. Probably such absolutely brilliant people are born once every thousand years. Michelangelo was probably such a person—a sculptor, artist, architect and poet. Almost five centuries ago he wrote:

> *What a joy to sleep, more joyful a rock to be.*
> *No, in this shameful and reckless age,*
> *Not to know, not to feel, —is an envious fate.*
> *Oh touch me not. Dare not wake me from my sleep.*

Five centuries ago. And how timely....

Upon returning from Kislovodsk to Moscow I went to school. At this time classes were already being held, it is true, but there were many experimental programs: the brigade method, the Dalton plan and some other method. History, as a subject, was not taught. The old had been discarded, and the new had not yet been written; instead we were taught social science.

We were very lucky at our school, for we had wonderful teachers. Geography was taught by the former director of the Popova and Kirpichnikov gymnasium, Poliksena Nilovna Popova, and despite all the various methods, her lessons were very interesting. Our sworn enemy, the Menshevik Vasily Alekseyevich Efremov, was a superb mathematician. Thanks to him, and once again in spite of all the experiments, we knew our mathematics. I remember our literature teacher, Anna Evgenievna Petrova, with particular warmth.

I am deliberately giving their first names, surnames and patronymics. Let my memoirs at least stand as a testament to these people, who, during a very difficult time, did their duty honestly and conscientiously. How necessary this was, and how much they gave to us, we began to understand only many years later.

In the summer of 1920, father was conducting peace negotiations with the Poles in Riga, and he invited me to visit him. Since his wife and their child had gone to Petrograd, we were left alone. He, as usual, was busy for days on end, and only in the evenings did we manage to talk a bit. In addition, we both suffered from insomnia. He was taking sleeping pills, and he gave me some in the proper doses, but nevertheless we both were unable to sleep. But in return, what conversations we had!

Many years later I happened to read Aleksandra Brushtein's novel

The Road Leads into the Distance. She wrote how, when she was a child, she was at a cemetery with her father, where she asked, "Papa, will you also be here someday?" He said, "Yes, my daughter, and you will come to see me. You will come and say: 'It is I who have come, your daughter. I am already grown up, I live honestly, I work and good people respect me.'"

If it were necessary in the most compressed form to tell what my father tried to instill in me for my future life, then I think that it would be expressed in precisely these same words.

Among the members of the diplomatic mission conducting negotiations with Poland, which my father headed, were several interesting people.

Father's deputy was Leonid Leonidovich Obolensky, a former prince, descendant of a Decembrist and a Bolshevik.

His son, also Leonid Leonidovich Obolensky, is a famous actor. Now he is very old, but he still acts, and when I see him on the screen, I always remember the elder Leonid Leonidovich.*

Larisa Mikhailovna Reisner came to visit for a while. She fell ill, and they sent her to Riga for treatment. She was a very beautiful woman and a wonderful storyteller. Her stories were very imaginative, and she called everything by its real name. When she came to the most interesting place, my very correct father would send me "for cigarettes," since he couldn't bear to have such things said in the presence of his daughter. It seems to me that she was even somewhat defiant with a certain amount of cynicism. "I know they say about me that I have lived with all the people's commissars. No, I swear, not with all of them."

As a writer, she never appealed to me, since she was deliberately florid. And, in fact, her works have not withstood the test of time. Now no one reads her at all. What has remained is a semilegendary figure of a heroic woman, the prototype of the commissar in *An Optimistic Tragedy*. She died at a very young age, only thirty.

I returned from Riga to Moscow and life resumed as before: friends, school, the Komsomol.

* L.L. Obolensky died in 1991.

How innocent it sounds: "school, the Komsomol...." But if I think things over, how many sins lie upon me. How much we annoyed our wonderful teachers with politics! And then there was the "Komsomol Easter." We would assemble in a mob outside the Church of Christ the Savior (which no longer exists). To the ringing of bells and accompanied by marvelous music, people would enter the church with candles in their hands, and we would stand there, dancing and singing as loud as we could: "Down, down with monks, rabbis and all priests, we'll climb into the heavens and drive out all the gods."

Many years later I had occasion to come into close contact with believers, in prison cells and in camp barracks. They were called religiozniks. They conducted themselves very well, although, of course, there were exceptions.

In the barracks where I lived in Magadan with the women's brigades, there was a group of sectarians who were, I believe, Seventh Day Adventists; in any case, they refused to work on Saturdays. They worked very well, always fulfilling the norm no matter where they were sent. But every Saturday they arose with roll call, put on everything warm which they had and went straight to the lockup cell. They were somewhat reserved, but if someone addressed them, they always answered warmly and willingly.

Of course, they had it easier than we did. Everything which happened to them they looked upon as a trial sent to them by God.

My personal attitude toward religion is complicated. At a very difficult period of my life, when I had to reconsider much of what had seemed to be so unshakable and so indisputable, I suffered a great deal.

I saw how many people whom I respected had come to religion in different ways. And so I thought, "Perhaps, after all...."

I began by conscientiously reading all four of the Gospels. Then I talked with several serious people who were believers. And I understood—this was not for me. Probably the ability to believe is also a gift of some kind, one which I do not have.

I think that to be guided by the beautiful commandments "thou shalt not steal, thou shalt not lie, or kill and so forth," one need not be a believer—it is enough to be simply a decent human being.

However, I have been led far away from my narrative. Let us return to my chronology.

In the spring of 1921 I finished the fifth grade of secondary school. As I already have written, school lasted seven years, and I still had two years to go.

I was bored with school, and at the age of fifteen I felt myself to be grown up. I felt like starting real life more quickly and decided to pass from the fifth grade directly into the seventh. When I announced my intention at school, my long-running political enemy, our mathematics teacher, told me point-blank: "I know that you are able to pass in mathematics, but nevertheless I am going to flunk you. People like you should not be let out into the world even one year earlier than need be." I was no coryphée in math and understood that he, of course, could very well flunk me. So I took the path of least resistance: I passed the exams in another school and immediately enrolled in the seventh grade.

In the spring of 1922 I was sixteen and I finished my secondary education.

My mama very much wanted to live abroad, and friends arranged work for her among our trade representatives in Berlin. I went along with her for a month in order to relax after my school exams.

Berlin at that time was experiencing the most severe inflation, and the mark was falling with dizzying rapidity. Only foreigners could live there normally (those who had dollars lived there practically for nothing). The unfortunate Germans received their pay on a daily basis, and during their lunch break went running to buy things because the mark fell every day. What was striking in Berlin at that time was the number of immigrants, mainly Russians. Russian could be heard everywhere—on public transport, in stores, on the street. A sad joke was making the rounds: on Kurfurstendamm (in the center of Berlin) a German hanged himself because he was so homesick for his native land.

After a month I returned to Moscow.

Father was in Tokyo, mother was in Berlin and grandmother, who lived with us, was visiting her son in Baku. I was alone in our apartment—ideal conditions for my independence.

At about this time I began to earn my first pay. I was introduced to a young actor, Fedor Mikhailovich Nikitin. He had a large apartment on Triumfalny (now Mayakovsky Square), and, together with a few other enthusiasts, he organized a children's theatrical studio which was called The Toy Ring (Poteshnoe koltso). The fellows there were mostly homeless children — at that time they wandered the streets in large numbers, selling cigarettes, toffee candy or simply stealing. He would pick them out on the street, take them to his apartment, have a conversation with them and insist that they give up their former way of life. Some of them didn't want to do so and they disappeared, but the majority remained.

And what capable children they were! But they had to be fed, and the leaders of the group couldn't subsist on naked enthusiasm, as The Toy Ring was formed under the aegis of one of the workers clubs. The leaders began to be paid, which included me, since I conducted the circle studying social science in the club. I don't remember how many millions I received, but it was enough so that I could use the streetcar.

The Toy Ring began to become rather well known in Moscow, and our members were even able to perform, not just anywhere, but at the Bolshoi Theater. They put on a great show, but the authoritative commission from the Commissariat of Enlightenment found that their repertoire was not adequately consistent from an ideological standpoint.

After this, the "Ring" practically fell apart. Nikitin left for Petrograd, appeared in many films and became one of the "stars of silent film." I don't know why he had little success when movies began to be made with sound. Not long ago he appeared in the film *Life, Tears and Love*, in one of the leading roles.

In the summer of 1923 I went to Japan to see my father. The steamship traveled from Vladivostok to the Japanese port of Hokkodato. It was an enormous oceanliner, which had a movie theater, swimming pool and dancing. And the passengers' lounge — table d'hôte — was an enormous room, with an enormous table in the shape of the Greek letter Π. At the center of the crossbar of this letter sat the captain, a smart, thin, very elegant Englishman with an impeccable part in his hair and an impeccably pressed naval uniform.

We left Vladivostok during the daytime and at dinner all places at the table were taken. Stewards scurried about the tables in blindingly white jackets, people drank wine and the room was filled with noise and merriment. That night the liner began to roll severely, and at breakfast there were many empty places at the table. The tossing of the liner grew stronger, and by lunchtime only ten people showed up. By dinnertime, the unperturbed captain sat at his place, and at the other end of the table I took my place. After dinner the captain walked up to me, shook my hand, and said something in English. I, of course, didn't understand a word, but it was obvious that he had paid me a compliment.

Japan is an incredibly fascinating country. My memories go back to 1923, and since then much, of course, has changed, but at that time I was struck most of all by the combination of developed technology and that which belonged to antiquity. On the streets, rickshaws ran alongside the most wonderful modern automobiles. An electric-powered train went from Tokyo to Yokohama (at that time we had no electric trains traveling beyond the city outskirts). But from the window of this electric train one could see rice paddies where people worked using the most primitive hand methods, standing up to their ankles in water. And what amazing items the Japanese craftsmen made! From elephant tusks they would carve a rickshaw with a carriage and passenger, and all this would be the size of a walnut.

There my father developed what is now called a hobby—Japanese miniature gardens. The largest would be about a square meter and the smallest, the size of a teacup saucer. And trees would grow in these gardens. Over a pond the size of a tablespoon would bend a weeping willow the size of a finger, and next to it would be a cherry tree; when it blossomed, it would have tiny flowers as small as the head of a pin.

One relatively large, half-meter miniature garden, with roads and summer homes the size of match boxes, my father prepared as a gift for Lenin. Father wanted very much to obtain some kind of amusement for the stricken Ilyich. Since he was enraptured by these gardens himself, he felt that they would have to appeal to everyone else. They were in fact amazing; it is hard to convey in words their full beauty.

But Lenin then had another stroke, and he wasn't in a state to deal with miniature gardens. So father gave this marvelous garden to me as a gift. I brought it to Moscow and gave it to the Botanical Garden, for I didn't know how to take care of it. Later I inquired about its fate. It had dried up and died. Even the most renowned specialists at the Botanical Garden didn't know how to take care of it. This is an art which is passed among the Japanese from generation to generation, from father to son.

I was struck by how the Japanese maintain their traditions. Europeanized Japanese intellectuals receive their guests in rooms which are furnished in the European style; the rooms in which they live are furnished in the Japanese manner. When they go to visit Europeans, they dress in European clothes, but at home they wear kimonos and shoes with wooden soles.

In Japan my father became seriously ill; they said he had been bitten by a tsetse fly. Since he needed constant medical attention, a doctor was sent to him from Moscow. Father had rarely been able to apply his medical training in practice, but, to the extent that it was possible, he followed medical literature and stubbornly considered himself a physician. The first doctor sent from Moscow he rejected out of hand. This was some high-placed person's nephew, who, clinging to his "auntie's tail," was trying to travel abroad. Father very quickly sent him back.

After this episode, Dr. Ettinger arrived, a physician of high professional and human qualities. I cannot now recall why it was, but after a short while he was forced to return to Moscow. But I remember that in Moscow he often visited my father, both as one of the Kremlin doctors and simply as a good friend.

Later he was involved in the famous "doctors' plot" and perished in prison.*

After Dr. Ettinger left, father received the permission of the CC to invite a Japanese to serve as his regular physician; this was the son-in-law of Viscount Choto, then lord-mayor of Tokyo, a very influen-

---

* In 1953, several Kremlin doctors were accused of preparing to kill Stalin and other leading government officials. The frame-up was discontinued when Stalin died in March 1953.

tial figure in Japan and a major adherent of close Japanese-Soviet relations. His son-in-law received his medical training at the Sorbonne, practiced in Paris, knew three European languages very well and enjoyed the reputation of being a knowledgeable doctor. But what led father to trust him the most was the fact that he belonged to the clan of the Viscount Choto, who, as I already said, was a proponent of close Soviet-Japanese relations.

Despite the efforts of all the physicians, both Russian and Japanese, father's health took a sharp turn for the worse. He had to return to Moscow without finishing his diplomatic mission.

In Moscow he was placed in a sanitorium. And for me a new stage in my life began—higher education.

4

I enrolled in the economics department at the Plekhanov Institute of People's Economy. For some reason this institute is nowadays considered a trade institute. At that time it had nothing to do with trade (except that in the economics department there was a trade sector among all the others).

There were three departments at the institute: economics, technology and electronics. It trained engineers: engineer-economists, engineer-technicians and electrical engineers. On my diploma it reads "engineer-economist."

There was a very interesting contingent of students at that time in the institute. First of all, their age was noteworthy. The average age was around thirty. Many were participants in the civil war, some having learned to read when they were adults, and the majority came from workers' courses.

There were only a few of us, like my friend Difa and I, who had come straight from school. There were also "former" students, those who had not finished their studies during the stormy years of the revolution and were resuming their studies now.

I remember how I was once slow in getting on the streetcar. The No. 3 stopped right in front of the institute. I felt someone nudging me from behind, and a voice said, "Move along, colleague." I turned around. He saw my Komsomol badge and corrected himself, "I'm sorry,

... comrade." Even the word "student" was unpopular; we said vuzovets.* But how they studied, these vuzovtsy! Each resembled a person who has been given a valuable crystal vase. He carries it joyfully, with pride, but carries it carefully, understanding the full value of what he has in his hands. They not only attended seminars, but they went to all the lectures, although attendance at lectures at that time was far from mandatory. They paid the closest attention to the most boring subjects, such as statistics or some theory of commercial accounting. These were courses which Difa and I never went to once, but before exams we would sit there cramming and take the exams earlier than the others. By the way, as the experience of practical work would later show, it was precisely these "boring" subjects which we needed the most, and not the history of the party or dialectical materialism, which we studied with great seriousness.

These students, or to be more precise, the vuzovtsy of our class, later became the very cadres who were responsible for all the Magnitkas, Dnepostroys and other hydroelectric stations.† (Some of them were the directors of these projects; others were the prisoners who did the actual construction.)

My first year at the institute remains in my memory as the most carefree time I had as a student. The classes were not difficult, and they were interesting (and those that were not interesting we didn't take). The friends we chose were very entertaining—they loved poetry and often visited the "Young Guard" dormitory on Pokrovka, which later produced such famous poets as Svetlov, Utkin and Zharov.

We never missed the debates at the Polytechnical Institute, and we were equally interested in life on Mars, in Mayakovsky's poetry recitals and in Lunacharsky's debates with Archpriest Vvedensky.

By the way, at one of the debates the following interesting dialogue took place. In his concluding words, Vvedensky (a very erudite

* Student at an institute of higher learning.
† Magnitka—the giant steel works at Magnitogorsk; Dneprostroy—the hydroelectric station on the Dnieper River.

man) was developing the idea that everyone needs God and is searching for God in his own soul. He said, glancing snidely at Lunacharsky: "Even my esteemed opponent at one time also was searching for God" (hinting at the fact that in 1908-10 Lunacharsky was an advocate of God-searching).

In his concluding remarks Lunacharsky touched on a whole series of questions, and then also glanced snidely at Vvedensky, and said: "My esteemed opponent recalled that I once engaged in God-searching. Yes, in actual fact, there was such an episode in my biography. As I now remember, V.I. Lenin told me at that time: 'Anatoly Vasilievich, why waste your time on such nonsense! The time will come when some miserable little priest will reproach you for it.'"

While I have Lunacharsky in mind, I would like to tell of one more incident which is connected with him. Since the majority of students then lived very modestly, a special commission was created—the commission for improving the life of students, called CUBS for short. It organized lectures, reports and concerts, the proceeds from which went to benefit the students. I was sent into this CUBS, in order to strengthen the party-Komsomol contingent, which was very small there.

One time Commissar Lunacharsky agreed to give a lecture for the benefit of the students. A car was sent to pick him up containing the chairman of CUBS, Volodia Tomsky, and myself. At the appointed time we drove up to his apartment building, and Lunacharsky didn't make us wait for a minute. He came right down and got in the car. We drove along. He was silent and so were we. Then he straightened his glasses, coughed and asked, "Eh-h-h, pardon me, I have somehow forgotten, but what is the theme of today's lecture?" Volodia and I looked at each other in amazement and answered together, "Thomas Campanella, Anatoly Vasilievich and *City of the Sun*." "Eh-h-h, thank you very much."

Within ten minutes we had arrived. For an hour and a half he spoke of this very same Thomas Campanella and spoke brilliantly, both in form and in content. He gave the impression that he had spent a long time carefully preparing.

But we not only studied serious problems, we also had a good time. Our favorite place to relax was a bar on the Arbat, which was simply called Arbat, 4. It was fully within reach of a student's budget; you could sit there the whole evening over a single mug. And no one resented us for doing so. On the contrary, the doorman of this establishment proudly declared, "We have a great clientele — students and prostitutes."

We were great fans of the theater. Perhaps we sat in the gallery, perhaps we stood, but we saw every production. And what theaters there were in Moscow! This applies not only to the short period which I am now describing, to 1923. Such epochal productions of, for instance, *Princess Turandot* at the Vakhtangov took place in 1922, *Days of the Turbins* at the Art Theater in 1926, *Forest* and *The Mandate* were directed by Meyerhold in 1925 and *Phaedra* at the Kamerny was in 1922. Every theater had its own profile. And its own spectators. Even the studios of the Art Theater, and there were several, differed in some ways from each other. Theaters such as Meyerhold's and the Kamerny were absolute antipodes in the theatrical world. I am only talking about theaters which everyone has heard something about. Who now remembers the theater Semperante, the theater of improvisation? Who remembers the Goleizovsky ballet? Or Baliev's miraculous *Fledermaus* in the basement of Gnezdikovsky Alley?

They say that elderly people always feel that everything was better when they were young. I do not know if the theaters during the time of my youth were better than today's. Perhaps they were not. But today, even fine and talented actors quietly go from one theater to another. I simply cannot imagine that in the 1920s an actor from the Kamerny could have gone over to Meyerhold's theater, or that an actor from Meyerhold's could have gone to the Art Theater. After all, doesn't this mean something?!

But enjoying ourselves, or going to the theater or even reading great literature were not the main things in our life. What was most important was work on the social front and most of all — studies. It is true that we didn't always study what was needed, but we always worked earnestly and with great passion. Most of the time we studied in the reading room of the party's Moscow Committee, on Bolshaya Dmitrovka (now Pushkin Street). There you could find any textbook, and instead of resting, read an interesting book. Admission was only for those with party or Komsomol cards. If only I could convey the mood, the spirit, the atmosphere of those years and of that circle. There was an amazing "feeling of comradeship," in the highest sense of this word. A feeling of being certain that you were surrounded by comrades and could depend on each of them, and that each of them would understand you in the way that you would understand him. It wasn't important that each had his own character, his own level of development, his own tastes. What was important was the most fundamental—the greatest and most supreme goal. We wanted nothing for ourselves; we all wanted just one thing: the world revolution and happiness for all. And if it were necessary to give our lives to achieve this, then we would have done so without hesitating.

In January 1924 Lenin died. At this time a Congress of Soviets was being held in the Bolshoi Theater. Although many already knew about his death, it was officially announced from the tribune of the congress.

I happened to be at this session and heard Nadezhda Konstantinovna Krupskaya speak. Without tears, but with a kind of strength that was permeated with sorrow, she declared: "Comrades, Vladimir Ilyich has died. Our favorite, our very own has died...."

I never had seen so many men crying. I myself broke into a flood of tears, and an unfamiliar middle-aged man, evidently a worker, put his arm around my shoulders and, wiping tears from his own eyes, said, "Don't cry, my daughter, it can't be helped."

Then we spent many hours standing in line to enter the Union House, where Lenin was lying in state. It seemed that all Moscow was standing in this endless line of sorrow. There was a terrible frost, and bonfires were built in the streets. All this was later described many times. Although we later learned to think critically (and this science cost us dearly), it is impossible to forget those days.

In the spring of 1924, I turned eighteen. I successfully passed my exams, enrolled in the second year and went to rest in the Crimea. There I met the man who would become my husband and the father of my three children. We lived together for about fifteen years. And if we didn't happen to live together longer, it was for reasons beyond our control. But I will write about that later on.

5

The second year at the institute began much like the first. But nevertheless, it was not quite the same. Then there had been the joy of learning, pride from being part of the tribe of students. Now we had already extended our roots, made friends and begun to feel ourselves longtime inhabitants. The institute had become, to a certain degree, our home.

Among my acquaintances was the young composer Anatoly Neviarovsky, who wrote music for Esenin's poetry. It was through him that I met Esenin. I don't remember whose apartment it was, and besides Esenin there were two other young men. I never found out who they were, and perhaps Esenin didn't know either. Then we all headed for the cafe on Tverskaya which was called Pegasus's Stall. The crowd there was mostly literary or close to literary circles. Everyone knew Esenin, and from all sides they cried out, "Seriozha! Seriozha!" begging him to recite some poems.

He sat on the edge of our table, tugged at his collar and tie, and with a surprisingly forceful degree of sincerity, began to declaim, "Years of my youth with reckless glory, I poisoned you myself with bitter poison...." It seemed that he wasn't reciting poetry, but lodging a complaint.

During the same period I happened to meet with Mayakovsky as well.

33

Here is what concerns that period. For the reader of my notes, I would like to express a few reservations here. Everything that I write is the truth, or, as they say in the English courts: "The truth, the whole truth and nothing but the truth, so help me God."

But all this happened very long ago, and some of the dates may have shifted in time. It seems to me that all these events—the meeting with Esenin, being introduced to Mayakovsky, happened in the beginning of 1925, but perhaps it was at the end, or even at the beginning of 1926. I think that this has no practical significance. And people will forgive me....

I came into contact with Mayakovsky in two ways. I sometimes visited my distant relative who lived on Vodopyany Alley. The Briks rented their apartment from her. There I met Mayakovsky. Besides this, the older sister of my closest friend Difa was Malvina. They were half-sisters with the same father—Difa's mother was Malvina's stepmother. Malvina lived separately, not as part of their family. For a certain period she used to meet with Mayakovsky, and through her, we saw him too. At that time I very much loved Mayakovsky as a poet.

I stopped liking him when he became the "best," "poet of modern times," according to the remarks of the leader, who, as is well known, was a great authority and lover of poetry. I understood that Mayakovsky was not to blame for this, but nevertheless I could no longer like him. Then they turned him into a monumental figure (similar to the one which stands on the square bearing his name); he became an irreproachable tribune and fighter. In reality, he was nothing of the sort.

First of all, he was far from "irreproachable." He loved to play cards, he loved to drink and he loved women. Indeed he described himself as "entirely made of meat, completely human." Despite his declamatory style and external coarseness, he seemed to me to be a man easily offended and easily wounded. I think that it was precisely these qualities which led to his tragic end.

Once I was introduced to a very interesting household, which was headed by someone called Mama Lily (I cannot remember her real name).

I remember well how things were arranged in her room: two or three couches with a multitude of pillows and a few small tables. If one of her regular visitors brought a new guest, before being allowed into the room, he would be led to the kitchen and asked a couple of questions. They asked me: What was Kant's categorical imperative and which of the Moscow theaters did I like most of all?

I studied in a philosophy circle at the institute and more or less knew who Kant was. Then I understood that you didn't have to know; what was important was simply giving a clever and witty reply. In this circle they admired not so much erudition as sharp-wittedness and resourcefulness.

In reply to the second question, I said Meyerhold's theater, which was clearly not in my favor. In this refined circle they preferred the Kamerny.

Mama Lily's husband at that time was a certain Nespelov (or perhaps Pospelov), who worked at Gosizdat. He wrote acceptable verse and many parodies. He was credited with a cycle of poems devoted to Trotsky. Or to be more precise, they were not devoted to Trotsky, but they were an imitation of how various poets, such as Esenin, Mayakovsky, Igor Severianin and Vera Inber, would have written about Trotsky. I used to know them all by heart. Now, when I try to remember, it seems that I know only the ones à la Mayakovsky and à la Severianin. I want to record them before they are forgotten. That would be too bad, because, after all, they give a certain flavor of the times.

Here is the imitation of Mayakovsky:

> *Can a Bunsen burner replace*
> *A thousand volt Osram?*
> *Who is Frunze? After Trotsky,*
> *Frunze is just a shame.*
> *Why is it only now*
> *We know that Frunze, too*
> *Tightened the Wrangels' screws*
> *And made the Kolchaks shudder?*
> *Now, when the last and lousy*

White Guard lies in the grave,
We find that at Perekop
It was not on Trotsky we placed our hope.
I—from Lily, coddled by Krasnoshchekov, *
You—from the heroes of handing out quartermaster rations,
We both really got it in the neck
Most respected Lev Davidovich....

And here is the imitation of Igor Severianin:

Lev Davidovich, how painful it is,
Lev Davidovich, I am sad, Lev Davidovich, can it be
You have played your role....
Lev Davidovich—is a symbol, Lev Davidovich is a genius,
Lev Davidovich for the people is a slogan and a password.
How much glory, how many armies,
How many girls and fronts,
How much cannon thunder, how many shining autos,
No one will condemn you
For the wretched quintessence
Of the viscounts you created,
Both noble and wretched.
Lenin is splendidly enshrined, I thought you were his inheritor—
The uncrowned king of portraits everywhere.
But the Kremlin hears the hiss of those envious and pernicious
Confirming that you must go to Tyrolian Kavkaz.
Where diamond-glistening waves
Pound on Sukhumi's own Ostend,
The white-marbled hotel is Bonapartly Sainte-Hélène.
Sorrow not, Lev Davidovich!
Pour another sherry brandy!
I'll hurry to you in my limousine
And we'll share a friendly cocktail....

Here are four lines à la Vera Inber:

---

* Krasnoshchekov at that time was chairman of the Prombank; it said he was having an affair with Lily Brik.

... Now he has left these walls,
Filled with lofty thoughts.
But Sukhum will go down in history
As the Isle of Sainte-Hélène.

The spring of 1925 arrived, and along with spring came a busy period for all students—test sessions. For a number of purely personal reasons, I had not studied particularly hard for a whole year. So I had even more cause to apply myself rigorously during the testing period. I passed my tests with some success (we didn't have full-fledged exams, only tests), but I felt very badly. I began to tire very easily (which had never happened before), in the evenings I was feverish, and finally, in the course of two weeks I coughed up blood three times.

The doctors found that I had an active form of tuberculosis. I nevertheless passed into the third year at the institute, and then my studies broke off for two years.

6

In the spring of 1926 I began to work in Vesenkha (the Supreme Soviet of the People's Economy) in the economic planning directorate (EPD), doing what was closely related to my future specialization. After a while I was elected secretary of the Komsomol organization at the EPD. A short time later, the Komsomol organization recommended me for acceptance into the party. I successfully made it past all the organizations within the Vesenkha—not only the party bureau, but the general party meeting of the EPD and the general party meeting of the entire Vesenkha. All that remained was confirmation by the regional committee, which usually amounted to nothing more than a formality. But at that time there was a general party-Komsomol meeting, which discussed the "antiparty position of Comrade Trotsky" and which passed the corresponding resolution.

I voted against this resolution, and that was the end of my party "career"—before it had even begun.

I would consider my task unfinished, and these notes incomplete, if I didn't write here about Lev Davidovich Trotsky.

For many decades not a single other political figure has been subject to more public defamation than Trotsky.

His activity during the prerevolutionary period was either ignored or distorted. His role in the October Revolution and in the civil war was either ignored or distorted.

The French historian Pierre Broué wrote and published in France a book of more than a thousand pages, in which he gathered an enormous amount of factual material about the life and activity of Lev Davidovich. Another book, somewhat smaller, has also been written by the French historian Jean-Jacques Marie. Isaac Deutscher's book *The Prophet Outcast* is of great interest. How good it would be to see these books translated into Russian and published here.*

Recently in Russia a few articles have begun to appear where Trotsky is treated the way he deserves. To be sure, these articles are very few. And even now some of the stereotypes about him from the 1930s still creep in.

For instance, he is given the attribute of being fond of "the luxury of the grand princes." I was often in his apartment and can testify—they lived very modestly. What was characteristic of Trotsky was precisely a complete indifference to the trappings of a "luxurious" life, such as an apartment, furnishings, delicacies and so forth. And his children were raised in such a spirit.

His older son, Lev Sedov (who took his mother's surname), enrolled in the institute, left home and lived in the student dormitory. He didn't want to enjoy any of the advantages which his father's famous name could have brought him at this time, and he didn't want to receive any special treatment which would separate him from his friends and peers. At home, his parents were in agreement with this decision.

In other instances, Trotsky is depicted as a "man in boots," as an ideologue and, at the same time, as a child of war communism, somewhat as an opposite to the civilian Lenin, who didn't wear boots, but "worn-out shoes."

In reality, Trotsky was a thoroughly civilian person, and no boots had the power of turning him into an "old soldier," even if he had wanted to become one.

His first position in the Soviet government was commissar of foreign affairs.

I remember how surprised my father was (he was in Germany at

* A Russian edition of Isaac Deutscher's book, the third volume of his biography of Trotsky, was published in Moscow in 1991.

the time) when he found out that Trotsky had been appointed commissar of defense and chairman of the Revolutionary Military Council.

He was a brilliant polemicist, an authority on the international workers movement, a literary critic — anything you like, but not a military man.

However, the situation in the country at that moment demanded that he become a military figure, and he became one.

Gorky says in his recollections of Lenin, "Striking his fist on the table, he [Lenin] exclaimed: 'Show me another man who would be able in a year to organize almost a model army; yes, and win the esteem of the military specialists. We have such a man.' "[1]

As for the assertion that he was supposedly the ideologue of war communism, none other than Trotsky was the first to support Lenin's idea of shifting over to the New Economic Policy. It is no accident that his last job was as the leader of the Chief Concessions Committee. This work was not, of course, on a scale appropriate to him, but, I repeat, this appointment was no accident: He was an advocate of cooperatives, concessions, free enterprise and so forth, none of which fits within the framework of war communism.

Very much has been written in its time about the disagreements between Trotsky and Lenin. There were, of course, disagreements. Two such extraordinary and outstanding figures could not have always thought the same way about everything. But I recall the following, seemingly minor, incidents. Once when L.D. was visiting us, I don't remember for what occasion, he told father about a conversation which he had held with Lenin in 1918 or 1919. Lenin asked him, half in jest, "What do you think, Lev Davidovich, if they kill the two of us, will Sverdlov and Bukharin be able to manage?"

In July 1919 Lenin gave Trotsky the following document on a blank piece of paper from the Soviet of People's Commissars: "Comrades! Knowing the strict character of Comrade Trotsky's orders, I am so convinced of the absolute correctness, expediency and necessity for our cause of the order issued by Comrade Trotsky, that I fully endorse this order. V. Ulianov-Lenin."

Is this not an indication of absolute trust? And Lev Davidovich always spoke of Lenin not only with great respect, but with genuine human warmth.

I am trying to remember if he ever spoke about Stalin. He mentioned him several times, but it always seemed to be incidentally and with a certain feeling of disgust.

Many people have asked me, "Why was it, nevertheless, that Trotsky, who was undoubtedly more intelligent, talented and erudite than Stalin, and much more popular than him when Lenin was alive, in the final analysis (if it can be said in that way) lost the battle to him?"

I think—and this is my deeply subjective opinion (and not even an opinion, but more likely, a feeling)—that it was precisely this sense of disgust which prevented him from winning. I think that he was simply incapable of lowering himself to Stalin's level, to act using Stalin's methods.

And for Stalin, all methods were allowed.

So what, therefore, was Lev Davidovich Trotsky really like—chairman of the Petrograd Soviet in 1905 and 1917, one of the most active participants and organizers of the October Revolution, the person second in significance and popularity in the whole country under Lenin; and yet a "spy," "saboteur" and "agent of the Gestapo" under Stalin?

As Trotsky himself wrote in his autobiography *My Life*, he was born in the village of Yanovka in the Kherson Province. His father was a small farmer whose holdings grew. In the Kherson and Ekaterinoslav provinces at that time, there were about forty Jewish farming colonies with a population of about 25,000.

"My childhood," wrote Trotsky, "was not one of hunger and cold. My family had already achieved a competence at the time of my birth. But it was the stern competence of people still rising from poverty and having no desire to stop halfway. Every muscle was strained, every thought set on work and savings. Such a domestic routine left but a modest place for the children. We knew no need, but neither did we know the generosities of life—its caresses.... Mine was the grayish childhood of a lower middle class family, spent in a village in an obscure corner where nature is wide, and manners, views and interests are pinched and narrow."[2]

In this village L.D. lived until he was nine years old. Village life and peasant labor he knew, as they say, with his mother's milk.

When he was nine, they sent him to study in Odessa. In secondary school he studied eight years, and a year after he finished he had already been arrested. Thus began his life as a revolutionary. The main content of his life—excepting the civil war years—was (as he said himself) party and literary activity. In 1923 Gosizdat began publishing thirteen volumes of his works. Their publication was stopped in 1927 when the campaign against Trotskyism intensified.

My personal memories of Trotsky relate to my very first memories of life.

Beginning in 1908, the newspaper *Pravda* was published in Vienna. All its publishers—Parvus, Skobelev, Trotsky and Joffe—met constantly, and their families had friendly relations. Trotsky's older son, Liova, was my age and became my childhood friend.

I remember the following episode. Liova and I—we were both either three or four—were sitting at the table eating kasha. I had already eaten mine, but Liova was dawdling, acting up and throwing his spoon. Lev Davidovich walked in and asked, "How are things going, kids?" I immediately gave him a full report (I must have been a real stinker) about how I had eaten my kasha, whereas Liova wasn't eating, but fooling around. He looked at his son, and then very quietly asked, "So why aren't you eating your kasha?" Liova grabbed his spoon and, looking at him like a rabbit looks at a boa constrictor, began quickly to cram in the kasha, coughing and choking. By the way, I can't recall a single instance when L.D. ever punished or even raised his voice at a child.

Here is another episode. I was sitting and looking at some houses and ships which my father had drawn for me. You can judge the quality of the sketches by the fact that when L.D. walked into the room and looked at them, he said, "Nadiusha, how well you've begun to draw." I indignantly told him that papa had drawn them. "Ah, your papa! They are beautifully done, I wish I could draw that well." I loved my father very much and remember how happy I was that even L.D. couldn't draw as well as my papa.

In 1912, father returned to Russia and soon was arrested. He was freed from his Siberian exile by the February Revolution.

He saw Trotsky again in May 1917 in Petrograd, where father had come from Siberia and Trotsky from emigration. Once again they were in the same "cartridge belt," in the group of Mezhraiontsy, which in the summer of 1917 joined the Bolshevik Party.

In the fall of 1918, after the expulsion of the Soviet embassy from Germany, I lived in Moscow, studied at the same school with Liova, belonged to the same Komsomol cell, and often visited their apartment. Lev Davidovich was rarely at home—most of the time he spent at the front, but nevertheless I saw him at home, saw him with his comrades, with people who were his guests.

I would like to shatter that stereotype which developed around his personality, that he was haughty and arrogant. This is not true. He was neither haughty nor arrogant. He was a complex man, with a complex character, and he didn't open himself up immediately as many others do. He was demanding of people, and this did not appeal to everyone. But he was also demanding of himself and of those close to him.

In the obituary written after the death of his son, he wrote that his relations with Leon were not "of an even and placid character.... I also displayed toward him the pedantic and exacting attitude which I had acquired in practical questions. Because of these traits, which are perhaps useful and even indispensable for work on a large scale, but quite insufferable in personal relationships, people closest to me often had a very hard time."[3]

Throughout his whole life, he probably had only two close friends, Rakovsky and Joffe.

But he was a true friend.

After the death of my father, we found out how much he had done in order to secure the necessary medical treatment. He wrote to Semashko (who was then commissar of health) in this regard, and then turned to various other leading personnel. This was in 1927, and I think that it was not always convenient or pleasant for him to turn to these "leading" figures.

Besides a few friends and devoted assistants (who remained faithful to him both in disgrace and in exile), he also had a devoted family.

Living before the revolution in emigration, he didn't see his daughters from his first marriage for many years. But when he returned, he immediately established contact with them, and they often visited him at home.

I was together with their mother, Aleksandra Lvovna Sokolovskaya, in Kolyma in 1936. Their older daughter, Zinaida, went abroad in 1932 to see her father, and while she was living there was deprived of her citizenship. This apparently combined with other circumstances, and Zina committed suicide.

Aleksandra Lvovna recited to me from memory a letter she had received from Lev Davidovich after Zina's death. I remember the first sentence: "Dear friend, I cannot understand why fate is punishing us so terribly." "Dear friend," in this case was not a form of address; she was indeed his dear friend throughout the course of his whole adult life.

He was very attached to his sons as well. The older, Lev, followed him into exile, leaving behind a wife and child whom he loved very much. He was for L.D. not only a son, but a friend and a faithful assistant in his life and in battle.

His wife, Natalia Ivanovna, can serve as a model of devotion, as a wife, a woman and a human being. In relation to him she was always unchanging: as the wife of an emigrant, with very limited means; as the wife of a prisoner, sitting in jail; as the wife of the second most popular man in the country; as the wife of a disgraced political figure; and, finally, as the wife of an exile, driven out and covered with mud by the entire Soviet press and the pro-Soviet press abroad.

He repaid her with the same tender devotion. From L.D.'s diaries which were published in America, it is obvious that after forty years of life together, he never stopped admiring her, her steadfastness, her love for music, the breadth of her interests.

On the day when he learned about the arrest of his younger son, Sergei, he wrote in his diary: "Poor boy ... and my poor, poor Natasha...."

Natalia Ivanovna deserves having a few words said about her, and not simply as Trotsky's wife.

Today much is said and written about the need to protect and preserve various relics and monuments of antiquity. Yet no one remembers that in the 1920s there was a special section of the Commissariat of Enlightenment which was called the Department of Preserving Monuments of Antiquity. It was headed by Natalia Ivanovna Sedova. She did a great deal to preserve these monuments. For at that time there were "enthusiasts" who wanted to show their "revolutionary spirit" by destroying everything that was old. Thanks to her, the chapel of the Iverskaya Mother of God, which stood near the entrance of Red Square, was preserved. Then it was later removed, under the pretense that it restricted traffic. At that time, Natalia Ivanovna defended many churches and monuments of antiquity, which later also were destroyed.

She died in 1962, having raised Seva, L.D.'s grandson and Zina's son, and then helping him and his wife raise their children. Seva's older daughter is called Natasha.

Natalia Ivanovna protected Trotsky's archives and handed them over to Harvard University.

She was remembered fondly by all those who knew her.

And now I would like to explain Trotsky's role in my father's funeral.

Here is what outsiders and witnesses have written about it. The crowd responded angrily at the speech given by Riutin, who represented the Central Committee at the funeral. (A few years later, this same Riutin produced a major political document, which has since been published, which criticized Stalin's regime and Stalin himself. And, of course, he was shot.) Riutin's speech was interrupted by indignant cries.

As if coming out of a dream, eyewitnesses say, Trotsky asked Sapronov, who was standing next to him, "Why are they shouting?" Looking at Trotsky, one might conclude that he had not heard the various speeches. Immersed in his own thoughts, he looked at the grave, and the muscles of his left cheek nervously twitched. When they said that it was Trotsky's turn to speak, everyone fell silent. Trotsky was the last orator, and it was his last speech in the Soviet Union. Coming from him, the word "bureaucrat" sounded like the name of a longstanding enemy. He called upon people to follow the example of Joffe's life, not his death. (Later, I will give the full text of his speech.)

Yes, he was a true friend, demanding and faithful. And people close to him knew this. And children loved him.

Tatiana Ivarovna Smilga recalls that when he visited her father, L.D. relaxed after serious conversations by playing with children. When, in Trotsky's presence, they arrested Smilga, his youngest daughter, five-year-old Natasha, who was in childish despair over the fact that strange people were leading her father away, ran to none other than Trotsky. She wept bitterly, holding onto his leg with her little hands.

They buried my father in November 1927, and in January 1928, they sent Trotsky into exile in Alma Ata.

On the day he was being sent into exile, when we found out about it we ran to his apartment (at this time he no longer lived in the Kremlin, but on Granovsky Street). But we didn't find him there, they had taken him away. At home were his daughter Nina and his daughter-in-law Anya (Liova's wife), with the year-old infant Lev (the third generation). They didn't follow him into exile. There were a few other comrades, much like ourselves. The GPU set a trap in the apartment. They let everyone in, but let no one out, so we sat there until morning. In the morning, they let us all go. Nina explained how this all happened.

When they informed Trotsky that they were sending him to Alma Ata, he said that he didn't consider this decision to be valid and refused to go. The oldest among the group which had come to take him away was clearly upset, and said: "Comrade Trotsky, understand, this doesn't depend on me, I am simply following orders, I am a soldier." L.D. replied: "I am also a soldier. But I am a soldier of the revolution, I am a conscious soldier. And you?"

He refused to go. He didn't budge from the spot. They carried him down the stairs in their arms and sat him in a car. Natalia Ivanovna and Liova went with him. His younger son, Seriozha, went along to accompany them. When he returned, he said that the car had driven not to the station, but to some railway siding, where there were almost no people. They also carried him out of the car into the coach. Liova went along after them, shouting: "People, look! Workers, look! They're taking Trotsky away!"

He spent one year in Alma Ata.

In 1929 he was sent to Turkey. His last emigration lasted almost twelve years: Turkey, France, Norway and then Mexico.

During this entire time he never stopped working. He wrote; when it was possible, he gave lectures; he kept up an enormous correspondence.

During the period of the Moscow trials, at which, although he was absent, he was in actual fact the main accused, he wrote the following:

"I am ready to appear before a public and impartial Commission of Inquiry with documents, facts, and testimonies ... and to disclose the truth to the very end. I declare: *If this Commission decides that I am guilty in the slightest degree of the crimes which Stalin imputes to me, I pledge in advance to place myself voluntarily in the hands of the executioners of the G.P.U....* I make this declaration before the entire world. I ask the Press to publish my words in the farthest corners of our planet. But, if the Commission establishes—do you hear me? do you hear me?—that the Moscow trials are a conscious and premeditated frame-up, I will not ask my accusers to place themselves voluntarily before a firing squad. No, the eternal disgrace in the memory of human generations will be sufficient for them! Do the accusers in the Kremlin hear me? I throw my defiance in their faces, and I await their reply!"[4]

Could Stalin have accepted this challenge? After all, it would be enough for one finger to touch this rotten house of cards, out of which the Moscow trials were built, for it to come crashing down.

On the subject of the trials, I would like to give one more quotation about Trotsky:

"He forecast 'another trial, a genuine one,' at which the workers will sit in judgment over Stalin and his accomplices. 'No words will then be found in the human language to defend this most malignant of all the Cains that can be found in history.... The monuments he has erected to himself will be pulled down or taken into museums and placed there in chambers of totalitarian horrors. And the victorious working class will revise all the trials, public and secret, and will erect monuments to the unfortunate victims of Stalinist villainy and infamy on the squares of a liberated Soviet Union.'"[5]

What a remarkable gift of prediction!

There is one more myth, about Trotsky's "careerism," about his yearning for high posts and thirst for power.

Today everyone knows how Lenin proposed that Trotsky become his deputy. This would have given him, in addition to his popularity, the even more official status of "second person in the state." No one could become first while Lenin was alive.

Trotsky refused.

Here is what he wrote on the subject of the "tragedy" of his nonexistent "career": "Since my exile, I have more than once read musings in the newspapers on the subject of the 'tragedy' that has befallen me. I know no personal tragedy. I know the change of two chapters of the revolution.... I can only express my astonishment at the philistine attempt to establish a connection between the power of reasoning and a government post, between mental balance and the present situation. I do not know, and I never have, of any such connection. In prison, with a book or pen in my hand, I experienced the same sense of deep satisfaction that I did at the mass meetings of the revolution."[6]

Nevertheless, in another sense, Trotsky is perhaps the most tragic figure of the Russian Revolution.

It was his fate to outlive all four of his children. And not one of them died a "natural" death.

His second daughter—Nina, whom he called "my cothinker"—died from a very rare disease, general tuberculosis; she was consumed within two months, when she was only twenty-six years old. His older daughter, Zina, committed suicide. Liova was murdered in Paris, and Sergei was shot in Moscow.

It was his fate to witness how all his friends and cothinkers left the Opposition. It fell to his lot to see them shattered, broken and then annihilated.

Until his last days he fought against Stalin and Stalinism. And until his last days he believed in the inevitability of the world revolution.

That is what can be said about his life. Now I will tell what I know about his death.

In 1940, when I worked outside the zone in a Magadan camp, I had a chance to read newspapers, not regularly, of course, but from time to time. One of the newspapers which fell into my hands was like an exploding bomb to me.

On the last page, in small print, it was reported that in Mexico, L.D. Trotsky had been murdered at home. About his murderer, it was said that he was one of his former cothinkers who had become disillusioned.

For me, of course, all these comments were beside the point. I knew well who the actual murderer was, or to be more precise, who the organizer of the murder was.

Many years later I saw an Italian journal from 1960 with a major article about this assassination. The author was a woman journalist who had twice interviewed the assassin in prison. I naturally read this article in translation.

If you remove the journalistic sensationalism and feminine sentimentality, then the facts are as follows. Ramon Mercader was born in Barcelona in 1914 and never had any relationship to Trotsky or Trotskyism. His mother was born in Cuba. In the words of the article's author, she was a "Communist fanatic" who abandoned her husband in 1929 to work in the "fifth column" of Communists in France and in other countries. Her son was raised with the same ideology. As a youth he had been brought from Spain to Moscow by a member of the "secret police" (evidently, the NKVD), Leonid Eitingen. He knew three European languages well and prepared to learn the methods of Soviet espionage.

The author of the article located in Mexico a former member of the Spanish Communist Party, Julian Gorkin, who left the party after Trotsky was exiled from Russia. In a book by General Sanchez Salazar that was published in 1950, entitled *Murder in Mexico*, Gorkin is quoted as stating that "Mercader had been forced to become an assassin," that "he allegedly knew that his mother had been arrested in Russia as a hostage for the assassination which he would have to carry out."

Later it was said that, at the time of the assassination, his mother was waiting in a car not far from Trotsky's house, in case Mercader managed to escape.

All this is clearly inconsistent.

When the author interviewed Mercader in prison, he said that he had no intention of killing Trotsky. But when he approached Trotsky, an argument broke out, and then he got into a fight with one of the "bodyguards." "We wheezed and threw ourselves at each other. I broke away and pulled the ice pick out of my pocket."

All this, of course, is absolute nonsense. As a result of the "brawl," not one of those fighting was injured, but Trotsky, who didn't take part in the brawl, happened to be murdered.

The simple fact was that Mercader in good faith carried out the assignment he had been given. He carried out the assassination and didn't say a word about who had put him up to it.

And for this he was later decorated.

In the words of the article's author, Mercader had a privileged position in jail. He had a "free regime," headed one of the many prison shops and had significant means at his disposal.

As such, this person is of no interest. He was simply the technical executor of the murder.

The real murderer was far away from Mexico.

Here are the recollections of Trotsky's grandson, Vsevolod Platonovich Volkov. His mother Zinaida, who was Trotsky's oldest daughter, committed suicide. Lev Sedov, who was living then in Paris, came to Berlin to pick up Vsevolod. After Liova's death, Lev Davidovich and Natalia Ivanovna had the young boy brought to Mexico, where they then lived. Since then and until the present day, he has lived in Mexico.

The first attempt on Trotsky's life was organized by the famous Mexican artist Siqueiros. Siqueiros had been a member of the Mexican Communist Party since 1924. He was directed, of course, from Moscow.

Seva recalled how once, at five in the morning, some people broke into their home. Seva was very frightened and hid in the corner. After firing more than two hundred rounds from a machine gun into Trotsky's bedroom, the attackers fled. This attempt on Trotsky's life was unsuccessful. After this, according to Seva's memories, Lev Davidovich would say every evening, "Well, we've lived through one more day." He understood that Stalin wouldn't stop at the first attempt.

Mercader managed to get to know those around Trotsky and chased after the sister of one of his secretaries. Penetrating into the house in this way, he asked Trotsky to edit one of his works, which he supposedly was getting ready to publish. Trotsky agreed.

At the time of the assassination, Seva was in school. He was fourteen years old, and, in his words, he remembers this day as if it were yesterday.

Later, Natalia Ivanovna explained:

"It was a very hot day, and Mercader came to us in a raincoat, completely buttoned up. N.I. asked, why was he dressed in this way, wasn't he too hot? He answered something along the lines that in Mexico you could never be sure of the weather, and he turned to L.D. with the request to look at his manuscript. L.D. sat at his desk and placed the manuscript before him.

"Mercader stood behind his back, took an ice pick out of his raincoat pocket and struck him in the head.

"Trotsky cried out and fell on the floor, bleeding profusely.

"When Seva came home from school, he ran into the room. Mercader had already been taken away, and L.D. lay there on the floor. They were holding a cold press against his head. He was, however, conscious, and when he saw Seva, he said, 'Take the boy away, this is no place for him.'"

After a few minutes, they took him to the hospital. For a while he was conscious and even tried to joke with the doctors and nurses. He continuously tried to cheer up, convince or calm Natalia Ivanovna. He then lost consciousness and died the next day. He met his death as he had lived, courageously and steadfastly.

7

In the fall of 1927, my father's health took a sharp turn for the worse. Apparently there was a recurrence of the infection which he had developed in Japan; this was on top of heart disease and a whole "bouquet" of other maladies.

The Central Committee ordered that the most authoritative and experienced Kremlin doctors hold consultations. According to their consultation, they concluded that there was no possibility of treating Adolf Abramovich in Russia, and that he immediately had to be sent abroad. The inner-party situation had become very sharp at that time, and A.A.'s Opposition views were, of course, no secret to anyone. This apparently was the main reason why the CC didn't want to send him abroad.

This whole unpleasant story is outlined by A.A. himself in the last letter before his suicide. But, running ahead, I would like to speak about one episode which I learned of much later, from comrades working in the People's Commissariat of Foreign Affairs (NKID, or narkomindel).

Some time after the death of my father, the Japanese ambassador in Moscow sent the following statement to the NKID: "According to information at our disposal, the family of the late Mr. Joffe is in a state of great material need. Mr. Joffe did much in his time to bring Japan and the Soviet Union closer together, and we would like to offer his family our hospitality if they wish to visit Japan, or any other form of material assistance." At the narkomindel, they replied to him that there was no reason to worry, because the family of the late Mr. Joffe was by no means in need and the state was taking care of them.

If you take into account that father's wife was at that time in exile in Central Asia, and that I was with my nursing infant in Siberia, then, of course, the state was "taking care" of us.

Meanwhile, my father's health was getting steadily worse. His illness was accompanied by torturous physical pain—father said that it resembled a strong toothache in every nerve of his body. He was a very courageous man, and I think that he would have dealt with this if there had been any possibility of getting well, of being able to get back on his feet, of beginning to work again. But he had no such perspective. He understood this both as a politician and as a doctor.

On November 16, 1927, Adolf Abramovich committed suicide.

He left a letter addressed to Trotsky. I don't know who passed the information on to the authorities, but when I ran home, the door onto the stairway was open, and many people were in the foyer. In the doorway to the room where my father lay there stood a policeman, and he was allowing no one in.

I don't know how I got past this policeman, but I think I hit him with my fists and screamed that my papa was in there, and that they had to let me in right then to see him. He let me pass. Father was lying on the divan, on which he usually would rest.

There was no letter. Later, when Trotsky demanded that they give him the letter addressed to him, they gave a photocopy not to him, but to Rakovsky. Thus, no one saw the original of the letter, written in my father's hand.

Here is what Trotsky wrote about all that transpired:

"On November 16, Joffe committed suicide; his death was a wedge in the growing struggle.

"Joffe was a very sick man. He had been brought back from Japan, where he was Soviet ambassador, in a serious condition. Many obstacles were placed in the way of his being sent abroad, but his stay there was too brief, and although it had its beneficial results, they were not sufficient compensation. Joffe became my deputy in the Chief

Concessions Committee, and all the heavy routine fell on him. The crisis in the party disturbed him greatly. The thing that worried him most was the treachery. Several times he was ready to throw himself into the thick of the struggle. Concerned for his health, I tried to hold him back....

"Joffe had been unable to complete his cure abroad, and his physical condition was growing worse every day. Toward autumn, he was compelled to stop work, and then he was laid low altogether. His friends again raised the question of sending him abroad, but this time the Central Committee refused point-blank. The Stalinites were now preparing to send the Oppositionists in quite a different direction. My expulsion from the Central Committee and then from the party startled Joffe more than anyone else. To his personal and political wrath was added the bitter realization of his own physical helplessness. Joffe felt unerringly that the future of the revolution was at stake. It was no longer in his power to fight, and life apart from struggle meant nothing for him. So he drew his final conclusion."

Later on, Trotsky wrote:

"An unfamiliar voice informed me over the telephone: 'Adolph Abramovich has shot himself. There is a packet for you on his bedside table.' ... We set off in haste for Joffe's. In answer to our ringing and knocking, someone demanded our names from behind the door and then opened it after some delay; something mysterious was going on inside. As we entered, I saw the calm and infinitely tender face of Adolph Abramovich against a blood-stained pillow. B., a member of the board of the GPU, was at Joffe's desk. The packet was gone from the bedside table. I demanded its return at once. B. muttered that there was no letter at all. His manner and voice left me in no doubt that he was lying. A few minutes later, friends from all parts of the city began to pour into the apartment. The official representatives of the commissariat of foreign affairs and of the party institutions felt lost in the midst of the crowd of oppositionists. During the night, several thousand people visited the house. The news of the theft of the letter spread through the city. Foreign journalists were sending dispatches, and it became quite impossible to conceal the letter any longer. In the end, a photostatic copy of it was handed to

Rakovsky. Why a letter written by Joffe to me and sealed in an envelope that bore my name should have been given to Rakovsky, and at that in a photostatic copy instead of the original, is something that I cannot even attempt to explain. Joffe's letter reflects him to the end, but as he was half an hour before his death. Joffe knew my attitude toward him; he was bound to me by a deep moral confidence, and gave me the right to delete anything I thought superfluous or unsuitable for publication. Failing to conceal the letter from the whole world, the cynical enemy tried to exploit for its own purposes those very lines not written for the public eye.

"Joffe tried to make his death a service to the same cause to which he had dedicated his life. With the same hand that was to pull the trigger against his own temple half an hour later, he wrote the last evidence of a witness and the last counsel of a friend."[1]

This quotation has turned out to be rather long, but it is, after all, the only "eyewitness account" of its type and it provides the memoirs of a friend.

As for Adolf Abramovich's letter, it must be taken into account that this was not an appeal to the Central Committee, either present or future, it was a letter to a friend. As Lev Davidovich correctly wrote, and A.A. himself stipulated, there are parts of it which are extremely personal and not intended for publication. Nevertheless, it is a political document and should be published. Here is the letter.

> Dear Lev Davidovich,
>
> Throughout my life, I have always defended the view that a political or public figure must also be able to exit from life as an actor leaves the stage, and that it is even better to do this too early, rather than too late.
>
> When I was still an inexperienced youth, and the suicide of Paul Lafargue and his wife Laura Marx raised such an outcry in the socialist parties, I firmly defended the principled and correct nature of their positions. I recall that I vehemently objected to August Bebel, who was indignant over these suicides, that if one could argue against the age at which the Lafargues chose to die — for here we were dealing not with the number of years, but with the possible usefulness of a political figure — then one could by no means argue against the very principle of a political figure de-

parting from this life at the moment when he felt that he would no longer bring any benefit to the cause to which he had devoted himself.

More than thirty years ago, I adopted the philosophy that human life has meaning only to the extent that and as long as it serves the infinite, which for us is humanity. If the human race is "finite," in any case, its end will occur at such a distant time that for us it may be taken as absolute infinity. And here, faith in progress as I believe in it can fully envision that even when our planet perishes, mankind will have discovered a means of traveling to other, younger planets, thereby prolonging its existence even then. This means that all that is done for the benefit of humanity in our time will be reflected in those distant centuries. This gives the only possible meaning to our existence and to our life.

In this, and only in this, I always saw the sole meaning of life; and now, looking back over my life, twenty-seven years of which I spent in the ranks of our party, I think I have the right to say that for all of my conscious life, I have remained faithful to my philosophy, that is, I have passed through my life in a meaningful way, working for the good of mankind. Even years of prison and exile, when a man becomes detached from direct participation in the struggle and in service to mankind, cannot be stricken from the number of purposeful and meaningful years of life, for, being years of self-education and self-training, these years assisted the improvement of later work and therefore, they can also be considered to be among the years in service to humanity, i.e., the years which have been lived with meaning; it seems that I dare say, that I haven't lived a single day of my life, in this sense, without meaning. But now, evidently, the moment has come, when my life is losing its meaning, and therefore, the necessity has arisen for me to leave it, to put an end to it.

For several years now the present leadership of our party, in accord with the general line which they have advocated, have not given work to Oppositionists; they have given me neither party nor Soviet work on a scale where I might bring the maximum benefit within my powers. During the last year, as you know, the Politburo has removed me, as an Oppositionist, from all party and Soviet work.

On the other hand, partly, in all likelihood, because of my illness, and partly for reasons which you know better than I, I have taken almost no part in the practical work and struggles of the Opposition throughout this year. With an enormous inner struggle and from the beginning with the greatest lack of desire, I entered into that area of work to which I had hoped to resort only when I had become a complete invalid, and I devoted myself wholly to research, to scholarly and literary work.

No matter how difficult this was at the beginning, I gradually undertook this work and began to hope that with this activity my life would nevertheless preserve that inner usefulness which it needs and about which I spoke earlier; only then, from my point of view, could I justify my existence.

But my health grew ever worse. On September 20, for reasons unknown to me, the medical commission of the CC demanded that I appear for a consultation with professors and specialists. This consultation determined that I have an active tubercular process in both lungs, myocarditis, chronic inflammation of the gallbladder, chronic colitis with appendicitis and chronic polyneuritis (multiple inflammation of the nerves): the professors who examined me categorically stated that the condition of my health is much worse than I had imagined, that I shouldn't think of hoping to finish my course of lectures at Moscow State University and at the Institute of Oriental Studies, and that, on the contrary, it would now be much more sensible for me to abandon all these plans, that I shouldn't spend even one more day than necessary in Moscow, nor spend one more hour without treatment, that I should immediately go abroad to the appropriate sanitorium, and that since such a trip would take more than a couple of days, they would prescribe for me some kind of medication and treatment at the Kremlin polyclinic for the short time remaining before my trip abroad.

In response to my questions, what were the chances that I would find a cure abroad, and could I be treated in Russia without abandoning my work, my professorship, they categorically replied, in the presence of a senior doctor of the CC, Comrade Obrosov, and one more Communist doctor, and a senior physician from the Kremlin hospital, A. Iu. Konnel, that Russian sanatoriums would by no means be able to help me, and that I should hope for foreign treatment, because I had not been cured over the last two to three months, and that now they themselves were insisting on a trip of no less than six months and perhaps more. Under these conditions they had no doubt that, while I might not be completely cured, I would, in any case, be fully capable of working for a prolonged period.

In the nearly two months since then, absolutely no steps have been taken by the medical commission of the CC (which initiated the consultation), not only with regard to my trip abroad, but also with regard to my treatment here. On the contrary, for a while now the Kremlin pharmacy, which had always previously given me medicine which I prescribed, has been forbidden to do this, and I have in actual fact been deprived of the free medical assistance which I enjoyed, and have been forced to buy the medicine I need at my own expense in city pharmacies (it seems that at the same time the ruling group of our party has decided, in relation to other comrades in the Opposition, to fulfill its threat to "punch the Opposition in the stomach").

While I was healthy enough to be able to work, I paid little attention to all this. But since I was becoming increasingly worse, my wife began to petition the medical commission of the CC and N.A. Semashko personally (since he is always, after all, calling publicly for the carrying out of the slogan: "preserve the old guard") about my being sent abroad.

The question, however, has always been pushed aside, and the only thing which my wife has managed to achieve is that they have given her a copy of the consultation's statement, in which my chronic illnesses are listed, and which states that the physicians insist on my being sent abroad to a sanitorium such as Professor Friedlander's for a period of up to one year.

Meanwhile, nine days ago, I took to bed for the last time, since all my chronic illnesses became worse and sharpened "as always happens" and, what is most horrible of all, my old polyneuritis once again assumed a sharp form, under which I have to endure absolutely unbearable and hellish pain, and I have been absolutely deprived of the ability to walk.

In actual fact, for the duration of these nine days, I have had no treatment, and there has been no talk of my trip abroad. Not one of the CC doctors has been to see me once.

Professor Davidenko and Dr. Levin, who have been to see me, prescribed for me some minor medicines (which, of course, do nothing to help), but in doing so they acknowledged that "they could do nothing," and that my immediate trip abroad was needed. Dr. Levin had once told my wife that the question was being dragged out because in the medical commission they probably thought that my wife would travel with me, and "this would be very expensive" (when comrades who are not in the Opposition fall ill, then everyone knows that they, and often their wives, are almost always sent abroad in the accompaniment of our physicians or professors: I myself know of many such instances and must also state that, when I fell ill for the first time with the same acute form of polyneuritis, they sent me abroad with my entire family, both wife and child, as well as Professor Kanebach: then, of course, there were none of the newly-established mores in the party).

My wife replied to this that, no matter how painful my condition was for her, she had no pretensions whatsoever that either she or anyone else would accompany me abroad. In response to this statement, Dr. Levin assured her that in this case, the question would be resolved more rapidly.

My condition continued to deteriorate. The pains have become so unbearable that I have finally demanded at least some form of relief from my doctors. Dr. Levin was here to see me today, and he repeated once again that they could do nothing and that my only salvation lies in an urgent trip abroad. In the evening, the CC physician, Dr. Potemkin, informed my wife that the medical commission of the CC had decided not to send me abroad, but to treat me in Russia, since the professors and specialists had been insisting on prolonged treatment abroad, feeling that a short trip would be useless. The Central Committee, however, is agreed to devote one thousand dollars to my treatment (up to two thousand rubles); it doesn't feel able to assign any more. As you know, in the past I have given not just one thousand rubles to our party, and in any case, I have given more than I have cost the party since the revolution has deprived me of my means, and I can no longer undergo treatment at my own expense.

English and American publishers have repeatedly offered sums of up to 20,000 dollars for excerpts from my memoirs (of my choosing, with one stipulation, that the period of the Brest negotiation be included); the Politburo knows very well that I am sufficiently experienced, both as a journalist and as a diplomat, not to publish anything which might injure either our party or the state; it knows that I was a censor both for the NKID and for the Chief Concessions Committee, and as ambassador for all publications in Russian in a given country. Several years ago I asked the Politburo permission to publish such memoirs with the proviso of giving the entire honorarium to the party, since it was hard for me to take money from the party for my own treatment. In response to this request, I received the immediate decree of the PB that "diplomats or comrades who are engaged in diplo-

matic work are categorically forbidden to publish their memoirs
abroad, or excerpts of their memoirs, without prior review of the
manuscript by the collegium of the NKID and the PB of the CC."
Knowing the kind of delay and tardiness which would occur with
such a double censorship, under which it would not even be possible to contact a foreign publisher, I then refused such a proposal in 1924. Now, having been abroad, I have a new proposal
with a direct guarantee of 20,000 dollars in royalties. But knowing how the history of the party and of the revolution is now being falsified; and considering that I cannot assist in such a falsification, I have no doubt that the image of the PB (and foreign
publishers insist precisely on the most personal character of the
memoirs, that is, on characterization of the people which appear
in them and so forth) will be so tightly restricted, that it will be
impossible to illustrate correctly the activity of either one side or
the other, that is, of either the true leaders of the revolution, or of
the leaders who have now been elevated to this office; thus, without directly violating the PB's decree, I don't feel that it is feasible
to publish my memoirs abroad, and consequently, I don't see the
possibility of being treated without receiving money from the CC,
which clearly feels that it can value my life and health, given my
twenty-seven years of revolutionary activity, at a sum of no more
than 2,000 rubles. In the state which I am now in, I am, of course,
deprived of the chance of doing work of any kind. Even if I found
the strength, despite the hellish pain, to continue giving my lectures, such a situation would demand serious medical care, being
carried about on a stretcher, assistance in getting the necessary
books and materials from the libraries and archives, and so forth.

When I was suffering from the same disease in the past, the
entire personal staff of the embassy was at my service, now, however, according to my "rank" I am not even offered a personal
secretary. Given the lack of attention paid to me, which during
the recent period has been observed during all my illnesses (right
now, as I said, I have been without any real assistance for nine
days, and I haven't been able to obtain even the electric heating
pad which Professor Davidenko prescribed for me), I cannot even
count on such a minor favor as being carried about on a stretcher.
Even if they gave me treatment and sent me abroad for the necessary length of time, the prognosis would remain highly pessimis-
tic: the last time I suffered from polyneuritis I lay motionless for
around two years, and at that time I had no other accompanying
diseases; meanwhile, all my illnesses have derived from this one,

and now I have about six different diseases. Thus, even if I were able to devote the necessary time to treatment, even then I would hardly be in a position to count on even a short period of life after this treatment. So now, when they feel that they cannot give me serious treatment (for treatment in Russia—in the opinion of the doctors—is hopeless, and treatment abroad—for a couple of months—would be just as useless), my life is losing any meaning. Even if I were not to proceed from the philosophy which I outlined above, it would hardly be possible to call somebody's life necessary when it means unbelievable suffering, lying motionless and with no possibility of carrying on any sort of work.

That is why I say that the time has come when I must put an end to this life. I know in general the party's negative opinion of suicide, but I assume that there is hardly anyone who, upon learning of my condition, would be able to condemn me for this step.

In addition, Professor Davidenko states that the reason for the return of my acute illness, polyneuritis, is the turmoil of the recent period. If I were healthy, I would find in myself the necessary strength and energy to fight against the situation which has been created inside the party.

But in my present state I consider such a situation in the party to be unbearable, when it silently puts up with your expulsion from its ranks, although I have absolutely no doubt that sooner or later a turnabout will occur in the party, which will force it to cast off those who have brought it to such a shameful state.

In this sense my death is the protest of a fighter who has been brought to such a state that he can react to so shameful a deed in no other way.

If I might be allowed to compare major and minor events, then I would say that the historical event of supreme importance, the expulsion of you and Zinoviev from the party, which inevitably will be seen as the beginning of the Thermidorian period in our revolution, and the fact that after twenty-seven years of work at responsible party and revolutionary posts, they have put me in a position where nothing else remains for me but to put a bullet into my head—this demonstrates from different directions one and the same regime in the party. Perhaps both these events— major and minor taken together—might manage or are destined to become precisely the impulse which will awaken the party and put a halt to its sliding along the path to Thermidor.

I would be happy if I could be sure that this will be so, for then I would know that I have not died in vain. But although I know with certainty that the moment when the party awakens will come, I cannot be sure that this will happen right away.

I nevertheless have no doubt that my death will be more useful now than my continuing to live.

You and I, dear Lev Davidovich, have been bound by ten years of joint work and personal friendship (I dare to hope). This gives me the right to tell you in parting what I feel is mistaken in you.

I have never had any doubts about the correctness of the path you have marked out, and you know that for more than twenty years I have accompanied you, since the time of the "permanent revolution." But I have always felt that you lack Lenin's refusal to bend or to retreat, his readiness to remain even alone on the path which he feels is correct, foreseeing a future majority, the future recognition by all that this path is correct. Politically, you have always been right, beginning with 1905, and I told you many times that I heard with my own ears how Lenin acknowledged that in 1905 it was you and not he who was right. Before they die, people do not lie, and I repeat this to you one more time now.... But you have often forsaken your personal correctness in favor of an agreement or compromise which you valued too highly. This is a mistake. I repeat, politically you have been right, and now you are more correct than ever before. One day the party will understand this, and history will definitely make the proper assessment. So do not fear if some even abandon you at this time, or, even more so, if others do not come to you as soon as we would like. You are right, but the pledge of the victory of your correct position lies precisely in the maximum refusal to retreat, in the strictest straightforwardness, in the full absence of any compromises, for this always was the secret which lay behind Ilyich's victories. I wanted to tell you this many times in the past, but decided to do it only now, in farewell.

Two words of a personal nature.

I leave behind me a wife who is little adapted to real life, a young son and a sick daughter. I know that you can do nothing for them now, and I can count on absolutely nothing in this regard from the present leadership of the party. But I have no doubt that the time is not far off when you will once again take your appropriate place in the party. Don't then forget my wife and children. I wish you no less energy and audacity than you have displayed up until now, and I wish you the speediest victory. I embrace you firmly. Farewell.

Yours, A. Joffe
Moscow. 16 November 1927.

P.S. This letter was written on the night of the 15-16th, and to-day, on the 16th, Maria Mikhailovna was at the medical commission in order to insist on my trip abroad, if only for one or two months. In response, she was told once again that, in the opinion of the professor-specialists, a short trip abroad would be absolutely useless. She then was told that the medical commission of the CC had decreed that I immediately be transferred to the Kremlin hospital. Thus, I have been denied even a short trip abroad, and the fact that treatment in Russia has no sense whatsoever and will give no positive results is acknowledged, as I said earlier, by all my physicians.

Dear Lev Davidovich, I regret very much that I didn't manage to see you, not because I have doubts about the correctness of the decision I have made and would hope that you would be able to convince me otherwise. No. I have no doubt whatsoever that this is the most rational and most sober of all decisions which I could make. But I fear for my letter; such a letter can't help but be subjective, and in the presence of such acute subjectivism it might lose the criterion of objectivity. Even one false-sounding phrase might ruin the entire impression from the letter. Meanwhile, I, of course, am counting on the fact that you will use this letter, for only in that case will my step be of some use. Therefore I not only give you the most complete freedom to edit my letter, but I even beg of you to exclude from it everything which seems to you to be extraneous, and add whatever you feel should be added.

Well, farewell, my dear friend. Be firm. You will still need much strength and energy. And don't think badly of me.

8

My father's funeral was scheduled for a workday and during working hours. Thousands of people followed the coffin, yet city transport ran as usual, probably so that it would be more difficult to walk along the streets. From out of the fog which enveloped me during those days, I suddenly recall certain small details.

I remember how a young man made his way out of a passing streetcar (the doors at that time didn't shut automatically and people usually hung on outside on the steps). He literally crawled over the heads of the people hanging on, waved his arms and shouted, "A final salute to Comrade Joffe!" Someone walking behind me muttered, "What a lunatic, he'll fall under the streetcar," and someone else replied, "Half of Moscow is filled with such lunatics."

When the procession arrived at the gates of the Novodevichy Cemetery, someone came out and said that only relatives and close friends could enter the grounds of the cemetery. The crowd began to grow angry, and then Trotsky's loud voice could be heard, "In that case, we will organize the funeral proceedings here on the street." The gates opened up, and the funeral was held around the gravesite.

Adolf Abramovich had never been expelled from the party, and he was officially buried by the Central Committee. Representing the CC at the funeral was Riutin, at that time a member of the CC and secretary of the Moscow Committee. This was the same Riutin who a few years later apparently understood what was going on, and then issued a bold and principled platform against Stalin. And, of course, he was shot. But I have already spoken about that.

The last to speak was Trotsky. This was his last public speech in the Soviet Union.

I would like to provide the full text of his speech:

> Comrades, Adolf Abramovich entered into the life of the last decade as a diplomatic representative of the first workers state in history. Here it has been said, it has been said in the press, that he was an outstanding diplomat. This is true. He was an outstanding diplomat, that is, a worker at the post to which he had been sent by the party and by the proletarian regime. He was a great diplomat because he was a revolutionary.
>
> Adolf Abramovich came from a bourgeois milieu, or to be more exact, from a wealthy bourgeois milieu. But, as we know, there have been examples of people coming from that milieu who have so completely, with flesh and blood, torn themselves away from this milieu, that in the future they were no longer in danger of being conquered by petty-bourgeois ideas. He was a revolutionary and remained one to the very end. Here people have spoken—and spoken correctly—about his high intellectual culture. As a diplomat he was forced to move in circles of intelligent, principled and malicious enemies. He knew this world, its mores and its habits, but he wore the mores of this world skillfully and subtly, as a full-dress uniform thrust upon him by his service status. In Adolf Abramovich's soul there were never any uniforms. Here it has been said—and said correctly—that a clichéd approach to any question whatsoever was alien to him. He approached every question as a revolutionary.
>
> He occupied responsible posts, but never was a functionary. He approached every question from the standpoint of the working class, which has risen from the underground to the heights of state power.
>
> He approached every question from the standpoint of the international proletariat and the international revolution—and in this lay his strength, which waged battle with his physical weakness. He retained the force and direction of his mental powers until the last moment, when a bullet, as we still see today, left a dark spot on his right temple.

Comrades, he departed from this life in a seemingly voluntary manner, but no one will dare to condemn or accuse A.A.,
because he departed at that hour when he told himself that he
could give the revolution nothing more than his own death. And
he departed just as steadfastly and courageously as he lived.

Difficult times never frightened him: he was just the same in
October 1917, as a member and then as chairman of the Military-
Revolutionary Committee in Petrograd; he was just the same outside Petrograd, when shells sent by Yudenich were exploding; he
was just the same at the diplomatic table of Brest-Litovsk, and
later in countless capitals of Europe and Asia.

It was not difficulties which frightened him; what forced him
to depart from this life was the impossibility of fighting against
difficulties.

Comrades, allow me to say—and I think that this thought
will fully correspond to the last thoughts and the final testament
of A.A.—such acts as the voluntary exit from life have an infec-
tious quality.

But let no one dare to imitate this old fighter in his death—
imitate him in his life!

We, his close friends, who not only fought but lived side by
side with him for decades, we are forced today to tear from our
hearts the extraordinary image of this man and friend.

He glowed with a soft and even light which warmed the heart.
He was the center of émigré groups, he was the center of exile
groups and he was the center of prison groups.

He came, as I already said, from a well-to-do family, but the
means which were at his disposal during his younger years were
not his personal resources, but the resources of the revolution.
He generously aided his comrades without waiting to be asked,
as a brother and as a friend.

In this coffin before us we have brought here the earthly remains of this extraordinary man, next to whom we were free to
live and struggle. Let us bid him farewell in the same spirit in
which he lived and struggled....

He lived under the banner of Marx and Lenin, it was under
this banner that he died, and we swear to you, Adolf Abramovich,
that we will carry your banner to the very end!

After my father's death and Trotsky's exile, we developed the
Opposition work with particular force. It must be noted that the most
irreconcilable Oppositionists to Stalin's growing regime were precisely

the young people, and especially the student youth. We were most of all impressed by the fact that the Opposition called for the free expression of opinions in the struggle against the spreading bureaucracy.

In the fall of 1927 I resumed my studies at the third year of the institute. It was at this time that my anti-Stalinist activity began. I must say, that of all the inner-party groupings, it was only the Trotskyists who actively fought. We did approximately what revolutionaries did in the czarist underground. We organized groups of sympathizers at the factories and in the schools; we issued leaflets and distributed them.

During my fourth and last year, I became a member of the so-called Moscow Komsomol Center, which contained representatives of the Opposition from all regions of the city. The strongest Opposition group was in our Plekhanov Institute. We, naturally, established contact with young workers, and due to this I became acquainted with many of their representatives. Their real names were not used. At one of these meetings I got to know Roman, one of the leaders of a "group of five." Somewhat later, I met for the second time with the man by the name of Roman. He said that in order to coordinate the work, a Moscow Komsomol Center had been formed, and the general opinion was that I should be sent there from our region.

Soon I was at the first session of this center. I don't remember how many people were there. Probably about ten or fifteen, but perhaps there were more. In any case, all the regions of Moscow were represented. We exchanged information—who among us was connected with what number of people and in what form. As far as I remember, no minutes of the meeting were taken. Nevertheless, a few years later, at one of my interrogations, the investigator read me a very detailed account of the sessions of the Moscow Center. And, after all, only the members of our center were in attendance, there were no outsiders.

At the second session the decision was made to issue leaflets and distribute them at the factories and institutes. We had the possibility of duplicating them either on a rotary press or on a hectograph, I don't remember which.

One young fellow and I were commissioned to write the text of the first leaflet. At the next meeting, each of us was to present his own variant, and then after discussing them, one leaflet would be made from the two versions. We were instructed to describe Stalin's personality and his role in the party situation which had developed. At that time he was not yet "the genius of all times and peoples," but he was clearly gaining strength.

I went home and sat down to write this first leaflet in my life. How should I write it? Behind me were the dispersal of the demonstration on the tenth anniversary of October, the funeral of my father and Trotsky's exile.

I remembered—in a political agitational leaflet, I shouldn't reveal the personal, almost physical revulsion which I experienced in relation to this man, but it was hard for me to maintain complete objectivity.

I got out Lenin's "Letter to the Congress," which was called his "Testament." As people know, it was not published after Lenin died, but we had it at home. My word, why was I wracking my brains—nobody could write better than this: "Comrade Stalin, having become General Secretary, has concentrated an enormous power in his hands; and I am not sure that he always knows how to use that power with sufficient caution." And further: "Stalin is too rude, and this fault, entirely supportable in relations among us Communists, becomes insupportable in the office of General Secretary. Therefore, I propose to the comrades to find a way to remove Stalin from that position and appoint to it another man who in all respects differs from Stalin only in superiority—namely, more patient, more loyal, more polite and more attentive to comrades, less capricious, etc."[1] Using Lenin's letter, I wrote my first leaflet.

At the next session, it was accepted without any changes. The following leaflet concerned the question of how Lenin's instructions on cooperation were being carried out, about the Workers and Peasants Inspection, and was written by me once again with a large number of quotations from Lenin's last works.

Of course, there were leaflets on other questions: about inner-party democracy, about the danger of the bureaucratization of the party apparatus. Here is an excerpt from a leaflet on this question:

"Does bureaucratism contain within it the danger of degeneration? It would be blindness to deny this danger. If allowed to undergo prolonged development, bureaucratism threatens to become cut off from the masses, to focus all its attention on questions of controlling, selecting and removing cadres, to narrow its field of vision and to weaken our revolutionary sensitivity."

This was written in 1928.

As for the theory of permanent revolution, one might agree or disagree with this fundamental thesis of Trotsky, but one cannot deny that its essence lies in an unbounded faith in the inevitability of world revolution.

The impossibility of building a full communist society in a single isolated country was denied by no one, let alone by Lenin.

"If we examine things on a worldwide historical scale, then there can be no doubt that the final victory of our revolution, if it were to remain isolated, if there were to be no revolutionary movement in other countries, would be hopeless."[2]

Opponents of the theory of permanent revolution have also, by the way, referred to Lenin: "The victory of socialism is possible in the beginning in a few, or even in one separate capitalist country. The victorious proletariat of this country, after expropriating the capitalists and organizing socialist production at home, would rise against the rest of the capitalist world, attracting to itself the oppressed classes of other countries and creating an uprising among them against the capitalists."

As the further course of events was to show, the central thesis of permanent revolution proved to be true, that is, the impossibility of building socialist society in a single, isolated country.

It cannot be built even in several countries, if it is introduced artificially, according to one model, and especially with the use of force. And this is just what happened in Hungary in 1956 and in Czechoslovakia in 1968.

But the main thing is that socialism, the shining dream of the best minds of humanity, proved to be discredited by the "socialism" which we have in our country. It has not attracted the "oppressed classes of other lands." The world revolution has not occurred.

We dreamed of putting out our own newspaper, even if it were the very smallest, but we had no chance of doing this at all.

By the end of the 1920s, we were already able to see sprouts of what would flourish in the 1930s: the dictatorship of the degenerated party, and therefore, of the state apparatus, and, finally, the dictatorship of one man, on the national scale in the form of the general secretary, and, lower down, in the form of the secretary of the area committee, regional committee and so on.

Despite the mass expulsions of Oppositionists from the party and Komsomol, neither I nor my father's wife were touched in this period; she wasn't expelled from the party, and I wasn't expelled from the Komsomol. Some think that this was out of respect for my father's memory. I think that here Menzhinsky, who was then head of the OGPU, played a role. He had worked with father in 1918 in the Berlin embassy and respected him very much. He undoubtedly was an intelligent man and, despite the post which he occupied, something human probably still remained in his character.

At our institute, where there was a particularly strong Opposition group, I turned out to be the only person who was not expelled, and I retained the right to attend closed Komsomol and party-Komsomol meetings. Indeed I not only attended, I sometimes spoke as well.

How terrifying it was! An enormous auditorium, filled with hostile faces and bitter taunts from those present. To my delight, the wife of one of our comrades, a member of the Komsomol, was transferred to our institute. She shared our views, but no one knew about it, and she was not expelled. She sat in the first row, and when it came my time to speak, I always looked at this Zoika so I could see at least one friendly face.

The leaflets, the meetings in private apartments—all this continued. But, I repeat, the forces were uneven.

In one of his prerevolutionary articles, Lenin wrote: "We are marching in a compact group along a precipitous and difficult path, firmly holding each other by the hand."[3] That was what it was like for us. We were going in a tight group along the edge of a precipice, which was not only deep but fatal for many of those who went.

At the end of 1928 they began to exile people in groups from Moscow, beginning with members of the Central Committee and ending with Komsomol members at my level. They were mostly sent to Siberia, Central Asia and Kazakhstan.

This wave of exiles coincided with the acts of repentance by Zinoviev and Kamenev.

In May 1929, Radek, Preobrazhensky and Smilga wrote a letter of repentance. A declaration—in, it is true, a somewhat more restrained form—was written by such an experienced Trotskyist cadre as Pyatakov. Whole pages of *Pravda* were devoted to the names of people who had placed their signatures beneath one declaration or another. Each who had "repented" in this way was returned from exile and reinstated in the party. A ditty was making the rounds: "If you miss your family and your teapot too, write a letter to the head of the GPU."

They arrested me in the spring of 1929.

I was seven months pregnant, and therefore, in those relatively liberal times, they didn't hold me in prison, but had me sign a note that I would not escape and then summoned me for interrogation.

I was questioned by Rutkovsky, an investigator of particularly special cases, who was later shot along with Yagoda. At this time I was finishing up at the institute and, besides my interrogations, was taking a series of tests (there were no formal exams at that time). I understood that if I didn't pass my tests now, I would never finish the institute. Despite my pregnancy and the interrogations, I nevertheless graduated.

The interrogations were not hard. I fully admitted belonging to the Opposition and denied only my underground work. Otherwise I would have had to name some names, which I didn't want to do.

When I finished at the institute, I received permission from Rutkovsky, who evidently was tired of useless conversations, to travel to Leningrad.

On August 20 I gave birth to my daughter and on October 20, after allowing me the legally required leave, they sent me into exile to Krasnoyarsk for a period of three years. As they used to say at that time, "arrivals regulate departures," that is, the more people who returned after signing declarations, the more harshly the authorities dealt with those who had not signed them.

But all these events were like "blossoms" compared to the "berries" of 1937....

I left for exile not with a group of prisoners, but in an ordinary railway passenger car, with my husband, child and nanny.

My husband Pavel took ten days off at his own expense in order to accompany us. The decision had been made that he (and the same applied to another group of comrades) wouldn't reveal himself openly as an Oppositionist, so that he could remain in the party.

9

In Krasnoyarsk, where I was sent, there was a colony of about seven or eight Oppositionists. Among them were two Muscovites. One was an acquaintance of mine named Samuil Yakovlevich Krol, chairman of the Central Committee of the food workers union, an extremely kind and good person, whom everyone liked and affectionately called "Krolik." The other was Lado Yenukidze, the nephew of Avel Safronovich Yenukidze, permanent secretary of the VTsIK (the All-Union Central Executive Committee). Avel Yenukidze had no children of his own, and for him Lado was not simply a nephew, but something of an adopted son.

When the "genius of all times and peoples" had not yet become a genius, but was simply an ordinary member of the Central Committee, he lived with Yenukidze in the same apartment; they were considered to be bosom buddies.

Avel Safronovich was shot in 1937. "Cain, where is thy brother, Abel?"

In exile we all worked at normal jobs, usually according to our specialization. Those who didn't want to work (and there were such people) were not forced to do so. Once every ten days we would report to the NKVD, and the head of Krasnoyarsk NKVD, a certain Tulyakov (an incredibly handsome man, but also incredibly stupid), would say, "I simply don't know how to talk to you. Today you are an

73

exile, and tomorrow you'll write a declaration and they might send you back to me as some kind of boss."

One day when I was reporting, I got to know an exile from another category, a genuine state, or perhaps privy, councillor, Dumbadze. He was the brother of Yalta's governor-general, the famous Dumbadze. I don't know what the Yalta Dumbadze was like, but his brother was a very cultured and interesting man to talk with.

Despite the considerable difference in our ages, he was happy to converse with me. He said, "I can see immediately that you are a girl from a good family." I answered, "Yes, from a good Jewish family." He was a bit offended and replied, "You know, Georgians have never been anti-Semites." He told what life was like at the court, how he personally knew Nikolai and the czarina and how he used to meet with Rasputin.

Stewing, as they say, from an early age in these circles, he understood the necessity of certain changes. He said that what was most difficult for him to bear after the revolution was not the loss of wealth, or even the loss of his social position, but the fact that he had stopped understanding.

"You know," he said, "it always seemed to me that I could understand everything. I understood Nietzsche and the French Encyclopedists, I understood Shakespeare and Beethoven, but I cannot understand what is going on now. The revolution was made in a peasant country. If that were bad for me and those like me, but good for the peasants, believe me, I would understand. But even in the times of the worst harvests and famines, the peasants didn't suffer as much as they do now. I simply cannot understand why this is so, and who needs it to be this way."

Collectivization was already under way. What could I say to him?...

I had a particularly difficult time in exile. It was doubly difficult. First of all, it was difficult at work because I was working for the first time in my specialty and immediately became convinced that the institute had given us little which helped in practical work. It gave us a general education, methodology and the ability to work with books. But, my word, how little all this helped me in my job as the economist for the Krasnoyarsk fruit and vegetable union, where I ended up due to the good graces of the local authorities. At the same time, having a higher education brought a great deal of responsibility. It was assumed that I should know everything and be able to do everything. Whereas I knew nothing and could do nothing. And there was no one to turn to. My immediate superior, who didn't even have a high school education, openly despised me. In his own way, he was right. What good were my culture and my erudition to him, when I had no conception whatsoever of the state of the fruit and vegetable economy in the Krasnoyarsk region? In general, I resembled a person who doesn't know how to swim, but who is thrown into deep water — flounder about and maybe you'll swim. So I floundered about. But it wasn't easy, particularly if you consider that I was all of twenty-three years old and had a rather high opinion of myself.

It was even more difficult at home. My loving relatives, who were in horror that I was setting off to such distant parts with a two-month-old infant, not having any idea of how to take care of her, provided me with an experienced, well-qualified Moscow nanny. She felt that her job was the child, and not once did she even wash a glass for herself. There could be no talk of my cooking at home. I ate at the cafeteria, and, as a supplement to her pay, gave her money every day for lunch, and then, when I came home from work, she would go to the cafeteria. At night she never got up with the child, and my daughter (no doubt in revenge for her stormy existence in the womb) cried constantly and didn't sleep for nights on end. When she was two or three months old, on the advice of a doctor, she was given special baths for insomnia, since normal children at that age sleep the greater part of the day.

I went to work without ever getting a good night's sleep, which also didn't facilitate my success on the service front.

This all came to an end in January 1930, when Pavel arrived (I'll explain later how he managed to come). He sized up the situation, immediately bought the nanny a railway ticket and sent her back to Moscow. Then he found a young girl to be a nanny. She was the daughter of the people in charge of my apartment. I simply breathed a sigh of relief. My new nanny had no high qualifications, but she was a wonderful, kind girl. In addition, she was helped out by her mother, who had managed quite simply to raise six healthy children.

It must be said that no one would take me into their apartment since I had a nursing infant. But two elderly Jews rented me a room; they had lived for forty years in Krasnoyarsk, but had maintained all the Jewish traditions. They took us in simply because I was Jewish. They felt that I was a person who had been lost for Judaism, which was, by the way, absolutely correct.

The entire family adored my Tuska (that's what we called Natasha at that time). The old head of the household would often sigh and say to me, "Just look, no matter what you are, your child is a real Jewish infant. How beautiful she is, how bright she is!"

For me, the Krasnoyarsk epic ended in March 1930.

At that time the party organizations in Moscow and Leningrad were conducting the "party mobilization," that is, Communists were being sent to work in the provinces. They were assigned to more or less leading positions, and not in some out-of-the-way backwater (some "Tmutarakan"), but for the most part a regional or provincial center. Nevertheless, the majority tried to find a way out and not go. Popular folklore took note of this phenomenon with the following ditty: "I want to live with my family and not as a stranger on the periphery," and so on.

Pavel went to his own party organization and asked them to send him to work in Siberia. Because of some lists, people were not being sent to Siberia just then, but they latched onto him and proposed that he choose either Central Asia or the Far East. He chose the Far East (at least it was in the same direction) and counted on finding something when he arrived at his destination. So, along the way to the Far East, he stopped for a week in Krasnoyarsk, straightened things out with the nannies and went on his way. He was heading for Khabarovsk, where he would be at the disposal of the area committee (obkom). The obkom sent him to work at the regional financial directorate.

During almost the entire civil war, he had been the commissar of a food requisition detachment and, of course, took part in battles. He could easily have served as a prototype for Joseph Kogan, one of the heroes in Bagritsky's works. Probably many recall the ending of *Thoughts about Opanas*: "Thus let me die at Popov Log, let me meet the same glorious death as Joseph Kogan."

He had very many chances to die "the same glorious death," or some other, not so glorious. But he stayed alive and after demobilization returned to his native Petrograd. His subsequent work, out of inertia, was connected with financial agencies.

The first thing he did when he arrived in Khabarovsk and received an appointment was to direct an appeal of the following character to the party obkom. His wife and infant child were in Krasnoyarsk, where she had been exiled for belonging to the Opposition. He was preparing to take measures to transfer her so that she could be with him in Khabarovsk and was asking the sanction of the obkom for this action.

What idyllic times these were!

For such an impudent declaration they didn't put him in prison, they didn't even expel him from the party. No, they asked him a few questions about me, primarily of an anecdotal character, and, when they found out that I was only twenty-three, they said, "Ai-ai-ai! That's only the age of a Komsomolka! Bring her here, we'll reeducate her."

Pavel replied that that wasn't my character type, and that he could give no guarantees about my reeducation. To which they replied, "But we'll try in any case." Therefore the petition for my transfer from Krasnoyarsk to Khabarovsk was approved by the Far East obkom. In March 1930, my daughter and I were already in Khabarovsk.

From Krasnoyarsk to Khabarovsk I traveled in a railway coach. It is true, I had an escort, in the form of one sergeant. He turned out to be a wonderful and helpful fellow; at the stops he would buy me yogurt and rolls. My neighbors in our compartment, a married couple, assumed that I was the wife of some high-ranking military officer, who had given me this sergeant as a servant. They looked askance at me the whole way and demonstratively paid attention only to my seven-month-old Tuska. From time to time, the wife even muttered to herself, "They've brought back officers' servants, just like it used to be." This angered me somewhat, although if I were in their place, I probably would have acted the same way.

As we approached Khabarovsk, I used the occasion when my sergeant left the compartment to explain to them what the real situation was. I will never forget with what amazed and enthusiastic expressions they looked at me. Each one of them shook my hand with both of his or her own, and the wife (who, evidently, was more emotional in nature) added, "Please, forgive us."

Pavel met us at the station in Khabarovsk. He wanted to arrange to greet us as well as he could, so he asked for an auto from an acquaintance in the regional executive committee (there were very few cars at that time in Khabarovsk). His friend said that he would do it with pleasure, but the auto that was at his disposal had been taken to the GPU — they were bringing someone in under escort, and all their cars were somewhere else. As it then turned out, I was the one being brought in under escort.

My sergeant took me to the Khabarovsk GPU headquarters, and for all the subsequent years of my exile, this was the first and last time I was there. I asked whether I had to report, and they said that there were no exiles here besides me, so I wouldn't have to report — "If we need you, we will find you." On this note we parted.

Pavel headed the budget department in the regional financial directorate. The budget of the region to a significant degree determined the growth of its industry and in general its economy, and if one considers that the Far Eastern region embraced a territory in which two Frances and a Luxembourg could fit, the volume of his work was rather large. I began to work in the regional council of the people's economy, leading a group engaged in "scientific research work." The entire "group" consisted of myself and half a statistician (one statistician served two groups). Having "floundered around" for a year and a half in Krasnoyarsk, I felt much more confident. The atmosphere at work was absolutely different; it was much more pleasant. Soon I grew so emboldened that I began to write articles for a local journal which dealt with questions of history, ethnography and the economy of the region. My articles were published and I was even paid an honorarium.

We managed to find a good nanny. A pretty good circle of friends formed around us and my status as an exile even gave me a certain additional authority.

But I nevertheless managed to ruin my husband's "career." After about a year's time, the post of first deputy of the director of the regional financial administration (kraifu) became vacant, and Pavel was the leading candidate. But this position was a nomenklatura position of the People's Commissariat, and it had to be approved by the regional committee (kraikom). As we later learned from unofficial sources, in the kraikom they "scratched their heads." "A year ago we supported his petition about transferring his exiled wife to join him. For a year, the exiled wife has shown not the slightest intention of repenting. And now, we're supposed to give him a promotion. No, it isn't worth the trouble...."

The head of the kraifu was Shalimov, who had known Pavel at the front and very much wanted to have him as his deputy. He tried to intervene, but got nowhere. The deputy, on the recommendation of the kraikom, became a worker who was promoted to the administrative post. Pavel said that, in general, he didn't want to work in the administrative apparatus and asked them to send him to any other region. Shalimov replied that, of course, this would be correct, for a while it would be better not to plague them with his presence, "and there he would be visible."

So we left for Spassk. This was the same place which is mentioned in the song: "Nights of fighting in Spassk, days of fighting in Volochaevka." There had been no nighttime battles for a long time, and the days were very boring. I went to work in the branch of the state bank. I went there very reluctantly, there simply was no other choice. But it turned out that I worked for many years in the state bank system and even got my pension from this system.

Fortunately, the Spassk epic did not last a long time. Pavel was clearly not suited to be a worker at the regional level and soon was transferred to Vladivostok. It should be said that in the regional system Vladivostok was something like "the free city of Novgorod." It had its own planning indices and accounted for them directly to Moscow, although administratively it was part of the Far Eastern region. In general it was a very unusual city.

Although Khabarovsk was considered the capital of the region, it was much more provincial than Vladivostok. That was probably because Vladivostok was a typical port city: ocean liners at the dock, a mass of sailors and foreigners and an amazingly colorful bazaar, at which you could buy everything you wanted at unbelievable prices, from black caviar to Chinese collapsible paper toys.

According to Pavel's position in Vladivostok (head of the city financial department, deputy chairman of the city executive committee, member of the bureau of the city committee), we belonged to the "Great Soviet" elite. And I, most of all, was struck by the daily life of this elite. I remembered starving Moscow of 1919-20. I remembered how my mama and I lived; I was often at the Vorovskys (my mother was friends with his wife), I was at the Trotskys. People who occupied the number one posts in the state were fed just a bit better than the average inhabitant of Moscow.

Pavel recalled how in 1920 he had been deputy commissar of supplies in the city of Odessa, and his wife, who had just given birth to their child, lived mainly on cucumbers, which were sold for practically nothing, and the baby had diarrhea from hunger.

It was widely known that Tsiurupa, the people's commissar of supplies, fainted from hunger at a session of the sovnarkom.

This was clearly another epoch.

At the Vladivostok cafeteria for members of the city committee, at lunch one could have any appetizers in an unlimited quantity. There were wonderful cakes, pies and whipped cream for dessert. There was also, of course, a special, closed distributor for members of the city committee. There, for very reasonable prices, you could buy the best imported things which had been confiscated as contraband.

That was how life was for all the responsible personnel throughout the entire periphery of our vast homeland, without, perhaps, the contraband, which was probably made up for by something else.

Despite this "feast during the time of plague," the first secretary of the Vladivostok city committee, Vladimir Verny, was a man of high personal principles and modesty. When Verny's wife needed a car, she would hide this from her husband and ask for it from one of the comrades; Verny didn't allow the city committee car to be used for personal matters. They had a daughter, Inessa, who was then seven or eight years old. She was very sickly and needed some kind of supplementary food. He said quite firmly that she would get only what was stipulated by the law.

Pavel and he immediately found much in common and established contact not only at work, but had warm, personal relations.

In Vladivostok I worked for a while in the state bank and then went on pregnancy leave. In July 1932 my second daughter, Kira, was born. Pavel had his regular vacation coming, and we set off for Moscow.

Although the official three-year term of my exile had already ended, it was clear that they wouldn't allow me to work in Moscow. I always loved Moscow very much. It was my native city, but at that time even I didn't have any great desire to remain. As Nekrasov wrote: "they can't entice me to enter that wasted forest; where once the oak trees reached high into the skies, now only stumps stick up from the ground...." Pavel's vacation ended and he left for Vladivostok, whereas I remained for a bit with the children in Moscow. While we had been gone, major changes had taken place.

Verny, the first secretary of the city committee, had been transferred from Vladivostok to Blagoveshchensk. This was a clear demotion. Evidently his principled nature and modesty in everyday life had stuck in the throats of others there.

The behavior of the first secretary set the tone. It is no accident that they say, "Like priest, like parish," and the "parish" clearly didn't want to live in that way.

Verny proposed that Pavel go with him, and my husband agreed.

Therefore, when I left with my children from Moscow, our journey lay not in the direction of Vladivostok, but of Blagoveshchensk. But the trip was no shorter, and I had with me three "fellow travelers": Yura, the ten-year-old son of Pavel and his first wife; Tala, who was three and a half; and Kira, who was eight months old.

I didn't have to complain of being bored on this journey. But everything comes to an end, and this did as well. Pavel met us at a station with the funny name of Yerofei Pavlovich (it turns out that these were the first and middle name of Khabarov). From there a branch of the railroad went to Blagoveshchensk.

Blagoveshchensk was such a deeply provincial town that Vladivostok by comparison was Paris. But even this town had its own special features. It was situated on the banks of the Amur, and on the opposite side was the Japanese buffer-state of Manchukuo. The border ran down the middle of the river. Along the entire riverbank, on

both sides, were border posts. Because of this, there were many incidents, both humorous and serious. One of the members of the city
committee had a rendezvous with the wife of another member of the
city committee. The affair happened in the summertime. They walked
for a long time along the riverbank and were looking for a comfortable place to "touch down." At last they found one. But apparently it
was too close to the river and the border guards caught them. They
were taken to the outpost and it quickly became clear "who was who."
Of course, they were immediately released, but there was a scandal in
both the "noble families." A second incident was more tragic. It also
happened to one of the members of the city committee, a very friendly
fellow named Misha Volkov. He was a guest at somebody's place, got
extremely drunk and set out for his home late at night. In
Blagoveshchensk at that time, there were almost no streetlights; only
the main square where the bazaar was located had lighting at night.
And Volkov lived right next to the bazaar. He apparently stumbled
along the dark streets for a long time and finally came upon a clear
space with bright lights. He headed for the lights with the full certainty that he was crossing the bazaar square. In actuality he was crossing the frozen Amur, and the lights which he saw were the lights of
Manchukuo. How he made it past the border guards is inexplicable.
The Japanese first beat him and then informed our authorities. They
bought his release for hard currency and then sentenced him to prison.
That's how the good man Misha Volkov ended up in prison for nothing at all.

At the end of 1933 there was a party purge. It was conducted in
Blagoveshchensk by a plenipotentiary from the regional committee in
Khabarovsk—one of those who once objected to my transfer from
Krasnoyarsk.

Pavel was expelled from the party "for contact with the active
Trotskyist Joffe." Not having yet lost his sense of humor, Pavel said
that this was probably the only time that the word "contact" was used
in the most literal sense.

He was removed from his job immediately; a nonparty figure, much
less someone expelled from the party, could not occupy such a position. The temporary substitute of the head of the city finance depart-

ment (gorfo) became his replacement. But for a whole month, while we still lived in Blagoveshchensk waiting for the decision of the kraikom, all the workers at the gorfo came to see Pavel at home, since he had not been able to convince them that they shouldn't.

Upon arriving in Moscow, Pavel sent an appeal to the Central Control Commission. He took Yura to his mother in Leningrad, and we all lived with my mama.

The Central Control Commission, of course, confirmed the expulsion with the same formulation.

Our friends from Leningrad and the Far East, Tolya and Esya, had at that time made their way from Khabarovsk to Moscow. Tolya worked as the head of the planning department of glavdortrans, an organization which supervised automobile transport throughout the Soviet Union. The head of glavdortrans was also from the Far East; he had been deputy chairman of the regional executive committee and knew Pavel. They proposed that he work as a nonparty specialist. But to do this he needed a Moscow residency permit. At that time, the internal passport system had already been established (we received our passports in Blagoveshchensk) and residency permits were strictly enforced. I could be given such a permit under one "minor" condition: that I write a declaration acknowledging my mistakes. I had already mentioned that such declarations had been written and signed in vast numbers during 1929-30. Later they were also written and signed, but not in such great quantities.

It is hard to imagine what pressure was put on me to sign. It started with my family: first of all my mama, her brother and my favorite grandmother. My father's family joined in: his sister and brothers. Pavel's family added to the pressure: his sisters Asya and Olya came to visit us from Leningrad, Asya's husband came as well. Our friends insisted, too: Tolya, Esya. My friends from the Opposition who had already signed and returned to Moscow joined in applying pressure. In short, everyone was trying to persuade me. With the one exception of Pavel. And the main argument everyone gave was the example of the older comrades whom I respected, former active Oppositionists who at that time had left the Opposition. In reply to this I always answered, "And Rakovsky?" It so happened that just at that time, like a bolt from the blue, Rakovsky's statement appeared in the newspapers. It was written in the most restrained manner: "I committed mistakes.... I ask to be returned to the party...." approximately like that. But nevertheless it was a statement. And Rakovsky had written it. If it had been anyone else but Rakovsky ... Rakovsky, who was Trotsky's great friend, Rakovsky, who was the friend of my father, who had been in the funeral commission as the representative "of friends."

So I began to reflect. Perhaps I truly didn't understand something, for you couldn't compare my political experience with that of Rakovsky, a man who had been engaged in revolutionary activity for forty years. In Bulgaria and in Romania, in France and in Russia. I couldn't suspect him of lacking principles. And although I felt that I could not write a statement, he had written one. That means, one of us was mistaken. Which one? According to all objective evidence, there could be no doubt. But nevertheless?...

I called him on the telephone and he immediately said, "Come on over."

He lived at that time on Tverskoi Boulevard. When I arrived, his daughter Lena and her husband were with him. Lena was the daughter of his wife, but he had adopted her in childhood, and she bore his patronymic and last name. At home they called her by the amusing Romanian name Kokutsa. Her husband was the famous poet Joseph Utkin. We very much admired his poems, "Red-haired Motele" and others, and I would have been glad to get to know them. But at that moment he was not the purpose of my visit. They left, and I remained to have a talk with Christian Georgievich. He spoke with me very well, seriously and confidentially. His basic thoughts were that we had to return to the party in any way possible. He felt that there was undoubtedly a layer in the party which shared our views at heart, but had not decided to voice their agreement. And we could become a kind of common sense core and be able to accomplish something. Left in isolation, he said, they would strangle us like chickens.

Apparently, there was no political experience which could provide an idea of what lay before us....

At the end of our conversation I asked him, "What do you think, if my father were alive, would he agree with you?" He didn't answer at once. He thought for a while, and then said, "He was an intelligent man and a sober politician. I think that he would agree with me."

The following day, I signed a brief statement, "I request that my signature be added to Comrade Rakovsky's statement."

They gave Pavel and me a residency permit in Moscow, and he began to work, first as a nonparty person in the planning department of glavdortrans, the director of which was his friend Tolya Gorenshtein.

After a while I too began to work, in one of the branches of the state bank. We lived in our old apartment on Sretensky Boulevard, in a large room which my grandmother had maintained for us. It was crowded, of course, with four of us in one room, and a babysitter too, but what could be done....

I became very close to my brother. Vladimir, Volya, was my brother through our father. He was eight years old when father died and ten when his mother was sent into exile. She didn't take him with her, since she felt that it would be better for him not to go.

By the time he was fifteen, he was not your average boy. He was completely apolitical and never even joined the Komsomol. He loved poetry very much and wrote his own poems, which were unusual for someone his age. I think that he was talented. I can never forgive myself for not having memorized a single one of his poems. He showed his poems to Dolmatovsky, a rather well-known poet at that time, who said that my brother's calling in life was poetry.

Like the majority of boys his age, he was in love. The object of his love was a pioneer leader in school, a woman much older than he was. There was nothing surprising about this—boys of fifteen often fall in love with older women. But Volodya's feelings far exceeded the usual infatuation of an adolescent. And he, in general, did not fit the pattern of a boy his age.

At the beginning of 1936 he was sent from Moscow; they sent him to his mother, who was then in exile.

Soon after he left, they arrested me. I spent the next ten years in Kolyma and learned almost nothing about Volya.

Maria Mikhailovna, his mother, served her prison camp term in Vorkuta. Where he was, and how he lived at that time, I do not know. Later, during my second exile, I met people who had known Maria

Mikhailovna. I tried very hard to find something out about Volya, but the information was contradictory. Some said that he had enrolled in Tomsk University, had passed his exams with distinction, but had not graduated "for biographical reasons." Others said that he died in prison; according to some, he had been shot; according to others, he had committed suicide. If that had happened in 1938, that means he would have been nineteen years old.

When Musya (Maria) returned to Moscow, on papa's gravestone in the Novodevichy Cemetery (on which were indicated my father's full name and the years of his birth and death), one more line was added: "In memory of Volodya Joffe, son, born in 1919."

On December 1, 1934, Kirov was murdered.

The first announcement in the newspapers was very laconic: He was murdered in the corridor outside the doors of his office. The murderer was a party member, Nikolaev.

Of course, every kind of rumor immediately began to circulate spontaneously. Some insisted that it had been an act of personal revenge on the part of Nikolaev, since Kirov had stolen his wife. Among our acquaintances there were people who knew Kirov personally; they said that this could very well be. But after a few days, a more lengthy article appeared, stating that the organizers of the murder were Zinoviev and Kamenev. We no longer had any doubts; we knew who needed this and for what purpose.

Running ahead, I would like to add something more. In 1956, when those of us who survived returned after rehabilitation, my friend Boris Arkadievich Livshits (I will say more about him later) was in Leningrad visiting the wife of his old friend Pyotr Smorodin. In the 1920s, Smorodin had been secretary of the Central Committee of the Komsomol, and Boris had worked in the apparatus of the Central Committee. At the time of Kirov's murder, i.e., in the 1930s, Smorodin worked in the Leningrad area committee (obkom), where he was one of the deputies and a friend of Kirov. Pyotr was shot in 1939, but his wife returned from exile in 1956. And this is what she told Boris, repeating, of course, what her husband had told her.

Kirov returned from Moscow after the Seventeenth Party Congress, at which he was elected to the Central Committee almost unanimously, whereas Stalin was last on the list and had barely gathered the necessary number of votes. Kirov thus said to Smorodin, "Petro! I haven't long to live, he will never forgive me for this." And he did not forgive. He never forgave not only Kirov, but the entire congress.

At the congress there were 1,956 delegates; 1,108 were arrested and accused of counterrevolutionary activity. Of the 139 people elected at that congress to membership or candidate membership in the CC, 98 were shot, or 70 percent. Of the members and candidate members of the CC who were shot, one had been in the party since 1918 and one other since 1920. All the rest had been members of the party since well before the revolution.

At the beginning of 1935 a wave of repression began. Within two months Pavel was summoned to see the director of glavdortrans. In a very mild form he was asked to tender a statement about being relieved from his job for personal reasons. "That way it will be better both for you and for us." Pavel said that he would submit no such statement, that he had no desire to resign "for personal reasons." "If they need to fire me, let them fire me," he said to me. "It will be interesting to see what formulation they use to do so." Just recently he had received a commendation in his department, and his photograph hung on the Board of Distinction.

But he nevertheless submitted a statement: because of Tolya. If he left of his own volition, everything would be calm and quiet—who knows what reasons a man has. But if he were fired and a scandal ensued, things would have to be called by their real names, and the question would inevitably arise: "Who recommended him? Who accepted him?"

Someone would remember that he and Gorenshtein had been friends for a long time. All this would bring Tolya major unpleasantries. That is why, for his sake, Pavel handed in his resignation. Of course, he immediately began to look for work, first in his specialty and then any office work. Then, any work at all. At a factory, in a shop, as a nightwatchman at a warehouse. They wouldn't hire him anywhere. He wasn't hired at the last jobs because he was "too much of an intellectual."

During this entire time I continued to work at the bank, and they didn't touch me. Inscrutable indeed are the ways of the NKVD!

Hard times fell upon us. Four people lived on my meager wages. From time to time, mama took care of her favorite Tala for a few days, but this didn't save the situation. By the way, once she helped us in a very appreciable way. In the summer of 1935, she arranged a free stay for me and my children at a children's sanitorium in Anapa. Since her husband worked at the People's Commissariat of Public Transport, the trip there was free as well.

I was very reluctant to leave Pavel alone, but for the sake of the children, I, of course, had to go. We spent six weeks in Anapa and returned to Moscow in September. Our friends surreptitiously found Pavel whatever work came their way: financial accounting, proofreading, annotating books. Since we had for a long time been without a babysitter, Pavel and I shared the housework together; he spent a great deal of time with the children.

But all this came to an end. Unexpectedly and horribly.

On April 11, 1936, they arrested me.

PART 2

1

The evening that they arrested me, we were at mama's, telling her how we had taken our younger daughter, Kirochka, to the hospital, for she had come down with scarlet fever. Fortunately, our older daughter was in a forestry school outside Moscow. We were sadly recalling how our younger child had cried when they took her from us.

After eleven, the bell rang. Two men came in wearing NKVD uniforms. They didn't present any arrest order, they just very politely asked me to go with them to the Lubyanka, "for twenty minutes, or a half an hour at the maximum." Pavel said that he wanted to come along. Our "guests" glanced at each other, "Well, all right. Please, come along."

We went down the stairs. By the entrance stood a passenger car, not a "raven" (paddy wagon), but an ordinary car.

At the Lubyanka, they led me away, without even giving me the chance to say good-bye. They produced the arrest order there. Then they led me to a cell, where I spent the night in solitary.

The cell resembled a hotel room of average quality: good bed, clean linen, a side table next to the bed. Later I became convinced that the more cleanliness, quiet and order there is in a prison, the more terrible it is....

They let Pavel return home and made a search of our apartment. A year later, in 1937, when every third person awaited arrest, people prepared for searches and destroyed everything extraneous.

I was among the "first swallows," and we didn't expect to be arrested. At home we had Trotsky's collected works, which had come out in the twenties, with the author's inscription to mama. Not long before, my mama had married. When she moved to a new apartment and began her new life, mama left all this with me.

There was also "seditious literature" which belonged to me personally: a book by David Borisovich Ryazanov, with the inscription: "To an old Komsomolka from an Old Bolshevik." There were a number of documents relating to the death of my father. In general, there was plenty of work for those conducting the search. At the interrogation I, of course, said that everything in our apartment belonged to me.

In the morning they took me to Butyrki Prison in a "raven." There they went through the whole procedure: fingerprints, photograph, body search, shower. They took away my garters, the belt to my skirt, shoelaces and hairpins.

I remember how I was struck by the degradation and absurdity of all this. What could a person do with hairpins? Even if the absurd idea popped into someone's head to hang himself by his shoelaces, then how could this actually be done? They simply had to place a person in a revolting and humiliating position, where one's skirt would fall down, stockings would slip and shoes would shuffle.

So there I was in the cell, one of the four cells of the women's "political corridor." In the cell there were 200 people. Along the walls were bunkbeds. My journey started in the corner near the slop bucket. As the population of the cell changed and places became free, I moved closer and closer to the window, and the women who arrived after me, in turn, began their journey at the slop bucket. Order was strictly kept by the cell's elder, a certain Nonna (I don't remember her surname). Nonna, as they explained to me, was the most splendid prostitute in Moscow, and among her "clients" were high-placed officials and foreigners. That is why she fell under Article 58 (betraying the motherland).

At this time Butyrki held a large group of young people, organizers from the park of culture and recreation, almost all of whom were in the Komsomol. They were charged with counterrevolutionary propaganda. I was joined in my cell by Klava Gushchina, the wife of the "leader" of this group, Arkadii Tokman. Arkadii was later shot; what Klava's fate was, I don't know.

I was very troubled when I met a German communist who had escaped from a fascist camp. With enormous difficulty she had made it to the Soviet Union, to her socialist fatherland. The socialist fatherland greeted her ... with prison. She didn't speak a word of Russian, and simply couldn't understand what was going on. It seemed to her that there was some kind of monstrous misunderstanding. She was very glad to see me, at last she could clear things up in German. But I couldn't explain anything to her.

Pavel was seized ten days after I was. He brought me one package and divided his time between the Botkin hospital, where Kirochka lay, and Butyrki prison. He had grown so exhausted from anticipation that for the first time in ten days he slept soundly on the Butyrki bunks, next to the slop bucket. All that could happen had already happened.

The energetic fellows from the park of culture arranged correspondence throughout the entire prison and immediately organized contact for us. I found out about the arrest of my husband the next day. Pavel was a very good father, caring and affectionate. The thought that he was with the children was very comforting for me. Now, even this comfort had been taken away.

The investigator Rogov didn't resemble my first investigator Rutkovsky in any way. The latter had been a Chekist trained by Dzerzhinsky, with all the resulting pluses and minuses: he was intelligent and spiteful, educated and cruel. While he lost out to Rutkovsky in many ways, Rogov had, by comparison, one unarguable and decisive plus: he was humane. At that time, an investigator still could be humane.

At the first interrogation I declared that I would say nothing until I had been provided with information about the status of my sick child. And every time that I came to be questioned, he handed me the phone and I talked with the physician on duty.

On May 14, the day I turned thirty, he arranged for me a meeting with Pavel—we were both called in for questioning at the same time. Pavel gave me his own gift, a piece of chocolate bought at Butyrki .

The interrogations were directed for the most part at my Oppositional activity in 1927-28, and proceeded rather blandly: "Do you know so-and-so?" "No, I don't know that person." During my questioning I understood that a whole number of comrades who had been connected with me during that period had been arrested.

The women's "political corridor" in Butyrki consisted of four cells, and they didn't put people involved in the same case in the same cell. It is true, there were incidents which were both somewhat curious and somewhat sad. All of the former wives of one of the arrested Trotskyists had also been arrested. It turned out that there were five of them, but only four cells, so two of the wives wound up in the same cell. They were both, by the way, former wives, and they got along very well.

A person gets used to everything. Even prison life, with all its monstrosities, becomes routine. Friends appear. The fate of people who only yesterday were strangers is felt with the same acuteness as the fate of the people closest to you.

From the party layer in the cell I remember Alya Chumakova, who ended up in Vorkuta, Berta Gurvich (her fate is unknown) and Liza Osminskaya, whom I later met in Kolyma. I will talk about her later. The overwhelming majority in the cell were the "idle chatterers" or "joke tellers," who were there according to Article 58.

I remember the very kind and sweet Shurochka Zakharina. She had a friend, "so respectable, cultured, so attentive." She went with him to the theater, to the movies. She expressed various opinions about the plays and films. Apparently, these opinions didn't always coincide with the official point of view. When they arrested her, the basis for the charges was precisely those opinions, which had been expressed tête-à-tête to the "respectable" and "attentive" "friend." I don't know why they had to imprison poor Shurochka. Probably her "friend" had to fulfill a "plan."

I remember a sixteen-year-old girl, Asya. She worked on the Chinese-Eastern Railway Line. When this railway was sold, all its personnel returned to Moscow. And they put them all in prison. When

Asya was summoned to her first interrogation, she immediately fainted. She wasn't pretending; she genuinely lost consciousness out of fear, out of horror, out of not knowing what to say and what not to say.

In the cell there were a few people who had been transferred from the internal prison of the NKVD (the Lubyanka), where I had spent my first night of imprisonment. They told how a certain Meshkovskaya was being held there; her first husband had been a Trotskyist in the twenties. She had separated from him long ago. Her second husband was an official in the party's CC and recently had been ambassador to Mexico.

Meshkovskaya studied Spanish and upon returning to Moscow worked in the Spanish section of the Comintern. It must be said that at that time quite a few of the Comintern workers had been arrested, especially those connected with Spain (the rest were rounded up in 1937).

Meshkovskaya was interrogated for whole nights in a row, and often was brought back only toward morning. The first time she was relatively calm, since she felt that she was guilty of nothing and even hoped to be released. But after about a month, her mood changed drastically. Now she was convinced that she was just as guilty as all those who were around her. She admired the talent of the NKVD operatives, who were able to find crimes where she didn't even suspect they existed. For hours on end she would sit there, deep in thought, trying to imagine someone else she should name from among the ranks of the party who had committed (or might have committed, in her opinion) a crime against the party.

Once, when she had returned from questioning, she joyfully announced that her husband had been arrested. "What happiness! Now we will be together."

The women listened to her in horror. I think that she had simply gone mad, perhaps with some help from the investigator, who apparently knew how to influence her unstable mind. And her husband was nothing short of director of the organizational department of the party's Central Committee. I know nothing about her further fate.

My interrogations were not particularly difficult. The "active methods" were not yet being employed. I turned out to be the "luckiest" among all the unlucky: I was one of the first to be arrested and therefore escaped the "active" interrogations of 1937 and managed to be set free before the war. Those who were charged according to the same article, but who were taken in later and received the same five years, remained in prison another four years after their sentence was up.

But I understood all this only later. Then I thought only about the fact that they had arrested me and my children were left behind.... I comforted myself with the thought that they were with my mama, that it wouldn't be so bad for them there, but, my God, what small comfort this was.

Everything is relative. Later, when my daughters were entirely on their own, how happy I would have been to know that they were with mama....

After two months my interrogations ended. Rogov summoned me for the last time. They read me the decision of the special board: five years of corrective labor camps—in Kolyma, the northeastern part of Siberia. Five years in 1936 was the maximum sentence given by a special board. Those who went to trial, particularly if they appeared before a revolutionary tribunal, usually received ten years.

How naive we were! What little significance we gave then to sentences. Five years, ten years—what difference did it make! There will be changes, and we will all be set free, regardless of our sentences. But everything turned out to be much simpler and more ordinary: all, basically, were released according to their sentences. And those who later received an astronomical twenty-five years, and, of course, didn't believe that they were real, watched how people with ten years left the camps; they watched, and understood, that their sentence was quite real after all.

After the sentence was read, we were taken to a transfer point. This was in the former Butyrki church. There we all met, Pavel and I, our fellow accused, Difa Kagan and her husband, Zyama Shukhet, Olga Georgneburger and her husband, and my comrade from the institute, Sasha Teplyakov. It turned out that we all had been given five years in Kolyma, except Pavel, who received three years in some nearby camp. After his sentence was read, he filed a petition to be sent with his wife to Kolyma. "And if the difference in the sentences is an obstacle, I request that I be given an additional two years." I often think that if he had not done this, he would have finished his three years in some local camp and perhaps he would have remained alive. Of course, people died in nearby camps as well, but nevertheless, it was not the same as Kolyma, which was an extermination camp, especially for men. There were few women, and they had it easier; as for the men sentenced under our article, literally only a handful survived.

Pavel, however, had made his application. They didn't give him two additional years, but they sent him to Kolyma after all.

Before we left, they allowed us farewell visits. Pavel was seen by his sister, Asya, who traveled from Leningrad, and I was visited by my mama.

I don't know what Misha, the husband of my mother, said on this occasion. Probably he remained silent, just as he always remained silent when he didn't like something. Mikhail Ostrovsky was the director of the coach administration of the People's Commissariat of Transport (NKPS). Somewhat limited, very modest, kind and boundlessly devoted to his work (the coaches were the meaning of his existence), he never doubted the correctness of the party's general line. Even regarding the Stalin cult which was under way, he felt that "evidently it must be necessary." They said about people like him: "never was in, never belonged to, never was attracted by" (the Opposition).

They arrested him in July 1937. He displayed extraordinary courage during the interrogations and refused to sign anything.

In 1956, when we returned, the former director of the personnel department of the NKPS sought out my mother. After they imprisoned Kaganovich's deputy, Livshits (he was put on trial), they arrested all the directors of the departments of the NKPS in two rounds. First they imprisoned one group, then they arrested those who replaced them. They said that all this happened with the direct participation of Kaganovich himself.

The director of the personnel department was arrested almost simultaneously with Ostrovsky. In December 1937, they were brought face to face during questioning. He saw Misha, who was almost unrecognizable, with a broken arm and a swollen eye, which could see nothing. He began to shout, "Bastards, what have you done to this man?" They set upon him, and when he came to, he was in his prison cell.

They shot Misha in December 1937 in Lefortovo.

To this day, I cannot understand: Where did they find such a large number of executioners? For, after all, similar interrogations, involving torture, were going on everywhere, "from Moscow to the furthest reaches." Moreover, these methods were cultivated (if such a word can be used) and mechanized; special torture chambers were built.

I have met people who went through both Hitler's interrogations and ours. They stated that there must have been an exchange of experience, for the methods were very similar. Everywhere people were found who used these methods. Where were they from? And in such great numbers? I would have understood if these cadres had been taken from among "legal" criminals. Those I have seen and they are truly animals. They could calmly kill a person or they could lose someone's eye in a card game and then knock it out to pay off their debts.

Among the torturers and executioners, there may have been some former criminals, but, for the most part, no, they were drawn from some other sources. From where?

In 1937, my good friend Khava Maliar shared a cell with a woman who was a member of the Polish Communist Party. She was summoned for interrogation almost every night. She was completely black and blue from the beatings. It was difficult to imagine how a person could bear all this. When she became closer to Khava, she explained what gave her the strength to endure. The interrogations continued from evening until dawn, but the interrogators apparently had a normal workday; therefore, there were two: one for the first part of the night and another for the second part.

The first would beat her until she lost consciousness. Then the second would show up. He would throw a sheepskin coat on the floor and tell her, "Lie down." She would lie down in a semiconscious state. He would then walk around the room, throwing heavy objects on the floor, swearing loudly and, in short, simulating a high degree of activity. She, meanwhile, would lie on the coat and somewhat recover. Thus the second half of these many nights gave her the strength to bear the first half.

I am telling this to show that if a man didn't want to be an executioner, then he didn't have to be under any circumstances. That means, however, that the rest wanted to be....

And now a second question. Why, in general, was all this necessary? Why did people have to put their signatures beneath the outlandish nonsense with which they were incriminated? Almost always people signed in a semiconscious state. Sometimes the interrogator himself guided the hand of the one who was signing. Of course, he could have just as well signed himself. For all practical purposes, this didn't change anything. Those who signed and those who didn't sign received absolutely the same sentence. In addition, there were always people to be found who were ready to write whatever was needed about any person they were told, without any torture being applied at all. Some felt that in doing so they were carrying out their duty as party members or as citizens, others simply did it for their own benefit.

Who, then, felt that all this was necessary?...

So our large Kolyma group of prisoners prepared to set out. Not receiving an answer to his petition, Pavel declared a hunger strike, demanding that he be sent to Kolyma. They immediately separated him from all the rest and locked him in a "doghouse" (an isolation box). From there he yelled to all passers-by that he had declared a hunger strike and asked that I be told.

Someone told me. I then refused to leave and demanded to meet with my husband. The head of the convoy said, "Why do you need a meeting, when you'll be traveling together?" I didn't believe him. I already knew that you couldn't believe them.

However, Pavel was indeed assigned to the same group with all the rest of us. And so, shoulder to shoulder, we stood in the group formation and for the first time in our lives we heard the famous formula: "Step to the right, step to the left—we'll shoot without warning."

In the Stolypin wagon we were in neighboring sections.

The Kolyma group was sent with a special convoy, i.e., the guards didn't change from Moscow to Vladivostok. We were never put in a single transfer prison.

Only in Irkutsk were we taken to a bathhouse, and what happiness that was! Our trip would be remembered as endless days of horribly stuffy air and the constant smell of fish soup.

All three of us, Difa, Olga and I, were in the same crowded railway compartment with an iron-bar door. Our husbands were in the next compartment, behind the wall; we were young and healthy, we didn't believe in the reality of our sentences and we had hope.... One theme was forbidden: children.

But at last, we reached the transfer point. At that time it was in Vladivostok (later it was moved to Nakhodka).

The territory of the transfer point was ringed with barbed wire, but conditions were not particularly harsh. We could go from barracks to barracks and talk with our comrades. The guards would bring us produce from the city paid for with our money.

Taking advantage of the good weather, we spent a great deal of time outdoors, we would talk and discuss the perspectives of our future life. We, the three married couples, were worried about whether husbands and wives would be allowed together.

How little we understood what our future would hold!

On August 20, on our Natasha's birthday, they loaded us on board a steamship. The *Dzhurma* was a large steamship, but we didn't get a chance to see much of it. We spent the entire voyage in the hold. It was good that I didn't get seasick, for many suffered miserably. In the hold, on bunks, we were all together: Difa, Olga and I with our husbands; there was a good comrade, an old party member named Lazar Sadovsky, the Kiev Komsomolka, Sonia Erkes and many others.

There it was—Kolyma, the Bay of Nogaev. Finally they allowed us to go out onto the deck. Since we weren't used to the fresh sea air, we felt a bit intoxicated.

We fixed our stares on the approaching shore. Everything was very desolate: naked cliffs, a low-hanging sky. The shore was already close by. The guards began to stir, they arranged us in fives and took a head count as if we were sheep.

Trucks stood on the shore. Once again they counted us and put us in the trucks. Men and women were sent separately. The three of us said farewell to our husbands. Our fears had been justified. When, where and how would we see each other again....

Magadan at that time was made entirely of wood. The only stone building was the post office and a school that was still being built, with all ten grades.

The camp was called the "women's worksite" (zhenkomandirovka). I remember how surprised we were that all the subdivisions in the camp were for some reason called "worksites."

Once again they counted us. And then, we were in the camp. The barracks was large, poorly lighted and the floor was cleanly mopped. Later I became convinced that for some reason the camp administration worried most of all about the cleanliness of the floor. And not only in our area, but everywhere. There were trestle-beds, and each person had a separate bed. After the bunks in Butyrki prison and the cramped conditions of the Stolypin wagon, here it seemed very spacious.

The "old-timers" immediately ran up; they had arrived several groups earlier than ours. After half an hour we already knew the ropes. You could walk freely about the camp. If you worked at your specialty, they gave you so-called free exit, i.e., we could go to and from work without a guard escort. That meant we could go to the stores or to the cafeteria for civilian hires.

Our men probably would soon be sent further in along the road. In general, everything would become known when Masevich, the head of the SPO (secret political sector), arrived. He wasn't in Magadan just then, and the camp officials didn't have anything to do with our affairs.

Masevich was the former head of the secret political sector of the Leningrad NKVD. He was sent to Kolyma after Kirov's assassination.

They sent all the leading officials of the Leningrad NKVD to Kolyma. This, of course, was understandable. They knew too much, they knew who the real murderer was.

In Kolyma they occupied high posts at that time. Medvedev was the head of the southern mining administration, Rappoport was his deputy, Zaporozhets was head of the northern administration and Masevich, head of the secret political sector.

For them, this was obviously an intermediate stage. In 1937 they were all shot.

Masevich showed up after two weeks. By that time, the "deployment of forces" in our group had been determined: ten people, headed by Tsilia Kogan, secretary of the party bureau in one of Moscow's factories, had expressed the desire to work on construction. "We don't want to eat our bread for nothing." Their wish was granted, for a few days already they had been carrying bricks. By the way, during this entire time, they were convinced that when the boss of the SPO arrived, their enthusiasm would be duly assessed and they would be sent to a good job. But people correctly said about Masevich: He didn't like toadies and didn't believe enthusiasts.

He arrived and said, "Insofar as you are already working and you chose work according to your own wishes, why should I disturb you? Keep on working."

Masevich, on whom, when all was said and done, the fate of every prisoner in our category depended, was, under the circumstances of Kolyma at that time, almost a legendary figure. In any case, the stories which they told about him resembled legends.

In 1936, when we arrived in Kolyma, conditions of life there for prisoners were rather liberal. The tone was set by Berzin, who was at the head of Dalstroy, the NKVD organization in charge of Kolyma. He shouldn't be confused with the other Berzin, the head of counter-intelligence. As far as I know, they weren't even relatives. However, they had much in common. They were both Latvians; both were old members of the party; both participated in the October Revolution. And both were shot in 1938.

Such were the conditions in Kolyma when prisoners of our category began to arrive. They immediately demanded work according to their specialties, cohabitation between husbands and wives, and not only for those, like us, who had been married before our arrest, but for those who had only become acquainted there and wanted to live together. In order to achieve this, people resorted to hunger strikes. When we arrived in Kolyma, hunger strikes had assumed mass proportions. In the majority of cases, they ended successfully for those who had gone without food.

Of course, all these "achievements" came to nothing when 1937 reached Kolyma, and new leadership came to power. More about that later. But at that time, Masevich had to deal with all such questions, and in this regard all sorts of legends were told about him. For instance, the following occurred. Two people who had come to know each other either in transit or in Kolyma insisted on living together. He was at one of the mining sites, and she was supposed to be transferred to him. But due to some kind of technical error, she was sent to an altogether different mining site and to another man. They both wrote indignant letters to Masevich. She, about the fact that it was absolutely not with this man that she intended to form her family life. He, about the fact that he had in general not asked for anyone to be sent to him, he didn't need this.

Masevich replied: "That's all right. Be patient." After a while they sent him a letter jointly signed, to the effect that the situation which had developed satisfied them both and they asked that they be left together.

A second incident: A woman was arrested when she was pregnant, somewhere in her seventh or eighth month, and endlessly turned to Masevich with all kinds of requests. Apparently he got tired of this and gave orders to place her in a hospital, in the maternity ward. She sent him an angry letter from there, stating that she still had another month to go, and that she had absolutely nothing to do in the hospital and so forth. He replied: "That's all right, have your baby." On the next day, she had a completely normal delivery.

Of course, everyone knows that it was a pure coincidence that the two at the mining site appealed to each other and that the woman simply miscalculated her due date, but all of this created something of a legendary reputation for Masevich.

And so, while our enthusiasts carried bricks to the building site, the rest of us received work: engineers and economists according to their specialization, while journalists, teachers and others received various office jobs.

I ended up in one of the administrative offices of Dalstroy. The conditions at work were not bad, and after a while I gained a certain authority. By the way, this wasn't hard. The contingent of civilian hires was not among the strongest when it came to work habits, at least in our department. The pay was 900 rubles, out of which 500 was retained by the camp, for full "board and lodging," and the rest went into my camp account. I wanted very much to send money to my children, but mama had warned me that there could be no communication between us because of Misha.

Many of my friends showed up at our location — Tanya Myagkova and Anya Sadovskaya. Anya responded to me with particular warmth. First of all, I passed on greetings from her first husband and good friend Lazar Sadovsky; and second, before being arrested I had become friends with her younger sister, Liuba, a Komsomolka from the town of Sharikopodshipnik. (Later Liuba died in one of the camps.)

Anya was a person of great principles and strong character. I never met anyone who reacted to her indifferently. People either liked her very much or couldn't stand her. I belonged to the first group.

I remember the Old Bolsheviks, Bliuma Solomonovna Faktorovich and Sofia Mikhailovna Antonova.

Bliuma Solomonovna was a bit gloomy and taciturn. In contrast, Sofia Mikhailovna was amazingly youthful in spirit, loved life and possessed a profound human tolerance. We, who were relatively young, called her our "camp mama." Still at large was her daughter, Koka, who had been born in a czarist prison. Koka helped her very much. Later she earned her doctorate and became a specialist on India.

I saw both Bliuma Solomonovna and Sofia Mikhailovna for the last time in Moscow, after rehabilitation. This was at the funeral of Anya Sadovskaya, who had died from cancer.

I can't help but recall still one more older woman, Aleksandra Lvovna Bronstein, Trotsky's first wife and the mother of his two daughters. Despite her simplicity and humanity, she seemed to me to be a figure from some ancient Greek tragedy. Having behind her forty years of party membership, czarist prison and czarist exile, she ended up in camp after being branded an "enemy of the people." How horrible to lose both daughters. Nina had died in Moscow, perishing in two months from tuberculosis. Nina's children, Leva and Volina, remained with Aleksandra, and now she knew nothing about the fate of her grand-children. Her elder daughter, Zina, went abroad to join her father, and left her daughter, Sashenka, with her husband. Zina committed suicide in Germany, leaving behind a young boy, Seva.

When I was leaving Magadan, and we were saying farewell, she told me: "If you ever read somewhere or hear that I have confessed to being guilty, don't believe it. This will never happen, no matter what they do to me."

Olga Ivanovna Grebner (from an entirely different circle) was a very kind woman. In the past, as Viktor Shklovsky's secretary, she had met many fascinating people. She was a typical representative of Moscow's intellectual Bohemia. Olga Ivanovna's downfall was her last name. The niece of her husband Grebner, Lily Grebner, was the first wife of Sergei Sedov, Trotsky's younger son. Olga Ivanovna separated from her husband and had no contact whatsoever with his niece and in general never knew Sergei. Nevertheless, she received five years in the Kolyma camps. She had an affair with a very famous film director. The night they came for her, he was at her place.

When they took her away, she asked him: "Don't abandon Valentina" (Valya was her sixteen-year-old daughter). We must do him justice — he never abandoned Valentina, he married her. They both helped Olga Ivanovna in the camps, with money and with packages. Valentina later married Kozinstev and wrote her memoirs about him.

From among the youngest women of my age, I remember the very sweet Sonya Smirnova, Dita (it seems, Arkanova) and Sonya Erkes, who was with me in transit.

From among those I'd shared a cell with in Butyrki I met Liza Osminskaya, an old party member from Leningrad. She knew my husband very well. At the women's mission I found her in the barracks with those on hunger strike. To find Liza Osminskaya among those on strike was completely unexpected. In Butyrki, she had been so orthodox that if anyone expressed the opinion that today's soup was poor or that the warden was coarse, she would take this as an attack against the Soviet Union.

That is how the camps "reeducate" people....

Despite working at my profession, and having living conditions which were not bad, I kept insisting on being sent to my husband. Pavel was at the mining site called Five-Year-Plan, in the southern district. Both Difa and Olya had already left to join their husbands, but Masevich kept refusing to send me. It is true that he gave me the chance to send food packages to my husband, and these packages went not by ordinary mail, but through field communications, that is, through the channels of the NKVD. At the mining site, Pavel would be called to the head of the camp, who would hand him the wrapped package and then politely ask if everything was in order.

An experienced campmate, Tanya Myagkova, was certain that Masevich had the following orders with regard to me: create certain conditions and hold her under observation. But evidently that wasn't the case. In the beginning of 1937, Masevich summoned me and said that my request had been granted, and that I would soon be on my way to meet my husband.

The winter of 1936-37 proceeded for me under the sign of the Moscow trials, first of the so-called Trotskyite-Zinovievite bloc and then of the "parallel center" and then of the rightists.

Of course, my friends and people convicted under the same article, who were generally members of the party, also suffered, discussed and made all kinds of suppositions. At that time we still had information, we read newspapers.

All this resembled some kind of monstrous play which the "directors" didn't even bother to make seem real. I don't think that anyone could have seriously believed what was taking place. Even people who are far from politics could have put two and two together. But for me, real live people stood behind all this.

Take Zinoviev. I never knew him personally, but my father knew him well. I remember he would tell how in 1919 in Petrograd, when Yudenich was almost on the outskirts of the city, Zinoviev, who was then chairman of the Petrograd Soviet, was absolutely distraught. His hands shook and he told my father, "I wish you would give me some of your composure." He had an unexpectedly frail, almost woman's voice, given such a solid build. He never evoked in me either admiration or sympathy. But nevertheless he was so close to Lenin. Together they put out the collection of articles entitled *Against the Stream*, and together they hid out in the Gulf of Finland.

And next to him was Kamenev. I knew him very well—a man of unusual intellect and a solid, experienced, sober politician. These were the main actors , the leading figures of the first trial.

And the others: Krestinsky, or Christian Georgievich Rakovsky, with whom I had so many ties. Trotsky's friend, father's friend, and only two years ago, what a good talk we had at his place on Tverskoi Boulevard. Out of all those in my father's generation, he and the late Krasin were the people who were closest to me.

And Doctor Levin, Lev Grigorievich Levin, the old Moscow physician and old Russian intellectual (although he was a Jew). I had known him since childhood, and he was our family doctor. His apartment on Mamonovsky Alley faced a small museum. All the walls were covered with photographs—the most famous actors, artists, writers, scholars—and all had warm and friendly inscriptions.

And Yenukidze, Avel Safronovich Yenukidze, whom everyone simply called Avel. Permanent secretary of the All-Russian Central Executive Committee, the ever-present chairman of all funeral commissions. Where is his grave? As children, we would run to him for complimentary tickets to the theater. He would very amusingly appear to be upset, "You are pestering me," but he never refused.

January 1937 witnessed the start of the trial of the so-called parallel center: Pyatakov, Radek and Sokolnikov. Pyatakov was a man who was close to Trotsky; Lenin wrote very positively about him and placed great hopes in him when he was young. He testified in great detail at the trial how, when he was abroad, he flew somewhere on a plane and met there with Lev Sedov, Trotsky's son. He even gave the exact dates. Nothing of the sort ever happened.

Radek. I knew him personally; he would come to visit father, and once, when we sat there very late, he escorted me home, from Leontevsky to Theater Square. Radek was a tireless sower of revolution. I remember a caricature drawn either by Deni or by Moor: Radek with a tattered briefcase, striding across houses and squares. The words beneath the caricature were: "a specter is haunting Europe, the specter of communism." A witty man, all the jokes of that time belonged, or in any case were ascribed, to him.

Stalin had often been wounded by Radek's barbs. People told the story of how Stalin warned Radek, after recalling him in 1928 from exile, that a condition of Radek's political rehabilitation was that he no longer tell jokes at his, Stalin's, expense. "After all," Stalin was said to have advised Radek, "you must understand that I am not only the general secretary of the Russian Communist Party. I am also the leader of the world socialist revolution."

"Koba," Radek shot back, "that's your joke, not mine!"

The directors of this monstrous spectacle never bothered about plausibility and, after all, how could there even be talk of plausibility? Drobnis, who came from a poor Jewish family living in the pale, was a bootmaker when he was young. Under Soviet power he occupied very high posts. Why would he need the restoration of capitalism? Simply from the standpoint of common sense, for what reason? In order to become a bootmaker again?

And the trial of the rightists! The leaders were Bukharin and Rykov; Tomsky wasn't at the trial since he had committed suicide. Why didn't he, when he had his gun in hand, kill a couple of the NKVD agents first? And then himself. Of course, they were grains of sand, they decided nothing, but at least they wouldn't have gone to arrest people as if they were going for a pleasurable stroll. They would have at least begun to fear arresting people — people, whose fingernails they weren't worth.

Rykov, who came from a modest intellectual family and never was wealthy or belonged to the nobility, when asked what was his work before his arrest, replied: "chairman of the sovnarkom." If he had been a self-seeker or an agent of the foreign bourgeoisie (and that was precisely how he was described by the prosecutor Vyshinsky), then why, once again, from the standpoint of elementary common sense, why would he have needed all this? Where, under what regime, could he have counted on more than being the head of the government in a land occupying one-sixth of the world's surface?

And Bukharin? Bukharchik, everyone's favorite, who felt himself at home at Lenin's, who called Krupskaya Nadya and who cried like a baby when Lenin died. I saw this myself. The things that he confessed to!

As I read the newspaper, I felt that my head would split open. When we discussed all that was taking place, the majority felt that they had made all these "confessions" under torture. I understood that under torture and in anticipation of even more terrible torture, many could be broken and might confess to anything. But they didn't simply confess: "Yes," "I was," "I said," and so forth. They went on at great length about their planned "crimes," as if they had rehearsed their horrible confessions.

I came to the conclusion that these weren't the real people, that the real ones had already been killed and that all the trials were simply monstrous dramatizations.

Finally, those attending these "open" trials were a specially selected contingent. If there had been people who really knew the accused well, who would have dared to say a single word?

They could always pick out the actors. But later I became convinced that they were indeed the real people. Unfortunately, they were themselves.

Their monstrous confessions to this day remain a mystery.

Of course, the opinion circulated that they had some kind of agreement with Stalin, that in return for their confessions they were promised that they would live and that those close to them would not be touched.

But could it possibly be that such intelligent people, such experienced politicians, didn't understand who they were dealing with?

So, in the beginning of 1937, I set out for the center of the southern mining administration—Orotukan.

They sent me in those liberal times without an escort, after giving me a large envelope stamped with sealing wax—my "dossier." Here I was, traveling alone on a bus with an unusual sense of freedom. I traveled 400 kilometers along the wonderful Kolyma highway, which was as straight as an arrow. Then it was 600 kilometers long and later they extended it an equal distance. How many people lay there along this highway, how many human bones went into its construction....

"Who built this road, papa?"

"The NKVD, darling...."

I arrived in Orotukan, in the "calico city," as the camp there is poetically called. The camp was for men, and there were only three women. They lived in a separate small barracks outside the compound.

One of the women was Lida Vorontsova, an eighteen-year-old from Leningrad, who taught at a drama school. She worked in a club at the port of Leningrad, danced the fox trot with foreign sailors and received ten years according to Article 58.

Here, she worked in the agit-brigade, the local theatrical collective. She was overjoyed to see me and decided that I would work in the agit-brigade. But this required traveling around the mining sites, which wasn't allowed according to the article I was arrested under.

The remaining two women, KRTDs,* were Liusya Charomskaya, from Magnitogorsk, and Danya Kievlenko, from Moscow. I lived with them for ten days, waiting to be sent to the mine. Of the two, Charomskaya was more intelligent, but Kievlenko was more of an intellectual, since she had somehow managed to finish two programs of higher education. She finished the pedagogical institute before the revolution and the oil institute after.

Charomskaya was a skilled party worker, an intelligent and reliable woman, but it seems to me that she didn't have an inner sense of what was going on. It seems to me that it would have been easier for her to find a common language with the camp administration or with the NKVD personnel, than with the prisoners. She said very little about herself, but Kievlenko told me the curious story of her arrest.

Liusya was the second party secretary in Magnitogorsk. The first was Lominadze, who shot himself in his automobile in 1934. I had heard about Lominadze's suicide while I was still in Moscow, but we didn't know that after this they arrested all the leading personnel at Magnitka. Among those rounded up was Liusya. In 1935 she received five years, along with Volfson, the chief engineer at Magnitka.

Her further fate is unknown.

Danya Kievlenko, whom I met later, heard that in 1937

---

* Those convicted of "Counterrevolutionary Trotskyist Activity."

Charomskaya was seen in Moscow in Butyrki. They once again accused her of something and gave her fifteen years.

As for Danya, she was the wife of an experienced Trotskyist, Yakov Kievlenko. She was very kind, sincere, but a bit sentimental and given to tears. In the camps, I came across her twice. The first time, which I am writing about now, was in Orotukan, and the second was a year later, also in Orotukan, but under entirely different conditions, on a special assignment.

But about that later.

After spending about two weeks at Orotukan, I finally ended up at Five-Year-Plan, the mine where Pavel worked.

At the mining site there were about 2,000 prisoners. I was the only woman. I made a devastating impression. On the first day of my arrival, as I walked with Pavel about the mining site, I simply couldn't understand what was going on. It was like in the fairy tale about Sleeping Beauty: Some man with a heavy bundle of wood on his shoulders would stop, completely hunched over, and stare at me. Out of the Corrective Labor Camp cafeteria, the cooks jumped out in their white hats in the minus-forty-degree weather and stood there gawking.

Pavel laughed, "Don't worry, everything is all right. They simply haven't seen women in a long time."

After this the more enterprising criminals went to the head of the camp, pounded with their fists and shouted: "They've brought in a broad for that lousy Trotskyist, and I'm supposed to just drop dead."

By the way, at the mining site there were two or three other women, the wife of the mine director, the wife of the chief surveyor and one other wife. They lived in separate small houses, in an isolated part of the village and almost never came to the mine.

About half of the mine were bandits and recidivists, who were deliberately sent farther away from Magadan into the taiga. The other half were KRTDs, party workers, scientific personnel, economists, students.

The urkas (criminals) lived as they knew how. They played cards (sometimes betting and losing live people), they drank (when something could be found), they stole (when there was something to steal).

They tried to form work brigades made of the criminals, but the latter hung signs on the wheelbarrows: "Barrow, barrow, don't be afraid of me, I won't touch you, so don't worry." And indeed, they didn't touch the wheelbarrows.

It is true that there were exceptions and some criminals worked. They were given the best places, awarded the highest percentages and written about in the local newspaper.

The criminals were divided into "honorable" thieves and "bitches." As a rule, the criminals "who honored the thieves' code" did not work and therefore despised the "bitches," those who worked.

The people working were mainly 58ers. They worked at the mine, fourteen hours a day, at forty degrees below zero. There could be no talk of working at one's specialty; such jobs were filled by the hires. They offered me a job in the cafeteria of the engineers and technicians ("easy work, good food"), but waiting on the "bosses." No. To their great surprise, I refused. Then they sent me to the cafeteria for prisoners. This was something altogether different.

I saw that, for my comrades in misfortune, both the "workhorses" and the "goners," it was simply pleasant to see a woman. Some would come to the distribution window and ask, "Sweetheart, say something, for two years I haven't heard a woman's voice."

I received satisfaction just trying to give slightly bigger portions or washing the dishes a bit (before me they weren't washed, the bowls were simply tossed into filthy, cold water).

I lived in a tiny room in the so-called san-city. The sanitary city was three kilometers from the main camp. Here was the medical aide, the dentist, the hospital and other medical bodies of a mine-site scale, and a dining area for the prisoners.

The dentist, Solomon Mikhailovich Kruglikov, a member of the party since before the revolution and a major businessman in the past, had received in czarist times the highest education available for a Jew from the pale—dentistry courses. Now this circumstance saved him from general work. The medical aide, an "honest" everyday criminal, was in prison for corruption. During the war in 1914 he had been an orderly in the military. He would receive patients approximately in the following manner: "Last name?"—"Ivanov"—"Breathe deeply. First name and patronymic?"—"Ivan Ivanovich"—"Cough. Year of birth?"—"1909"—"Take another breath. Article?"—"KRTD"—"Stop breathing...."

If the article was KRTD, that meant that the work category would be TFT, "hard physical labor," and that the prisoner would be released "five minutes before death."

Pavel lived in the barracks, but came to see me every day, and sometimes spent the night. The local authorities looked the other way at this.

A short while after I arrived at the mine, they brought Evgeny Ostrovsky and Musya Natanson. They were among the "Mariintsy" with the same article. The Mariintsy was a group of prisoners brought here from the Mariinsky camps. Ending up in Kolyma, they immediately stated a number of conditions: work according to their profession, cohabitation between husbands and wives and so forth. They declared a hunger strike, which lasted eighty days, the longest of all the Kolyma hunger strikes. They were force-fed. After a few days, Musya was too weak to resist, but Evgeny was a healthy man, and they fed him tied up until the last day. They won their strike. Or at least they were promised that their demands would be met. The hunger strike was called off, and they were immediately taken away to various mines. Evgeny and Musya ended up here. We lived with them on good terms, both I and Pavel in particular. For him they were, beside everything else, from Leningrad.

Once, at the end of April, at night, when Pavel wasn't present and we had long since fallen asleep, a knock resounded at the door. In walked a "koom" (an NKVD official) and a guard. They conducted a search and, of course, found nothing. Then the official told Evgeny and Musya to get ready to leave. With their things. The sacred prison formula: "with your things." It always meant a change in one's life. And rarely for the better. Then they were led away. As he was leaving, the official promised in a consoling voice: "Don't be bored, soon we'll come for you." I locked the door and remained alone, feeling absolutely crushed. I wanted to straighten things out, but I didn't have the strength to do so. I sat right in the middle of the room and tried to imagine where Evgeny and Musya now were. Probably I dozed off, sitting there on the floor, because I awoke to a terrible pounding on the door. The first thing that came into my head was that the official had returned for me just as he had promised.

But it was Pavel. Someone had told him that three people had been led away from the san-city, at least two and maybe three people. Before roll call, he ran from the main mine to the san-city; three kilometers into the mountains, running nonstop. When I opened the door, he couldn't speak, he was breathing too hard. He only reached out and touched me to make sure that I was truly there and then left. He had to be there for roll call.

I never saw Evgeny and Musya again. Then it became known that all the participants in the Mariinsky hunger strike had been shot. Among them was my comrade from the Krasnoyarsk exile, Lado Yenukidze.

At that time, Masevich arrived at the southern administration. After this, Pavel and I received genuine cohabitation rights. We were given a separate room in the general camp grounds. Pavel began to work as a timekeeper; I was put to work in an office.

But soon we almost lost all our "achievements." The criminals became very active. In Orotukan they brutally murdered the secretary of the Komsomol organization, Tanya Malandina. She had visited the mine, and I knew her to be a very admirable girl. First they gang-raped her and then killed her. They cut the corpse into pieces and hid them in various places.

At our mine they burned the senior mine surveyor and his wife. The little house in which they lived was covered with straw during the night, doused in kerosene and lit on fire. The building was wooden, dry and went up immediately, like a torch. They both burned, husband and wife. But their orderly managed to throw their three-year-old daughter out the window. And he himself jumped out. The orderly was from the criminals. He had already lived with them for two years and virtually raised the daughter. They said that he knew about the fire and perhaps even took part in it. It appears that this was the case. Neither the surveyor nor his wife heard a thing, yet he, in the middle of the night, managed to throw the girl out and get out himself. He was arrested.

Generally speaking, this surveyor was a real dog, but still it is terrible that people could do such things.

There was a court in the region. With all their might they tried to turn Tanya Malandina's murder and then the arson into political crimes. They said that everything had been organized by 58ers.

The "leading figure" at the trial, Sashka Orlov, who was nicknamed Eagle (Orel), put an end to this fabrication. There were two brothers who were very famous in the criminal world. The elder, Valet, had already been shot. At the trial Eagle declared: "All my life I have stolen and murdered. Let me go free, and once again I will steal and murder. I don't have anything to do with 58ers, and don't try to pin politics on me." Thus the political trial fell flat.

Sashka, the Eagle, treated me with great respect. He often would come to the cafeteria where I was working and liked to talk with me "about life."

I must say that these conversations were also not without interest for me. Like Miss Dartle in Dickens, I loved to find out what I didn't know. It turns out that in our country, right next to us, there existed a special world with its own traditions and laws. It was a kind of "antiworld." Here it was considered shameful to work, and thieves "who honored the thieves' code" didn't work. A man's qualities were judged by his ability to deceive, to steal and to rob. They had their own code of "honor": You couldn't take from your own, and if an "honorable" thief ended up in prison, then packages could be brought to him only by the woman whom he supported when he was free or with whom he had left his money and valuables. From a woman who owed him nothing, he couldn't accept packages, for a woman could earn money in only one particular way. Such packages were called "damp," and no self-respecting thief would accept them.

"I am surprised, Nadezhda Adolfovna," Sashka once said to me, "how can I be talking with you? I will tell you openly, I've had as many broads (that is, excuse me, women) in my time as there are hairs on my head, and I have never talked with a single broad (excuse me, woman) the way I talk with a man. I couldn't even imagine doing so."

Sasha was far from stupid. He was observant and understood that his life was not right, but he didn't know any other and generally didn't want to know one. He was quite content with being in the position: "Maybe it's only for one day, but it's mine." In addition, he was a thief "with authority," i.e., he enjoyed influence, his word was law and he valued his position (as, by the way, did many in our circle).

Once the following incident happened. When I left for work, I usually locked my room. One day, I ran home during lunchbreak and discovered that the lock was torn away and the suitcase with my things had been rummaged through. Nothing had been taken. Since there were no women at the mine, a woman's things were obviously useless for them. They did take Pavel's jacket, which had hung on the back of the chair, and a bottle of cologne.

When I returned to work, Sashka soon appeared. "What's wrong, Nadezhda Adolfovna, why are you so upset?" "Well, Sasha, something unpleasant has happened," and I told him. "The cologne is nothing, but I feel bad about the jacket. And it's not very pleasant that someone was digging around in my things."

Without saying a word, Sashka turned around and left. He came back after about an hour. He brought back the jacket. "You must excuse me, but I didn't manage to get the cologne. They had already drunk it. But in the future, Nadezhda Adolfovna, you don't even need to lock your door. The Eagle will answer for it."

It was this same Eagle who upset the Orotukan trial.

About two months after I arrived, it became clear that I was expecting a child. I was horrified: a third child and in such conditions.... But Pavel said, "Perhaps it's for the best. And perhaps, because of this they won't separate us. And just maybe, you might be put in somewhat better circumstances."

They separated us immediately after the birth of the baby. I won't write about what my "circumstances" were like. But, in general, Pavel turned out to be right: I hardly would have emerged alive from this meatgrinder if not for the baby.

Towards summer, the entire mine knew about my condition, it was obvious to the naked eye. The wife of the mine's director was expecting a child at the same time as I was. This didn't interest anyone, but the child which I expected was "our" child as far as the mine was concerned.

Among the prisoners there was a cabinetmaker who was a master at his trade. He was in prison for criminal activity, and we didn't know him at all. But he walked up to Pavel on the street and said: "The boss ordered me to make a crib for his infant. Well, of course I'll make it for him; he's the boss after all. But you, my friend, should have no doubts: for our child I will make a crib. And I will put my soul into it; no boss anywhere will have such a crib."

Everyone tried in at least some way to do something for "our" child. And it was simply impossible to refuse.

At Five-Year-Plan a priest was serving his sentence. I don't know the church hierarchy very well; but he was no simple priest, he occupied some high rank. He received an enormous number of packages from believers all over the Soviet Union. Even the most desperate criminals never took anything away from him. He himself distributed everything. He brought us butter, sugar and dried fruit. We tried to refuse, but he said: "You don't have to refuse because this isn't for you, it's for the expected baby." In leaving, he would cross me and say: "Every day I pray for you."

Perhaps his prayers helped me survive.... And how could we have refused the man who brought us some kind of towel. It had belonged to him when he was home and resembled a rag more than a towel, but he asked us in an embarrassed way, as if he were asking for a favor, "Please, take it. Perhaps it can serve as a diaper." And once I went into the camp laundry to wash something, and I began to feel bad, probably from the stuffiness and the steam. The men, ordinary criminals who worked at the laundry, walked me home and said, "Give us all your dirty things and we will wash them. And don't go there anymore; it's bad for the baby."

I am deliberately writing about this so that nobody will think that all people were rotten. This was not the case.

At the end of October they sent me to the hospital. The hospital of Ust-Taezhnaya was 403 kilometers from Magadan and 25 kilometers from the mine. Pavel remained at the Five-Year-Plan. We said goodbye next to the cart on which they took me away. He walked alongside the cart. When the driver turned onto the road and let the horse move at a trot, Pavel stopped and gazed after us for a long time.

I never saw him again. Neither living nor dead.

On November 1, in Ust-Taezhnaya, I gave birth to our third daughter.

2

The physician was the prisoner Andrei Mikhailovich Zhegin, KRTD; the midwife, Aleksandra Ilinichna, also KRTD (I simply don't understand how they managed to receive such an article. By the way, there were even more absurd instances.); even the orderly, Gosha, was KRTD; he was lame and this evidently saved him from general work.

My daughter was small and the midwife experienced, so all went relatively easily and successfully. When everything was over, I fell asleep, and Aleksandra Ilinichna did too. But when I awoke, I saw that she was sitting on my cot, and the first question which she asked was, "What did you dream about?" I had dreamt absolutely nothing and, in general, couldn't stand this prison habit of starting every morning with tales about dreams. But here is what she told me.

A few years before, her younger daughter Zoya gave birth to a child. She herself attended the birth and a healthy, normal child was born; everything had turned out fine. Zoya fell asleep, as did Aleksandra Ilinichna. In her dream, she saw Zoya walking toward her, saying, "Mama, I am going away. I don't want you to give my baby to Sasha (Sasha was her husband), he doesn't need the baby. Let him stay with you."

When she awoke, she walked up to Zoya, who was dead. She had died in her sleep, either from shock or a heart attack, I don't remem-

ber. Sasha, Aleksandra Ilinichna's son-in-law, was in such despair that
people feared he would commit suicide. He said that now he would
live only for the baby and that he wanted to take him right then. But
they talked him out of it—what would he do with a nursing child,
especially one being bottle-fed? He agreed to leave his son with the
grandmother for one year. Within six months he remarried, left to live
in another city and didn't even remember about the baby.

The infant grew normally. When he turned one, Aleksandra
Ilinichna once again saw Zoya in a dream. She said, "Thank you, mama,
for sonny. You've raised him for one year, and now I am going to take
him with me." On the next day, the child fell ill and soon died.

I never saw people more superstitious than in prison or the camps.
Very intelligent, well-educated people nearly always began to believe
in signs, in fortune-telling, in dreams.

At this time on the "mainland,"* 1937 had already reached its apo-
gee. Five-Year-Plan was an old mine, worked out, new groups of prisoners rarely came, and rumors reached us with great delay. But a certain time would pass, and we would be fully informed. We felt the new
"currents," as it were, on our own hides.

By November, when many naively expected an amnesty, 1937
reached Kolyma.

On November 6, although I was still quite weak, they sent me on
a special assignment. According to camp rules, during holidays all prisoners were supposed to be in the compound. They sent me to the same
camp where I spent a few days the previous year, before being transferred to the mine. At that time there were three women and they
lived in a small barracks beyond the compound of the men's camp.

In the men's camp compound, just as it had been at the Magadan
women's "worksite," people walked about freely. And how valuable it
was, even this small freedom! Returning from work, you could go outside to breathe the fresh air and look up at the sky. It was very beautiful—the vast, shining northern sky. You could go into another barracks,

---

* Refers sometimes to the southern part of Siberia, below the arctic circle, but
here to the outside world, as opposed to the camp world. Camps were felt to be is-
lands, set apart from "mainland" society.

talk a bit with comrades, you could go into the bathhouse and wash something. It seemed that you could do very much.

Twenty women now lived in one tent, on the doors of which hung an enormous lock. Next to this tent stood another. There was located a workshop where these women worked; they cleaned old jackets and coats. This tent was also always locked. Both tents were surrounded by two rows of barbed wire.

In the morning, the guard would open the lock, let out those on duty and take them to the main compound for bread and boiling water. Those on duty, two people under guard, would bring twenty rations of bread and twenty teaspoons of sugar, which would immediately be given out by the spoonful to each person.

After breakfast, one section of the women would go to the other tent, where they would again be locked up, and the other section would be accompanied by the guards to a knoll to prepare wood.

For lunch the women would be taken under guard to the main compound, to the dining area. By this time, the men had already left. After lunch there was more work. And in the evening, under guard, supper. Once a week, those in need of medical attention, once again under guard, would be taken to the medical area. The medical aide, like that at the mine who said, "Stop breathing," had no clear idea of where the heart is located, on the right or left side, but nevertheless, on the established days practically half the tent walked over to the medical area, for every chance to leave the compound was an event. Someone would meet somebody else, someone would learn something. Even scraps of a conversation accidentally overheard would be discussed and commented on a thousand times.

Besides me, there was one other woman with a child, Shura Nikolaeva, a Komsomolka from Moscow. Shura studied at the Communications Academy and at a Komsomol meeting voted against the expulsion of the cell secretary, whose brother had been arrested as an "enemy of the people."

She also received five years for KRTD. Shura had a six-month-old girl, Allochka. She had been arrested when she was pregnant. Her two twin boys remained at home. She didn't sew coats, but cleaned the barracks and went to fetch the boiling water.

Nadezhda Joffe's grandfather Abraham Yakovlevich Joffe c. 1900

Nadezhda Joffe's father Adolf Abramovich Joffe in 1918. He committed suicide on November 16, 1927.

Clockwise from top left: Joffe's older brother Alexander, Joffe, younger brother Konstantin, sister Vera in 1893

Joffe as a young man

Nadezhda Joffe's mother Berta Ostrovskaya in the early 1930s. She died in 1960 in Moscow at the age of 72.

During the negotiations at Brest-Litovsk in 1918. *Front row:* Kamenev, Joffe and Bitsenko; *back row, right:* Trotsky, Karakhan

The Genoa Conference in 1922. *From right:* Joffe, Chicherin and Krasin

Adolf Abramovich Joffe in the 1920s

Adolf Abramovich Joffe's grave in 1956 at the Novodevichy Cemetery in Moscow

Nadezhda and her mother in 1916

Nadezhda Joffe in the early 1950s

Nadezhda Joffe's husband Pavel Kossakovsky in 1925. He was shot in Kolyma on May 8, 1938.

Nadezhda Joffe and her daughters Natasha, Lera and Larisa

Her daughter Kira

Nadezhda Joffe in 1990

I tried to understand on what basis these twenty people were selected. It seems that there was none. Just as with everything else which happened, in this process there was neither rhyme nor reason. The majority of the women were Communists, but there were also completely accidental figures, and one, Lida Knysh, called herself a "hereditary, distinguished criminal." In the camps she was given Article 58, but why she ended up at this strange location, I don't know.

Even though we were locked up twenty-four hours a day and were located behind two rows of barbed wire, Lida was pregnant.

From my acquaintances I met Danya Kievlenko, with whom I had lived for a while in this same Orotukan the previous year, and Masha Shubovich, whom I knew at the women's "worksite." There was an older woman, an old member of the party, Nushik Zavarian; earlier I hadn't known her, but I had heard a lot about her. Liza Keshve was there, the sister of Nikolaev, Kirov's murderer.

There was one more Nadya, Nadya Gurevich. When they arrested her, her thirteen-year-old daughter was left behind. The girl had been studying to play the violin, and they considered her very talented, but she had poor vision in the form of extreme nearsightedness and suffered from headaches. She had no relatives and ended up in the Lefortovo isolator, a place where they gathered children and adolescents from everywhere, but mainly the homeless rabble. It was so terrible there that the girl ran away. But they caught her and put her in some orphanage. There could be no talk of music lessons. She completed her school lessons with great difficulty, since she had terrible headaches from the constant noise. In addition, the administration of the orphanage, who apparently saw that this was a fine girl with a good upbringing, gave her the "social responsibility" of watching over the bed linen. The orphanage ruffians constantly stole the sheets and sold them at the market. According to Nadya, the young girl always was known for an unusually developed sense of responsibility and suffered greatly from what was happening. Letters came from her infrequently, and every time—and I'm not just talking about the unhappy Nadya—all of us who had left children behind (and this was the majority) simply began to worry.

Evidently, big events had taken place somewhere. They removed our entire camp administration. The majority were not only removed, but put in prison. People said that the entire Leningrad leadership which had been sent in connection with the Kirov affair was arrested.

Such special contingents as ours apparently existed in other places. The hardening of the regime proceeded under the slogan: "That's the end of your Fillipov indulgences." (Fillipov was the former head of the administration of the northeastern corrective labor camps, USVITLag.)

Groups were continuously leaving the men's camp. Where they were going, we didn't know. Since I was washing diapers every day, I was allowed to go for water "out of order." Sometimes I saw how these groups were sent off: in the back of the truck people were standing tightly packed. Once I saw how one of the prisoners dropped his hat as he was getting into the vehicle. He remained with a bare head in the forty-below temperature, an old, gray-haired man. The hat lay on the ground, at the very feet of the guards. He asked them to hand it to him, but they wouldn't. Then the truck began to move. And he remained without his hat....

Once our Lida, who always knew everything, announced that a "big boss" had arrived at the camp, the new head of USVITLag, Colonel Garanin. That day I was on duty and walked to the men's compound for bread and sugar.

Garanin stood near the entrance. We passed by closely, and I glanced at him. He looked at the people walking by him as if they were glass—he looked through them. In the yard stood a group of prisoners. We stopped near the doors of the dining area, and I looked around. Garanin was approached by some prisoner, who was all bent over, as if he were hunchbacked. He shuffled his feet and coughed, evidently trying to gather the courage to say something. "Comrade director, I am very sick. I ask you to let them transfer me to lighter work, I beg you...." He seemed to say something else, but I couldn't hear what it was. Garanin suddenly came to life, gave a start, and only then did I grasp that it was he who had taken a revolver out of his holster. "You don't want to work...," followed by a string of obscenities. And he shot him point-blank. The man fell to the ground.

Our guard was upset and muttered, "Go on in, go on in, there's no need to stand here," and he pushed us toward the doors of the dining area.

The postnatal period in an almost unheated tent ended for me with a severe case of mastitis. I lay for a few days with a temperature higher than 40°C, and then they sent Lera and me to Ust-Taezhnaya, to the same hospital where she was born.

Andrei Mikhailovich, the head of the department, was an experienced surgeon and a good man. He kept me in the hospital for two months, although my mastitis had long since disappeared. He knew what our special assignment was like. I lay with my child in a separate ward, since there were no other women prisoners, and he wasn't allowed to keep us with the free-hires.

It is true that near the beginning of 1938 they brought in one other woman prisoner. She was called Zina Kapustina and she had poisoned herself. Andrei Mikhailovich immediately said that he couldn't do anything, and that she had only a few days to live. She died from uraemia.

They put her in a separate ward. Rather, it was not so much a ward as something like a closet, a small room without windows. I asked why she couldn't be put in with me. Andrei Mikhailovich didn't reply, he only said that it was better not to go see her. But I went anyway. I thought that perhaps it would be awful for her to die completely alone.

Zina Kapustina was twenty-five years old, but she could have passed for forty. She didn't respond to my greeting and silently stared at me. I asked, "Perhaps I can help you in some way?" She shook her head no, and, barely raising her hand, motioned with it in the direction of the door. When I had reached the threshold, she very quietly said, "Thank you."

The next day I was walking past the ward where Zina lay. They were cleaning her room, and the door was open. I don't know why I went in. She had changed dramatically in the course of just one day: she had a pale grayish face, the face of a corpse. Only her eyes looked alive. She asked: "Are you the woman who has a child here?" As she spoke, it seemed that every word was forced out with great effort. I said that, yes, I was the one. She looked at me—and perhaps this sounds savage—but this dying woman looked at me with pity and forcing out each word, said, "Yes, that's too bad. You can't even die. What can be done? Go on living." That night she died.

The whole hospital was filled with victims of frostbite. Andrei Mikhailovich performed several operations per day. He amputated frozen fingers and toes and at times entire hands and feet.

After evening rounds he sometimes came to see me; he was so exhausted that he could barely talk. He would sit silently for about ten minutes, say good-bye and leave.

In January 1938, as part of "strengthening the regime," they transferred him to general work, and he cut wood near the dining area. After a few days, they brought in some high official with a blocked intestine. They summoned Andrei Mikhailovich from the barracks, he performed the operation and the next morning he was back sawing wood. A couple of days before I was released, they brought in a free-hire woman with an attack of appendicitis.

They put her in with me, since the entire hospital was filled with frostbitten men and there were no free wards. The woman was very young. She tossed her head back and forth on the pillow and screamed, "Call the doctor-prisoner, let the doctor-prisoner do the operation." And once again they summoned Andrei Mikhailovich and he performed the operation.

I told him that, in my opinion, this was very stupid on his part. He should declare that for a surgeon, his hands were an instrument, and he couldn't operate after sawing wood for ten hours out in the cold. "Refuse to operate just once, and let them release you from the regular work." He smiled and answered: "How could I refuse, after all, I took the oath."

They then released me from the hospital. I never saw Andrei Mikhailovich again. But I heard that after a while they returned him to work in his specialty.

In general, the sole category of prisoners who almost always worked at their specialty was doctors. This was a great advantage, but also very hard for them. Every doctor naturally wanted to continue his work. But at the same time every doctor, if he was a true doctor and a decent human being, wanted to help the other prisoners. In this sense, it was most difficult of all for doctors at the campsites. The bosses demanded that as few as possible be freed from work, and yet the physician could see that every third, if not every second, prisoner needed to be given medical treatment.

I found changes at my assigned place. They had designated a corner of the large tent where coats were repaired and placed Shura Nikolaeva there with her Allochka and me with my Lera. The corner was tiny, with two beds, two cribs and in the middle, an iron stove. The tent was not heated. When the stove was alight, you couldn't bend over it, the heat was too much. If you leaned back, your hair would freeze to the canvas of the tent.

Then Shura fell ill with a cold. She lay there all flushed and at times lost consciousness. I went to the head of the camp, so that they would put her in the hospital. He said, "And so she'll die. The easy days are over." My milk had almost dried up. Little Lera was fed on kasha and kissel made from powder. We were supposed to get a so-called children's ration, but we only received half. The person who ran the shop kept part for himself, and we had to give part to the guard so that he would allow us to bring wood for our stove.

In the other tent, where the rest of the women lived, Galina Ioanova, a Pole whose surname I don't remember, went mad. She was a very cultured woman, a philosopher by training. She refused to eat and didn't recognize anyone. Once at night she almost smothered her neighbor, Lily Buravleva, a harmless and unremarkable person. She put a pillow over her face and leaned on it from above. It was lucky that Lilka managed to cry out, for the other women woke up. After this the bosses agreed to send her to the hospital.

One evening in the larger section of the tent steps could be heard. A man stood there in the opening. He was clean-shaven, well-fed and wore a leather coat. I immediately recognized him—it was Colonel Garanin. Behind him stood the head of our camp. And the entire camp council.

Garanin looked over our domicile: an iron stove in the middle, two tiny children, the feverish Shura, and then, looking straight through me with the same glassy stare as before, asked, "Any complaints?" I said that it was necessary that the tent be heated, that wood be regularly supplied, that the children receive milk and that the sick Nikolaeva be placed in a hospital. He turned his head and said to those standing behind him, "Write that all this be done." Then he turned to me, "Anything else?" Then I said that my husband was at a mine twenty-five kilometers from here, we had cohabitation rights and my things were with him. Besides this, he didn't even know that we had a new daughter. (Here, of course, I lied; I had written him a couple of times through the hospital. But my things did actually remain at the mine.) I said that I wanted to meet with my husband. He once again turned and said, "Write the name of the husband, obtain her things and arrange a meeting."

After this he left.

An hour later, the head of the work-dispatch office appeared and told me to gather my things. They were sending us to Magadan. There would be no arrangements, no things, no meetings—we were being sent immediately. This was a personal order from Colonel Garanin. Running ahead, I must say that when Garanin was removed and, according to rumor, shot, they said that he was by no means Colonel Garanin, but a simple bandit who had killed the real Garanin and taken his papers. I personally never believed this. First of all, he received his appointment to Kolyma in Moscow, where undoubtedly they would know what the real Garanin looked like. Second, he was a typical representative of the police organs of that period. Such Garanins, on a smaller scale and with fewer powers, were at every location, every campsite, in every prison.

We traveled in 45-below weather: the insane Galina, the sick Shura, two infants and myself. Of course, with a guard. They took Galina tied up. After the night when she had almost smothered Lilka, she had become violent. For the entire journey, about three days, she didn't sleep for a second and ate nothing. It was very cold, and at stopping places I tried without success to give her at least a few sips of hot water.

In Magadan they put her in the psychiatric division, and after a few days she died, probably from exhaustion. She absolutely refused to consume anything, even water.

They placed Shura and me in a women's division, in the "wet nurse barracks." The "wet nurses" were women who had children or were

nearing the end of their pregnancy. The majority were common criminals, for whom children were a good "business." For six months they
were given a ration, not forced to work, not sent out in groups, for
they fell under the so-called Krupskaya Amnesty for Mothers (this
didn't apply to those with our article). In general, it was completely
beneficial. There were a few 58ers there, but they somehow didn't fall
out of the "ensemble." Some of them were friends with the criminals,
ate with them and used the same criminal jargon. Others simply were
afraid of them.

While still at the mine, I had learned the price of the "romanti-
cism" of the criminal world, and the women in this world were much
worse than the men.

With regard to everyday life, the company of "wet nurses" lived
rather free and easy. They didn't work, they had "husbands" and since
there were very few women in Kolyma, some had more than one. These
"husbands" were rated for the most part from the standpoint of "content," but along with this, they had to have someone for their "soul."
Much like in Kuprin's novel *The Hellhole*.

The overwhelming majority of these "wet nurses" simply didn't
have any maternal instincts, but this didn't prevent them from raising
hell in the children's home if Alfredik's face hadn't been washed, or if
Gretochka didn't have a clean diaper. As a rule, the names of their
children were quite extravagant.

By this time I had already been in the camps for two years, but
this was the first time that I fell into such a circle. Never before had I
heard such foul language; everything was called by its real name; they
spoke in the greatest detail about the most secret and intimate sides of
life.

That is when I felt that I was truly alone. None of my friends from
the previous year remained. Some had been taken to the "mainland"
(Aleksandra Lvovna Bronstein, Tanya Myagkova and others), and
many had been sent along the way to other sites.

The camp contingent had changed greatly. With the tightening up
of the regime, many stool pigeons were cultivated. Here a few words
must be said about stool pigeons. Of course, they are not born, they are
made. And they are made in various ways. Some simply became stool

pigeons out of fear. They were summoned, yelled at and frightened, "So, you refuse to help us. Just wait and see! You have only yourself to blame. We'll send you to the back of beyond and give you a new sentence," and so forth. Many were broken by this and became informers.

In the majority of cases, however, informers simply wanted to make things easier for themselves—receive a good job, protect themselves against being sent away.

But the worst sort of stool pigeons were the "ideological" informers. Those who informed for their own benefit might conceal something from the authorities. They might not squeal on somebody because they were bunkmates, or because they came from the same area or simply because they liked someone.

For the "ideological" informer, such considerations didn't exist. The "ideological" stool pigeon felt that he had remained a Communist and that it was his party duty to expose all those who might be even potential enemies of the party and the state. Regardless of sex, age or friendly relations.

People told about one woman who was imprisoned in Moscow in the Lubyanka. She was summoned to the officials and they held approximately the following conversation with her: "Yes, you are temporarily isolated from Soviet society, you have been expelled from the party. But you yourself know—if you chop wood, the chips will fly. We understand the difference between you and real enemies. We believe that you have remained a party member, although without a party card. Isn't this so?" "Yes."

They gave her a list of twenty people. "Take these people—they are the real enemies of the party and the government. Believe us, we know this very well. But we have no material on them. Now you must give us this material. Sit down and write separately about everyone on the list; say that you heard their anti-Soviet views, that they told you about their counterrevolutionary plans and so forth."

They summoned her several days in a row. She wrote everything they needed, being certain that she was fulfilling her party duty. When she was done, the investigator said to her: "Well, that's fine. And now we're giving you twenty-five years for the fact that you knew all this and didn't tell us when you should have."

It was she who told this to her cellmate. She tried to commit suicide. I don't know what happened to her later. This, of course, was an extreme case.

But to inform a bit on one's cellmates, on bunkmates, on members of one's work brigade, and to think that in doing so this was fulfilling one's party duty—there were no small number of such informers.

After ten days of quarantine, they took the children, Lera and Alla, to the children's home. Within two weeks they had both fallen ill with inflammation of the lungs. Allochka was a fat, healthy girl, but she became very seriously ill. And there was nothing to be said about my baby! At that time she was skinny, dark as a worm, and so weak that she couldn't even cry properly, she only meowed like a kitten.

Oh, what a children's home it was! A real "angel factory." Children died there all the time; from dyspepsia, from anemia and simply from being worn out. Yet the conditions there could have been passable: the building was good, the food was also not bad. Everything came down to the way they were cared for. A 58er, as an "enemy of the people," wasn't allowed to work with the children. The ones who worked there were the criminals, the common, everyday criminals, the "socially close" elements. With rare exceptions these "socially close" elements didn't need their own children, let alone someone else's.

For them the children's home was a criminal's job, in the warmth, without guards and with good food. Here is how they worked. For hours on end they would stand under the stairway with their "husbands," or they would simply leave, while the children, unfed and unattended, would get sick and begin dying. Whenever there was the slightest epidemic, they would die like flies. Out of Lera's entire group, only three remained alive: Lera, Tamara, the daughter of a German Communist, Johanna Wilke, and Tolik, the son of a Moscow worker, Shura Ivanova.

And this, too, was one of the camp miracles. Why precisely was it these three who survived? After all, we, their mothers, could do nothing for our children. We simply wanted very much for them to survive. And they did....

After the lung inflammation, Lerochka returned to the children's home, and I went back to my worksite. But Shura's Allochka died. It was horrible to look at Shura, who within a few days had grown darker and aged by several years. But that wasn't all she was destined to live through.... They put Allochka in the morgue. I was allowed to go out through the gate and I walked to the cemetery to order a coffin and a grave. Our women in the flower shop made an arrangement for her of many beautiful flowers. Two women went with me to the morgue. They dressed Allochka and we adorned her with flowers. She had not been ill for long and lay there as if she were alive, such a big and beautiful baby. She could have been taken for three years old, but she was only a year and three months.

When I returned to the morgue (at that time it was a small building next to the hospital) I saw Shura sitting on a rock near the morgue. Her face bore such an expression.... I thought to myself—what more could have happened, for Allochka had already died. When I drew closer, she turned to me and said in a somehow very even voice: "Nadya, they raped my daughter." For a moment, I thought that she had gone mad. But she seemed to hear what I was thinking, "I'm not crazy. I am telling the truth. Go and see. I can't go in there." I went into the morgue. And the first thing I saw was the flowers. There were so many, and I had adorned her with these flowers myself. How beautiful she looked. Yet by now, everything had changed.

I went to the main physician. He apparently had grown used to not being surprised by anything. He went with me to the morgue. He looked at Allochka and summoned another physician. For two hours Shura and I sat on the rock near the morgue. It must be that they had simply forgotten about us. And then one of the doctors walked up to us and said that there had been a medical examination. They had established that the corpse had indeed been raped. It had been done by the person in charge of the morgue. He confessed that he often did this with the corpses of women. They led him away. Allochka was buried.

Life became a bit more difficult. Mothers were given a special ration for only six months, and Lerochka was already older. Naturally there was no help from home, and I couldn't earn anything by working. I lived the entire time on a ration of bread and prison soup (balanda). And, in addition, I fed my child. To make things worse, these accursed "wet nurses," among whom I lived, cooked and fixed things from morning until night. My head would spin from the continuous smell of food. At first they tried to treat me. But I simply couldn't find any rapport with them. I didn't want to, it was repulsive. It was repulsive to take advantage of their "kindness." It was repulsive simply to live with them. To hear their endless scandals: the prostitutes hated the thieves, since they felt that their (prostitutes') profession did no one any harm, and on the contrary, brought people pleasure. The thieves hated the prostitutes, since they felt that their (thieves') profession was filled with danger and risk, whereas the prostitutes were simply parasites. And both groups hated the noncriminals. At first I tried to somehow enlighten them. I remembered that at the mine, where there were absolutely no books, someone had brought me a fat notebook with an oilskin binding, and I filled it with poems I knew by heart. This notebook was in great demand. And not only among the 58ers. Among the criminals, too, there were lovers of poetry. I recalled this when I lived among the "wet nurses." I had no desire to read them poems. But someone dragged out a dog-eared volume of Chekhov's short stories. Without the beginning or end. But "The Lady with the Dog" was complete. I offered to read it aloud. I tried to read as expressively as possible, for it seemed to me that Chekhov's high degree of humanity would somehow reach them. They listened attentively, and when I was finished, there were a couple of minutes of silence. I looked at them almost with sympathy: "Did it get through?" Then one of them sighed heavily and said, "Yes, no matter what kind of a lady she was, they still fucked her." That was the end of my "enlightenment activity."

There were a few more 58ers besides me in the barracks. Some had been pregnant when they were arrested, others had affairs in the camps. But they tried not to sharpen relations with the criminals because they simply feared them. Life was more difficult for them than for me, although they were sometimes given some food.

You could never show the criminals that you feared them. And there were those who didn't fear them; they truly made friends with them, and felt that in this way it would be easier to serve out their sentences. There was Pana Sidorova, also KRTD. She was from a good family, a party member and before her arrest worked in the prosecutor's office. Here, however, she was no different from the criminals. In essence, she was worse than they were, for they simply didn't know any other way of life.

At first she tried to form a friendship with me: "Listen to me, the most important thing is to preserve yourself physically. Otherwise, you won't make it. You have to preserve yourself, if only for the children." (She had a daughter outside and a son here.) I heard this "preserve yourself for the sake of your children" not from just her. To preserve oneself at any cost was the most widely accepted means of inner self-justification. "To preserve oneself" meant to hob-nob with criminals, to attach oneself to those who had managed to get easy jobs and sometimes to simply "squeal." That was the price of "preserving" oneself.

At the beginning of 1938 in Kolyma, after the arrest of almost all the high officials, their wives were brought to the women's camps. Among these women I met an acquaintance, Olga Ishchenko, who worked as a nurse in the hospital. She had served out her sentence for a common crime and then married some kind of official. Then he was arrested, and she ended up in the camps once again. Zina Tettelbaum was one of these wives in our barracks. Why she ended up in a barracks for "wet nurses," I don't know.

She was nineteen, had finished the technical institute and asked to be sent to Kolyma. They had told her that there were few women there and you could find a good husband. She did indeed find a husband, but after ten days he was arrested. She spent their honeymoon at the women's camp.

Many of these women had children. The children were placed in the children's home. This was located on the second floor, and on the first was a kindergarten for children of the free-hires. There was only one kitchen, but different food was prepared. Once when they were repairing the kitchen, someone had the bright idea of taking those children and ours to eat in the dining area at the same time. For breakfast, theirs were given an omelette, bread and sausage, cocoa and rolls with jam. Ours were given oatmeal porridge and tea with milk. One of the new women had a little boy, Igor, a wonderful child with red hair, a button nose and a slight speech defect like Denisov in *War and Peace*, "Countess Wostova." They tried to convince him to eat his oatmeal, "Eat, Igorechek, it's very good for you." And he would cry, "No, this oatmeal isn't good for me, what's good for me is that Kwakow sausage and wolls with jam."

Soon they placed a few women who were in transit in the "wet nurse" barracks. Their children were with them, and within ten days they would have to be taken to the children's home. Once, late at night, when many were already asleep, two people came into the barracks. "Who is the elder here?" As our elder, we had a tall, heavily-built woman named Sonya, a Byelorussian. She had lived in a village near the Polish border, and her mother lived a few kilometers away on the other side of the border. When her mother fell ill, Sonya went to her place to milk the cow. She got six years PSh (suspicion of espionage). They arrested her while she was pregnant. She gave birth to a weak little boy. He was so feeble that he was obviously still alive only due to good feeding. Sonya had as much milk as the cow for which she received her sentence.

The people who came in asked where the woman was who had been brought the day before from the northern district. Sonya pointed her out. The woman was not yet asleep, but sat on her bed, holding her six-month-old son in her arms. One of the men went up to her. He was a fine-looking middle-aged man, wearing glasses. The woman looked at him in fear. But he turned so gently to the child, asked him what his name was and playfully waved two fingers at him, pretending they were a goat's horns. It was clear that the woman was a bit reassured. "Oh, what a wonderful fellow you are! What can I give you?" He pulled out of his pocket a set of keys on a key ring and began jiggling them. "Wonderful, wonderful fellow. He-e-re, come to me, little one, come to me." He beckoned to the little boy with both hands. The infant trustingly reached out and went into his arms. You had to see how quickly the man's face and voice changed. It was as if he were a different person. All his features became sharp, his voice became harsh and biting. "Elder, take the child." He shoved the child to Sonya and turned toward the woman. "Follow me." How she screamed! They dragged her to the door, but she tore away from their arms and reached for her child, screaming all the while. The two of them dragged her out of the barracks, and her cries could still be heard beyond the door. And in the arms of the distraught Sonya the little boy was wailing in a heartrending way. I don't even know who this woman was. She managed only to say that her husband worked in the party apparat somewhere in Ukraine, that she was also a party member and a teacher.

Sonya was sniffling. She put the child down to sleep and said, turning to me: "Well, you, after all, are party members, Communists. But why are they tormenting us?" Not a bad question twenty-one years after the revolution....

Once my neighbor bought some candy from the camp shop; they were sticky sweets, wrapped in a piece of newspaper. I naturally grabbed it. Evidently it was some kind of Far Eastern newspaper, perhaps the TOZ (*Pacific Ocean Star*). And—what a coincidence—in this bit of newspaper which accidentally fell into my hands I read that in Khabarovsk there had been a trial of the former leading officials from the Far Eastern obkom, who turned out to be "enemies of the people." Several names were mentioned, including Verny, Volsky and Kaplan, all of whom had been Pavel's friends at work in Vladivostok and Blagoveshchensk. All received the "highest measure." And "the sentence was immediately carried out."

All the Magadan wives were called into the work distribution office, where they read them the decision of the "troika" for Dalstroy— they all received ten years.

The next day, Olga Ishchenko hanged herself.

Zina Tettelbaum, who lived in the "wet nurse" barracks, paid for her family happiness at the rate of one year for each day: she had been married ten days and received a ten-year sentence.

They found Olga in an empty barracks. Earlier it had been used as a disinfection chamber and on the walls were hooks for the clothes. She was hanging by a belt from a dress, and was just like they describe people who have been strangled: all blue, with a protruding tongue.

Soon news came that she had been set free.

Lera had grown a bit, and they transferred me from the "wet nurse" barracks to the ordinary one. I wanted this to happen. Although the "wet nurse" barracks had separate beds and only twenty-five people, and in the new barracks there were two-tier bunks and one hundred people if not more, I was nevertheless pleased.

I was tired of these brutes, the "wet nurses." And it was hard to always be hungry and watch them stuffing themselves.

I learned that all my friends were sitting in a Magadan prison, people convicted for the same article and in the same case: Difa and Olga and Anya Sadovskaya and Sofia Mikhailovna Antonova and Danya Kievlenko. They were living under terrible conditions. It was crowded, filthy, they were fed only fish soup, water was limited and they were summoned to interrogations which were in fact hardly interrogations; they simply swore at them and insulted them with foul language.

It was a miracle that they didn't take me there. My friends later told me that when the key turned in the lock to their cell, they all looked at the door: "They're probably bringing Nadya."

Every night they took people away from the barracks in which I lived. In the middle of the night, the door would open and an official would come in accompanied with two other people. Heads would raise from the bunks: "Who were they coming for?..." And every night I waited for my turn. There were also endless nighttime searches.

When it got a bit warmer, they began to count the prisoners in the yard. All the women were arranged in order. The counting took two hours, and if the numbers didn't come out right, then it took even longer. And every day they read out orders: "By the decision of the Dalstroy troika ... for sabotage ... for refusing to work ... for pretending ... the highest measure of punishment." And every day dozens of names. And finally, "the sentence has been carried out."

Every day I waited for them to call out Pavel's name.... Every night I waited for them to come for me.... That is how the spring and summer of 1938 passed.

Towards fall, they let all my friends out of prison. Difa, Olga, Anya Sadovskaya and others returned to the women's camp.

They arrested Difa and Zyama (her husband) at the northern mining directorate. They ended up at Serpantinka, a horrible place of torture, a "torture chamber," where nobody came out alive. Difa was pregnant and was sent to Magadan. But this didn't save her from the Magadan prison. She spent almost her entire pregnancy there, fell seriously ill with pleuritis and received almost no medical attention. She was let out shortly before giving birth, with active tuberculosis. Soon after this they put her in the camp hospital and on October 6 she had a daughter, Zhanna. They took Zhanna to the children's home, and Difa worked at the women's camp in the flower shop. She always had good taste and learned to make very beautiful arrangements. She fed Zhanna after covering her mouth and nose with a gauze bandage.

The camp didn't make the treatment of tuberculosis any easier. She didn't get any better. In the summer of 1941 they once again placed her in the hospital, and freedom for her came in the form of being sent from a hospital for prisoners to the hospital for free-hires. With the first steamship, she and others who were officially declared sick were taken to the "mainland."

The steamship arrived in Vladivostok on the day war was declared. She never made it, of course, to Moscow. She spent another three years in evacuation and died, leaving behind her two children, Galya and Zhanna. The girls were raised by her sister Tamara, a rare person with a self-sacrificing soul who devoted her entire life to these children.

But I have jumped too far ahead. When she had returned from prison, Difa lay next to me on the bunks and told me in a whisper about Serpantinka. I have neither the words nor the strength to tell about the tortures to which people were subjected there. Difa met there Volodya Rabinovich, our comrade at the institute. Volodya was short, lop-eared, narrow-shouldered and red-haired, a typical child of the ghetto, although the majority of his life he had spent in Moscow. He was older than many of us, but we called him "Sonny." He was a person of great spiritual purity and had a high sense of comradeship. For comrades he was ready to do anything. When Difa saw him, he was completely crippled, almost couldn't walk and coughed up blood. He told her, "I won't make it out of here alive. If you sometime return to normal life, tell people about the way I died."

She wasn't able to do that. In her place, I will do it in these notes.

Serpantinka meant the death of an old woman and wonderful person — Nushik Zavarian. When the so-called Garanin period of "arbitrary rule" began, she wrote a statement to the head of Dalstroy: "To the governor-general of Kolyma from the Bolshevik-Leninist Nushik Zavarian."

They immediately took her to Serpantinka, and she never emerged from there alive.

In the children's home, the infants continued to die. It seems that someone noticed this shocking rate of infant mortality. They removed the doctor and replaced him with a new one who had arrived from Moscow. She was called Rozalia Borisovna Ginsburg. The first thing that she did was to go to USVITLag and declare that she didn't care at all what article the women working in the children's home were charged with, but she demanded that they be people who could be entrusted with children.

So they removed the criminals and put in their place older women imprisoned by decree, some under Article 58, point 10. In Lera's group Marya Ivanovna became the nanny, a wonderful old woman who was like the kind grandmother from a children's fairy tale.

Conditions in the children's home were completely transformed. The children almost never got sick anymore. Even the air seemed to become cleaner.

In the camp, the regime became a bit easier. This was first of all expressed by the fact that 58ers were allowed to visit the club. Our girls, who missed the cinema very much, went running to the first show. But at the club they were met by the teacher on duty. It seems that the new liberal atmosphere had not yet reached him. Or, to be more precise, it had reached him, but he didn't understand it. It is no accident that they say in the camps: "The old man had three sons. Two were intelligent and the third ... was a teacher."

In any case, he immediately drove the 58ers out of the club, and the girls, who were quite distressed, headed back to their barracks. Then some official arrived and apparently gave the "vigilant" teacher a real dressing down, for the latter jumped onto the club porch and plaintively called after those who had left, "Kontriki-i-i!* Come back!"

* Slang for those convicted of counterrevolutionary activity.

Just before the New Year, a large group of prisoners came to the women's camp, including many from Moscow. Among them I met some former workers at the NKPS, who knew my stepfather Mikhail Ostrovsky. From them I learned that Mikhail had been arrested in the summer of 1937, condemned by a tribunal and executed.

When I had been with Pavel, we had written his relatives and we even received photographs of our children. But since the fall of 1937, I had heard nothing about them. I tried to think that they were with mama, and consequently, that things weren't too bad for them. Mother didn't write me; she had warned that she wouldn't at our last meeting. And she asked that I not write to her or to any of our relatives. But I simply couldn't obey her wishes. I sent a telegram to my grandmother who lived in Baku with mama's brother.

After a week I received a reply: "Beba isn't here (Beba was a family nickname for my mother), the children are; they are healthy and feel well." Thus I learned about my mother's arrest. But, I have to confess, I was thinking more about the children. I knew that Vitya, mother's brother, was a well-known physician in Baku and earned a good salary. I knew that he was a generous and kind man, that he loved children, even other people's, and so he probably wouldn't be bad to mine. And they would be lovingly cared for by grandmother.

But my God, how much they had lost in their young lives! First me, then their father, then my mother.... How often they had to leave behind one group of people and get used to another.

Apparently nothing ever happens without leaving its mark. I felt the effect of sleepless nights, when they took people out of the barracks and they never came back. And every night, the anticipation: who will it be today, me or somebody else. And there were thoughts about my husband, who, most likely, had once been taken away like that. And the countless deaths of the children around Lera. And now this....

I had some kind of seizure—it was either my heart or nerves, and they put me in the hospital. I remembered this well, for this was my only sick leave during all the years in the camps.

In February 1939 they moved me once again.

Lerochka was fifteen months old, and I should have stopped feeding her long ago. But nonnursing mothers see their children twice a month, and Rozalia Borisovna, a kind soul, said that the infant was weak and needed mother's milk, although my milk had long since disappeared. She simply wanted to give me the chance of seeing my baby every day.

I had already begun to go to work. True, not to a permanent job, but to wherever I was needed, doing so-called light jobs. Oh, these "light" jobs in the camps! Washing barracks for 200 people, with double bunks; they were unbelievably filthy, covered with human waste in the most direct sense of the word. People were simply too lazy to go to the latrine. How many buckets of water I had to carry. Or to wash the floors in the apartment of some official, after it had been fixed up! The lime ate away at one's hands, and the floor had to be scraped with a knife.

True, sometimes they sent me to clean up in some dining area or in a store. For the entire year of 1938, I rarely managed to eat to the point of feeling full. But here they fed me. And I even figured out how to bring something into the camp for Difa and others.

When I was transferred, I ended up in Ola, a village of the fish industry administration of Dalstroy. In the beginning I worked on construction. The main brigade worked on building a school, whereas my fellow worker Ira (Irina) Bukmeer and I painted apartments throughout the whole village. Thus we walked about in quilted trousers with a bucket and brush. "Painter, need some bread? We'll shower you with loaves of white bread!" There was, of course, no white bread, but the food was much better than at the women's camp.

At least I had a steady job. I earned certain percentages. Even in this seventh ring of Dante's inferno, not all were equal: there were Stakhanovites, shock-workers, those who got 600 grams of bread, 800 grams, a thousand gradations. In order to be on some high rung, it was by no means required that you actually worked hard. You just had to be on good terms with the brigade leader, with various camp people assigned to the light work or simply fall into some needed position.

Irina was a very young Leningrad student. They had a group of several people. They would meet, go to the movies or the dances and, among other things, they read the stenograms of party congresses. Where they managed to get this "seditious " literature, I don't know. Nor did Ira know: "One fellow got his hands on it." They were surprised to find out that almost all the members of the Central Committee, Lenin's closest supporters, turned out to be enemies of the people. Then, it seems that one of them squealed. They all were sentenced. Some got three years, some five, some ten. Sometimes Ella Yegorova worked with us. Ella was my age and before her arrest was a geography teacher at a village school; her husband was director there.

Before some holiday they decided to decorate their school and, for lack of other resources, cut paper napkins out of old newspapers and covered the tables and shelves with them. A few of the newspapers had portraits of the leaders, and the leaders were therefore cut up.

As the director, Ella's husband got twenty-five years, and she received ten. They immediately enrolled in the camp amateur theatricals. Fortunately, 58ers were now being accepted. They convinced me to sign up as well, "You read poetry so well."

I agreed simply out of boredom, so that I wouldn't spend evenings sitting in the barracks. And to my surprise, I became the "prima donna" of the agit-brigade there.

The entire summer of 1939 I worked during the fishing season.

First there was the herring season, then came the Siberian and hunchbacked salmon. During the fish run, the entire camp worked on bringing them in. On some days, even the offices closed and all the free-hires were mobilized.

The fishing season is a curious spectacle! The fish move in huge schools, and if you stand in the water, they will knock you off your feet. I liked this work: the whole camp regimen amounted to nothing. There was no counting, no roll call. Everyone came and went at various times. In the morning, first would go the carvers, then the cleaners, then the salters. I worked at salting the fish. You work inside an enormous vat, wearing high rubber boots; you salt the fish and put them in rows. As the rows become packed, you pile them higher and higher, until the vat was filled to the brim. It sounds like the work wasn't very difficult, but at the end of the day, you could barely stand up. If you got the slightest scratch on your hand—and you got a lot of scratches from the fish gills—then salt would immediately get in it. We worked all the time with bandaged fingers. But then we ate as much fish as we wanted, and the very best.

At the end of the fish run, the head of the fish industry administration came to review the results. It turned out that our worksite had emerged with very good figures. The officials awarded bonuses, and a few prisoners were given bonuses. Including me. At the salter— 150 percent of the average and also the "prima donna" of the agit-brigade.

The camp is a kind of litmus paper, which shows a person for what he is. When I look back at my five years, I am not ashamed to recall them and I have nothing to blush about. There is only the question of the amateur theater.... Essentially, there was nothing wrong with it.... And yet....

Our distant ancestors, in approximately analogous conditions, hung up their lutes and said that they wouldn't sing in bondage.

My distant ancestors were the ancient Jews, the same ones who sat on the rivers of Babylon and wept, but they nevertheless wouldn't sing unless they were free. And yet we sang, and we were not free. Apparently, it was a different epoch and different people....

When they told me about the bonus, I went to the director and said that I didn't need any bonus, but it would be better if they let me visit my child, whom I hadn't seen for six months. He agreed. The administration of the fish industry is located in the village of Veselaya, which is six kilometers from Magadan. Some went to Magadan by bus, but most went on foot. Returning to Veselaya, the director took me in his own boat, without anything, without documents, in order to allow me to see my child and then return to Ola.

On the day after I arrived, they took me with a guard to Magadan, to the children's home. I spent about an hour with Lera. At first she didn't recognize me, but then she hugged me and cried so when I left. She had grown to look a lot like Kira, and it seemed to me that she, in fact, was Kirochka, which means that Talochka must be somewhere here as well....

I was supposed to be sent back to Ola in a couple of days, but there was no guard to escort me.

The day after our meeting, I put on my beige coat with opposum (participants in the amateur theatricals are allowed to keep their own clothes) and a fashionable cap made out of chenille, which they knit at the women's camp. I then put on lipstick, walked boldly through the village (fortunately, none of the local guards knew me by sight), got on the bus and traveled to Magadan.

I decided to go to the director of USVITLag, Captain Veshnevetsky. Garanin was no longer there. I was an old enough inmate to know that being absent without leave could always be qualified as an escape. But they had virtually taken away my last child, and I felt that there was hardly anything which they could do to me worse than that.

At USVITLag, I immediately went to Veshnevetsky's reception room. The secretary, a girl out of a fashion magazine photo, looked at me with an evaluating glance and said, "The captain today is only receiving prisoners." In actual fact, once a month, Veshnevetsky did receive prisoners. In order to see him, you needed permission from the head of the camp and the head of the directorate to which the camp belonged. Permission was given very selectively, in small numbers. Of course, there was no time to ponder, I knew that I would never have a second chance of being there. "Well, I am a prisoner." "A prisoner?" Once again, she looked me over from head to toe. "And does your boss know that you are here?" Without batting an eye, I replied, "He knows." "All right, go back into the corridor and I will call you." Thank God, she didn't ask for the camp name, which meant that she wasn't going to check.

In the corridor were fifteen male prisoners. Learning that I was a prisoner too, they began to take the most active part in my affairs. "A desperate girl." "Look out, you'll get in trouble." "What else could she do if they took away her child." I received a lot of advice, of all different kinds. But everyone agreed on one thing: I shouldn't have come in "free" clothing. Captain Veshnevetsky issued an order long ago that prisoners must only wear camp clothing. But of course in camp clothing I never would have made it through the village. What could be done? One of these fellows tore off my coat and gave me his own quilted jacket. I hadn't had time to decide whether that was right or not, when the secretary appeared in the doorway: "Young girl, come into the office." I went in. I was wearing a coat that was too large, the sleeves were dangling and I had a coquettish knit cap on my head; it's not hard to imagine what I looked like. The secretary went in after me and sat by the side of a small table; she kept notes during the reception. The captain sat behind a large desk. After Garanin he seemed to me to be fully human.

It would seem that I told the story of how Lera appeared on this earth rather coherently. The captain listened carefully and the secretary wrote things down. Then he turned to me, "We will check. If your child is not a camp child, but is from your husband, with whom you had cohabitation, we will give the corresponding directives to the head of your camp."

Feeling faint from joy, I went towards the door, when suddenly I heard the tender little voice of the secretary, "One minute. Tell me, please. Why did you come to sign in wearing such a good coat, and now you have such an awful jacket?"

Well, I thought to myself, now I'm finished. But the captain was apparently in a good mood. He smiled and looked at me, "You shouldn't cheat." All right. I leapt out into the corridor. I gave back to the unknown comrade his "lucky" jacket. Then I set out for Veselaya on foot, since I didn't have any money for the bus. It turns out that the captain worked very efficiently. By the time I arrived, there was already an order to leave me in Veselaya.

Thus began the next stage of my life in Kolyma, in the village of Veselaya. The group of prisoners there was small, there were about twenty women. Everyone lived in one barracks, without regard to the articles under which they had been convicted. About a third were 58ers, another third were "pure" minor criminals (embezzlers, bribe-takers) and the rest were serious criminals. Everything is relative. After the "wet nurse" barracks, this was simply a boarding school for girls of the nobility.

They sent me to work in the laundry. My workmate, Galya Khomenko, had in the past been a common criminal. Galya was the only person I met in Kolyma whom the camps actually reeducated. But credit for this should not be given to the camps. Galya was serving a normal sentence as a criminal, when she drank a bit too much and referred disrespectfully to the "adored leader." She received a "camp 58" (there were many such instances), after which they transferred her to the barracks for 58ers.

As she would later say, Galya saw a different way of life. Here lived people who didn't swear or fight, who were good to each other and who read books during their free time. When they recalled their past, these were recollections of a normal, decent life. All this greatly appealed to her. As "models,"' she picked several women whom she liked very much, and evidently, who responded to her well. She began to read books and gradually fell in love with reading. Arriving in Kolyma, she "mended her ways," broke all her ties with the criminal world and began to work for the first time (common criminals would not consider working).

Galya was a healthy, strapping woman. Work in the laundry, after a day of which I didn't even know where to lay my hands since they ached so much, wasn't hard for her. She had a serious romance with a fine fellow, Pasha Naumov, a motor-mechanic from the boat and an active participant in the amateur theatricals.

Running ahead, I will say that I met Galya and Pasha after I was released. They lived together and both worked. Galya was studying at night school. Once again, this was the only genuinely reeducated person I ever met in the camps. I met no small number of officially "reeducated" criminals, who occupied various posts in the camps. These were usually absolutely corrupt people, who fully retained their criminal nature, but who correctly understood that it would be easier to serve out their time if they were "reeducated." This gave them good living conditions, near immunity from punishment and sometimes even power over other prisoners. From their ranks came the cadres for the "pridurki," those who did light work. An amazing group, these "pridurki." Take, for example, the senior worker at the women's location, Vera Ziusko. She decided where to send each person to work. She decided whether a person would "turn up their toes" or "reach the end" doing heavy labor under guard, or else pretend to work doing some "cushy little job." She decided whether a camp inmate could go outside through the gates or whether they would sit in the camp compound and "get their ration for nothing."

In short, good relations with Vera were a guarantee of good prison life.

Vera had everything she wanted. She lived in a separate tent, had her own helper (or more simply put, her own housemaid). Even the greatest of the "great-Soviet" Kolyma elite could not compete with her wardrobe. She was served by the best cleaners in the laundry and the best seamstresses in the sewing shop. Everything that appeared in the stores she received before anyone else (if not the main director, then a salesclerk always lived with some prisoner and was interested in making sure that his passion be allowed through the gates without any problems). Vera was at that time a young, good-looking blonde, who was far from stupid and had a character of her own. She loved to read books, predominantly romances. She respected 58ers for "being learned" and sometimes allowed them little indulgences. Not, of course, unselfishly. Women gave her their foreign scarves, sweaters, belts and any other "vestiges of their early luxury" which they managed to bring with them into the camps. Vera was not a bad girl and at the women's location they liked her. Another in her place would have taken away their clothes and done absolutely nothing for them, or, in any case, would have done very little, only for show.

But Vera was "an honest bribe-taker." But woe to whomever she didn't like! There was no one to whom one could complain about her. The head of the work assignment office was a free-hire, and she wrapped him around her finger whenever she wanted. Thus at the women's site, Vera was highest authority and the last word.

I discovered all this, of course, when I ended up once more at the women's site. By the way, such "Veras," in one form or another, were at every campsite.

I remember the work-dispatcher at the mines: a healthy fellow, with a fat, insolent physiognomy, whom everyone respectfully called Anatoly Ivanovich. At the mine he was both czar and God, to an even greater degree than Vera was at the women's site. In the most literal sense, human life depended on him. I remember how he once was sitting on the steps of his office (at that time I was working in the office), and an old man walked past him, one of the KRTDs whose name was Feldman. He was wearing an old patched coat, completely worn out, and hobbled along, leaning on a handmade cane. Feldman was an Old Bolshevik, who had been in prison several times, escaped from exile and then lived in emigration.

Anatoly Ivanovich was sitting there with his stuffed face, smoking a fat cigarette and said, after Feldman walked by, "Why does our government bother with such people? If it were up to me, I would personally shoot every one of these yids and kontriks."

Veselaya also had its amateur theater brigade. Since I was already an "experienced" actress, they immediately recruited me. I played the main role in Shkvarkin's comedy, *A Stranger's Child*, in Karatygin's vaudeville, *Dear Uncle on Three Legs*, and in various concert programs.

The theater group at Veselaya was directed by a very interesting man, Nikolai Nikolaevich Osechkin. He was serving ten years, but under a relatively light article, without the letter "T" (in KRTD), and he worked as an economist in our office. On the outside he was a great economist and had nothing to do with the theater. He simply loved the theater, had seen much in his life and read a lot. In the camp he enjoyed great authority. In general, things had worked out well for him.

My friendship with Nikolai Nikolaevich began over walnut preserves. In some mysterious way known only to the suppliers, the local store received a few boxes of this walnut-based jam. Someone then said that this was Comrade Stalin's favorite preserve. Nikolai Nikolaevich, who was sitting next to me, noted under his breath, "That means this is the only case where I agree with the tastes of our adored leader." I already had enough camp experience and the necessary camp intuition to know that in the given instance I could rule out a provocation.

I understood that we had the same attitude toward walnut preserves and our "adored leader."

Nikolai Nikolaevich possessed a great sense of self-dignity and conducted himself very independently. The prisoners listened carefully to his opinions. And the authorities didn't like this.

As a result he ended up being transferred to the Lazo mine. From there I received one letter from him. The rest I learned later on from people who had been at that time at Lazo. Nikolai Nikolaevich also worked in the office there. He organized something of an underground "mutual aid fund." Those working in the office who received aid from home, and even some of the free-hires, gave a part of what they had, either money or food, and in this way supported "those on their last legs" who were doing common labor.

Despite all efforts to maintain the conspiracy, somebody squealed. Several people were arrested. Nikolai Nikolaevich was shot.

From among my old acquaintances, Ella Yegorova showed up at Veselaya. She worked at Ola with a circular saw and her leg was injured by a heavy chunk of wood. She spent time in the hospital and now was doing "light work," various jobs in the women's barracks.

During this whole period, approximately once a month I wrote a statement asking about Pavel's fate. I wrote to the USVITLag (administration of the northeastern corrective labor camps) in Magadan and to the GULAG (main camp administration) in Moscow. His three-year sentence should have ended in April 1939. If he had been freed, he naturally would have found me. That meant that he had received a new sentence, if he were alive at all. As it became clear later, the so-called Garanin sentences were in the majority of cases annulled. Of course, those who had been shot had been shot. But of the Magadan wives who had received ten years, soon almost all were set free. Except Zina Tettelbaum, whom I met later on in a camp. She served out her Garanin ten-year sentence. From the KRTDs, Sonya Erkes, who came in the same group as I did to Kolyma, also served out such a sentence. Why these two?

As with everything else taking place, there was neither rhyme nor reason to it all.

In January 1940, it became known in Veselaya that among the women, the only ones to stay on would be a few minor criminals in the camp administration. The rest were going once again to Ola.

I decided not to go see Veshnevetsky for a second time. I wrote him an official letter through the camp administration. Once again the captain rose to the occasion. They didn't send me to Ola, but to Magadan. Thus, for the third time, I found myself in the women's group.

While I was gone, a group of "tiurzaks" came to the camp. These were people who received in 1937 not a camp, but a prison, sentence. They had spent two years in political isolators in Yaroslavl or Suzdal.

According to the unwritten camp constitution, this article was considered even more odious than ours.

The physician at the women's mission, Anna Izrailovna Ponizovskaya, was also among the tiurzaks. They said that later she played a very unseemly role at the camp trials, which for a few participants ended with the supreme penalty. And the sentence was "carried out." Thus ended the life of Katya Rotmistrovskaya, who had worked at the children's home in Lera's group.

But all this was later, after my release from camp. In the barracks in which I ended up, I found Niuta Itkina. While a young girl she had taken part in the revolution. My father knew her and regarded her very warmly. I also met Olga Efremovna Kogan, one of the leading Leningrad personnel. Pavel knew her at work, and at one time had said a lot about her.

Vera Popova and I stared at each other and tried to remember where it was we had met. Either at one of the sanatoriums of the CC or at some transfer point....

Olga Shatunovskaya also lived in our barracks. After rehabilitation, she was a member of the presidium of the party control commission.

The tiurzaks were arrested for the most part in 1937 and almost always received ten years; some even received twenty-five. Those of us who had been imprisoned in 1936 were given no more than five years because at that time the special board didn't give more than five years. And we came under the lettered articles (that is, by letters of the alphabet) precisely according to the special board.

It should be added that active participants in the Opposition were arrested in 1936 and a few even in 1935. But in 1937 came the mass "recruitment": people were arrested who had nothing to do with any Opposition. They were almost always hard-line Stalinists who had once fought against the Opposition.

Thus it happened that completely obedient people who belonged to no groups whatsoever received sentences that were twice as long as those who actually did something.

And in the camps the tiurzaks, as I already said, were considered to fall under a more odious article than ours.

From among the tiurzaks, only physicians worked at their profession.

At the women's mission they immediately sent me to general labor under guard, to the warehouses in Nogaevo. But I was lucky. I ended up at a fish warehouse, which was subordinate to the fish industry authorities. There they knew me well, both from Ola and Veselaya. They even appointed me brigade leader. Thus I became, albeit on a small scale, part of the "administration" nonetheless. My brigade was very large and consisted mainly of KRTDs, tiurzaks and various other 58ers, as well as a few petty criminals who had been sent there for various offenses committed in the camps.

Here I encountered the basic difficulties of working as a brigade leader. There were many more women at that time in Kolyma (especially in Magadan) than in 1936. But nevertheless "demand" clearly outstripped "supply." In order to "have a fling" with some woman from the brigade, it was first necessary to establish contact with the brigade leader, so that she would look the other way. And why waste time and money, wouldn't it be easier to have a fling with the brigade leader herself? It doesn't make any difference who she is — "a broad's a broad."

As a result, I immediately came into conflict with the work-dispatcher there. My predecessors at the post of brigade leader, as a rule, were not able to close the books. He did this for them and received their thanks "in kind." Of course, I very quickly mastered this simple arithmetic and closed the books myself. Later this cost me dearly.

I engaged in the amateur theatricals at the women's mission, and in a completely unexpected genre: operetta. Through the girls from my barracks and from my brigade, I ended up in the amateur theatrical collective of the GKO, the city communal department. The camp of the GKO was a large men's camp, larger than ours, the women's.

According to an agreement between the "patrons" (the head of our mission, Gridasova, and the head of the GKO mission, Neiman), a few men took part in the women's theatricals, and, correspondingly, a few women participated in the men's.

At the GKO there was good jazz and several experienced professional musicians and actors. And, what was most important for me, there was a good collective: many Muscovites, with many common memories about Moscow, Moscow theaters and concerts. Amongst ourselves we recited poems by heart or excerpts from plays, and all this brought us very close together. I don't want to draw too close an analogy, but I can't help but recall the former Baroness Engelhardt who, when she was released from prison, married a former Petersburg cabdriver. She swore that what first strongly drew them to each other was common memories of Petersburg. They remembered the same restaurants, the same routes of trips outside the city (true, from different positions).... In general, the amateur theatricals were a great outlet for me in prison life.

And later they rescued me from general labor. The point is, my career as a brigade leader ended rather poorly. The work-dispatcher whom I already mentioned got even with me. He established that, in my books regarding the snow removal on the territory of the fish warehouse, I indicated more cubic meters of snow than had fallen in all Magadan during the whole winter, and the number of sacks repaired at the storage warehouse exceeded the maximum possible by ten times. This was completely true. In general, I couldn't have cared less about either the snow or the sacks. I wanted these women, who for the most part were KRTDs and "tiurzaks," to have somewhat better food and to earn enough at least for the shop. (In the prison shop, you could buy some butter, sugar or candy at your own expense.) Along the way it became clear that, in addition to all this, I allowed women who were having affairs to meet with their partners. This, too, was the truth. And I, meanwhile, would run off to the children's home, to see Lera.

In short, I was removed and transferred to heavy labor.

I was sent to a brigade which cleared the snow from the streets of Magadan. This was considered a strict form of punishment. In the freezing weather, in the wind, for ten to twelve hours a day we would work outdoors. It was not very pleasant. In addition, this was truly work under guard. They took my former brigade to and from work under escort. But on the territory of the warehouse, there were no guards. Here, the guards were constantly fooling around on the street near the women who were working. One would run around, while the other would sit in the office, where it was possible to smoke and warm up a bit near a hot stove. From time to time, the women of the brigade were also allowed to warm up, but not very often and not for very long. This was carefully watched by the brigade leader, a middle-aged Armenian woman, who had been a party worker in the past known by the nickname of "tough old man Anush." Every five minutes of smoking beyond the established time limit she was inclined to view as an attack against the Soviet regime.

After a while, when the impression of my "criminal" activity in the post of brigade leader had softened somewhat, they transferred me to another job, at the wood warehouse.

At the wood warehouse there were two kinds of jobs. Some of the women worked at the circular saw, dragging logs and cutting them into firewood. Then this firewood was loaded onto trucks. The work was very hard and much more difficult than clearing snow. The other, more privileged, section of the women worked on the trucks. The wood warehouse supplied fuel for all of Magadan's boilers. Several trucks were assigned to the warehouse, which distributed this firewood. A woman traveled with each driver. The job of these women was to unload the trucks at each place. This work was a pure sinecure. When the sides of the truck were let down, most of the wood fell out by itself, and the rest would be shoved out with our feet. All that remained was to pile the wood. Here the driver would usually help in a knightly manner, in order to ease the work of his own "sweetheart" and guarantee that time was left for personal matters. As a rule, each driver was accompanied precisely by his "sweetheart."

This was done very simply. Each driver would look for a woman who suited his own tastes. Then he would give a certain sum to the brigade leader (sometimes this was money, sometimes "borzoi puppies"—clothing or food), and she would assign to him that particular woman.

On the second day of work, I was chosen by a certain driver named Misha, who the women said was "independent" and didn't drink. They thought that I was lucky.

For several days Misha had conversations with me, from which it was clear that he knew everything about me which he needed to know: that I had a child in the children's home, that I didn't have a "muzhik" and that my sentence ended in a year. He said that he had the most serious intentions and would wait until I was free. He earned good pay and was ready to care for me and my child. I must say that I was very tired and wanted, as much as possible, to delay the final outcome. I answered that I had come to Kolyma with my husband, that I still hoped to find him, and if I didn't find him, then I would see and so forth. But abstract conversations were enough only for a short while. The scandal erupted after about a week, when Misha displayed extremely "active behavior." For the first time in my life, I swore a blue streak, remembering all the folklore which I had heard from the "wet nurses."

The "independent" Misha was evidently so shocked that he silently returned with me to the warehouse and I was never assigned to him again.

The enraged brigade leader made me a helper at the circular saw. For ten to twelve hours a day, I dragged logs and loaded wood onto the trucks.

I didn't take part in the amateur theatricals at this time. I didn't have the physical strength to lift myself up from the bunks. But it was just then that they assigned me to this activity. I never learned what my comrades at the GKO had done, what way they had found to get to Verka the work-dispatcher. But one fine day after roll call, when I was gloomily taking my place in the wood warehouse brigade, she waved her hand, "Step to the side." With the second group (which had one other advantage: getting up at 5:30, not at 5:00), she sent me to the GKO. At this men's worksite, where I worked in the theatricals, a small brigade of women, eight people, were assigned to the laundry and two or three to the seamstress shop, repairing linen. A few more women worked in the camp dining area, but they had nothing to do with our brigade. They answered to the camp cook, or, as he called himself, chef cook Akhmet. At the GKO they soon once again made me brigade leader.

The books here played no role, since they gave us good enough percentages and fed us in the dining room of the GKO, with the pridurkas, that is, by camp standards, very well. During this entire period I was not only full, but I also regularly took food for Difa. Groups of prisoners often came to the GKO, sometimes from distant camps and sometimes from invalid worksites. First they were sent to the bathhouse, which was located in the same barracks as the laundry, only the entrance was from a different side.

One of these groups (as it later became clear, it consisted mainly of KRTDs) stood around for an hour in the yard before the people were sent to the barracks. They, of course, talked with the local inhabitants, the prisoners. What an amazing "party geography" lesson this was! "Hey, friends, is there somebody from Novocherkassk? Here's your first secretary." "Anyone from the Cheliabinsk Komsomol Obkom, please answer!" And so forth.

It is terrible to recall how they looked. These men were thin, unshaven, with pale gray faces. We gathered up all our rations and tried to give them surreptitiously to some of the men on their last legs. Once I met a comrade who had arrived in the same group of prisoners as me. In the past he had been the director of a factory somewhere in the Moscow area and his name was, it seems, Georgievsky. He had been a tall, imposing and healthy man. Now he was a mere shadow of a human being. I would not have recognized him if he had not called out to me. He had worked for three years in the mines, become an invalid, been allowed to recuperate a bit there, and then they had driven him here. Right before the head of our workplace I handed him some bread and tinned goods received from the shop. The boss didn't say anything, he only asked, "A relative of yours?" I said, "Yes, a relative." I tried to find him later at the worksite, but they had sent his group somewhere else the next day.

This was typical for men convicted under our article: first excessive labor without enough food turned them into invalids. At the invalid worksite, they fixed them up a bit and then sent them again to common labor. Here they reached such a state that even assignment to an invalids' worksite didn't help. They simply began to die off.

I had friends not only in the theater group, but at the men's worksite. The head of the medical station there was a certain Dr. Khurgel. In the past he had finished the Sorbonne, knew how to speak French fluently and knew well the French Encyclopedists, French literature and poetry. Despite some strange traits, he was a very interesting person to converse with. He was serving a sentence for ... robbery. He was a drug addict and when he worked in the hospital, he used the entire supply of morphine and pantapon.

For a while in the camp there was a man who worked in the philosophy department at Tomsk University before his arrest. He said very little about himself or about his previous life. In the camp he agreed to do work which even those being specially punished refused to do: he cleaned the latrines. Of course, doing this work he was always alone. This suited him fine, no one and nothing interfered with his thinking.

Every day, when he had finished his job, he would go to the bathhouse—this he was allowed. As I said earlier, the bathhouse was located in the same barracks as the laundry. Therefore he and I often met and talked.

This was an amazing man. A person all to himself, he lived some kind of intense inner life. The repulsive work, all the other properties of camp life—all this passed right by him. He probably could have lived like Diogenes, in a barrel. By this time, I was already an old and experienced camp inmate. I knew that there are topics which could only be discussed with well known and tested people. And although I hardly knew him, I had the distinct impression that I could discuss anything at all with him. Unfortunately, he soon was transferred somewhere else, and I never heard anything more about him. He probably didn't live very long. He was already getting along in years and was ill.

Khava Maliar, from the tiurzaks, worked with me in the theater group. She didn't play any parts, but she knew how to sew a bit and was something of a theater costume designer. For her, as for me, the amateur theater served as an outlet.

She and I became friends. We often would meet later in Moscow, after rehabilitation, and we lived on the same street. Since her only son died in the war, she was alone and was ill. She didn't have much of a chance to enjoy her freedom in Moscow. After a few years she died. For my children, she remained for all time as a standard of great honesty, courage and adherence to principles.

I had other friends, too, apart from the theater group.

There was Anya Bolshakova, the wife of the writer Bolshakov, who produced a wonderful book about Lermontov with a very long title: *The Escape from Captivity, or the Story of the Suffering and Death of the Lieutenant of the Tenginsky Infantry Regiment, Mikhail Yurievich Lermontov.*

There was Nadya London, an intelligent person who was interesting to talk with.

There was Zhenya (Kotliarevskaya, I think), a tiny, skinny girl who looked like a bird. She was amazingly joyful, although it is difficult to find a "planet" less "outfitted for merriment" than a prison camp. They called her the "cockatoo."

There was Frida Stolova, a prisoner in our category, who was an intelligent and good comrade. She was expecting a child and dreamed that it would be a little boy, whom she would name Aleksandr. That was the name of her husband, whom she loved very much and who had died at the Solovki prison camp. She gave birth to a little girl, but nevertheless she became Sasha.

Our operettas enjoyed great success in Magadan. Camp amateur theatricals were felt to serve the camp population, and we, indeed, performed at all the Magadan campsites. But as a rule, the first rows were occupied by free-hires, and to a large extent, the various camp administrators. As our artistic director, Nestorov, would say, "If we could sell the tickets at the gates to the camp, how much money we would make." In the past, Nestorov had been a professional actor in operettas. He was serving time for being homosexual, and as a result, women didn't interest him at all. There was no small number of such people in the camps. Of course, to place them in a men's camp was like putting a fish in water. But ... who cared: a sentence is a sentence. And, when all was said and done, you couldn't put them in a women's camp, could you?! In general, Zhora was not a bad fellow. He was kind, very talented and knew the operettas which we performed by heart. Our concert director, a serious musician named Pavel Albertovich Peltser, wrote down the score as Zhora sang. Thus, we were able to perform the complete versions of *Marketplace of Brides*, *Rose-Marie* and the concert portion of selections from the operettas *Dona Juanita*, *Kholopka* and others. In *Marketplace*, I played Bessie and in *Rose-Marie*, Wanda.

One of the plays I will never forget. We were performing *Rose-Marie* at one of the women's worksites. Everyone was ready and had make up on. My make up was particularly complicated. In order to portray an Indian, I rubbed my face and hands with some substance which gave my skin a reddish color. (Since one of the components of this substance was alcohol, it was kept under lock and key.)

Just before the performance began, a girl who was obviously upset ran to the club from the work-dispatcher and said that Wanda (i.e., me) was being summoned to the NKVD. Orders were to immediately take her there under guard. What could we do? Everyone had already been made up. I quickly wiped off my "Indian" coloring, hoping that no one would notice how my hands were shaking.

An urgent summons to the NKVD a few months before being set free was not very pleasant.

But up walked the head of the KVCh (the cultural-educational section), a very significant figure in the camp. She began to shout that the hall was filled with all the administrative personnel, that the play couldn't be canceled and that we must immediately put our make up back on, and she would go to call the NKVD by phone. She was certain that the summons would be postponed.

Once again everyone put on their make up, once again I smeared on my horrible red paint. And as soon as we were again ready, the head of the KVCh returned all upset, saying that nothing had worked out, the NKVD was insisting that I immediately be taken there. Once again I wiped off the make up. And then (like in a nightmare), Gridasova, the "very" head of the women's worksite walked up. She declared that she personally had just called the NKVD, and the investigator Volodin who had summoned me agreed to delay the summons until tomorrow. "Immediately put on your make up. The show must begin in ten minutes."

By now I was like a squeezed lemon. I couldn't perform, I was in no shape to do so. What were we, serfs performing for our masters?

But she had a trump card. She said, "You have a child in the children's home. And you can be transferred at any moment." In short, I put on my make up for the third time. I don't even know how I performed. I only remember that when it came time to do the tango with a fan—Wanda's crowning number—I broke the fan. It was enormous and at the end of the dance was supposed to cover me entirely. Behind the scenes, Zhora whispered something along the lines that I probably needed an iron fan. But I didn't care at all.

The next morning they took me under escort to the NKVD.

The cleaning women throughout the building at the NKVD, all prisoners at the women's worksite, were all Gypsies for some reason. As it turned out, they had already seen *Rose-Marie* several times and particularly liked Wanda. Perhaps they felt that the Indian girl had something in common with Gypsies? Especially an Indian girl who abandons her wealthy lover and then stabs her own husband? I don't know. In any case, when they took me to the NKVD and my guard went to find out what to do with me, they all gathered around me. They were extremely interested in knowing why I had been brought here. I said that I myself didn't know, and that some investigator named Volodin had summoned me. Their brigade leader, an older, heavyset Gypsy, squatted next to me: "Ay, my dear, what have you done? He's the most terrible investigator!"

When I went into Volodin's office, I immediately understood why they had summoned me. Before him on the desk lay one of my many letters inquiring about Pavel's fate. After a few preliminary questions he gave me the official response to my letters: My husband had received ten years in the special designation camps, without right of correspondence.

In actuality, there were no camps "of special designation." This was the standard way of referring to people who were no longer among the living. But I still tried to find something out. I asked, "If he cannot write to me, then perhaps I can write to him at least once—if only to tell him about the birth of our daughter." He replied, "Not allowed." I tried to say something else. He leaned across the desk and said, "Listen to what I am going to tell you. You are still young, put your life in order."

Nonetheless I learned exactly what happened to Pavel. When we were set free. Difa was transferred from a hospital for prisoners to a hospital for free-hires. There she was put in a ward with a girl who had worked in the administration of the USVITLag, where she maintained a card catalog of those who had died. She felt very sorry for

Difa. When the girl was released from the hospital, Difa asked her to find in the card catalog the names of Zyama and Pavel. The girl turned out to be very obliging. She came to visitors day in the hospital after about a week. She had found both names. They both had been shot.

My activity in the brigade at GKO soon came to an end. This time the action was not directed against me personally, it was simply that they removed the entire women's brigade from the GKO. It seems that there had been some kind of conflict between the bosses at both worksites. After a little while, they removed women from the theatricals entirely. This was done, of course, on the initiative of our boss, who had become angry with Neiman at the GKO over something.

The head of the women's worksite, Aleksandra Romanovna Gridasova, had once been the Komsomolka Shurochka, who had come to Kolyma after finishing the technical institute and taken a modest position as the inspector of the housing department.

In this capacity she caught the eye of Nikishev, who was then the director of Dalstroy (after Berzin was shot, the director of Dalstroy had been Pavlov and then Nikishev).

At first, Shurochka was his semi-official lover, and then Nikishev (who was more than twice as old as his passion) sent his family to the "mainland"—he had a wife and two grown children. Shurochka then became his legal wife and enjoyed unlimited influence. There were times when Nikishev would return late at night from a trip somewhere and in the morning would issue various orders, "Remove so-and-so, appoint so-and-so." This was the result of Gridasova's nighttime "work."

She was not malicious, Shurochka, she simply was out of place and didn't know how to conduct herself. Then she gave birth to a child. The happy and proud Nikishev was getting into his car and boasted to his driver, "Just look at me, my friend. Here I am sixty and I've produced another baby." "Ah, comrade director," the driver replied without thinking, "the baby is not yours, but mine."

Nikishev conducted an investigation, and everything turned out to be as the driver said. He sent Shurochka and the driver to the mainland, and the first child was followed by a second, and then, it seems, by a third. The driver drank, Shurochka lived in poverty and walked around during the winter in canvas shoes. She borrowed money (in the majority of cases, without returning it) from former prisoners. As far as I know, no one ever refused her.

But I am running ahead.

3

N ext to me on the bunks at one time lay the former petty criminal and camp 58er Tanya Kiseleva.

Unexpectedly I received some curious information from this Tanya about the death of Nadezhda Sergeyevna Alliluyeva, Stalin's wife.

Tanya's "muzhik" (to use the camp terminology) had once been one of Stalin's personal bodyguards.

Apparently at a moment of extreme openness in bed, he told Tatiana what had happened on that memorable night. As she put it, Tanya "didn't need" this story, but she was impressed by the chance of telling me something sensational which I didn't know and which, undoubtedly, would interest me.

By combining the testimony of this former bodyguard with the much later testimony of Svetlana Alliluyeva ("24 Letters to a Friend"), the following picture emerges.

As is now well known, at some kind of banquet, Stalin very coarsely shouted to his wife, "Hey, you. Sing!" With tears in her eyes, she replied, "You can't say 'Hey, you!' to me." She got up and left. She was accompanied by her closest friend, Polina Zhemchuzhina, Molotov's wife.

Many years later, Zhemchuzhina told Svetlana that Nadezhda Sergeyevna was very upset, but that gradually she calmed down (ap-

158

parently, her husband's rudeness was no longer anything new to her) and their conversation shifted to other topics. Alliluyeva spoke about her plans connected with studies at the Industrial Academy (Promakademia), about some kind of literary work and about her children.

They parted after a couple of hours, according to Zhemchuzhina, and Nadezhda Sergeyevna had completely calmed down, she was her own self again.

It was impossible to imagine that a few hours later this person would shoot herself in the heart.

Now come the recollections of the bodyguard. After his wife left, Stalin remained at the banquet until four in the morning. The bodyguard was naturally with him.

When he returned home, Stalin didn't go to his own room, but to his wife's—they had separate rooms, separated either by a corridor or by other rooms.

Stalin went into his wife's room and since not even the bodyguard was allowed into the couple's bedroom, he sat on a chair in the room whose doors led into Alliluyeva's bedroom. Since it was about four in the morning, naturally, he began to doze.

He was awakened by the sound of a door slamming. Jumping to his feet, he saw the scowling Stalin, who wasn't looking to either side or paying any attention to him, walk past to his own room.

With that, the bodyguard's duties were over, and Alliluyeva was found dead the next morning.

Once, when he was "four sheets to the wind," and, in Tanya's words, "his eyes were wide with fright," the bodyguard told Tatiana about all this and added "in a strange whisper," "But their doors didn't slam, the boss couldn't stand it if the doors slammed. What I, being only half awake, thought was the door, was a gunshot. He killed her, do you understand?"

A few days after this, the bodyguard was transferred somewhere else and after a while longer, he ended up in Kolyma.

I am telling this story the way Tanya told it to me, changing the words ever so slightly. As they say, "I haven't added a thing...."

I am personally inclined to think that the bodyguard was right, that Stalin actually killed his wife. And if he did not kill her, then he said something so terrible that his wife, who just a few hours earlier wasn't even thinking about suicide, put a bullet into her chest.

Apparently as an experienced participant on the bathhouse-laundry front, they sent me to work in the large laundry in Nogaevo. The work there was in two shifts, first ten days, then ten nights. The washing was done by machine, in large drums. The women worked in various auxiliary jobs, but chiefly at ironing. I worked at drying the clothes. The drying area was a long, large room, along the left side of which stood wide tables where linen was folded. Along the right side were drying ovens, twelve driers.

Each such drier was a tightly closing container, a meter or more in width and two meters deep, with criss-crossed poles, on which the linen dried. The person working here had to periodically open these containers, take out the dry linen and hang up wet material. By the time you got to the last one, you had to begin again from the first. I don't remember what the temperature was in these driers, but I remember clearly the sensation of true asphyxiation—these were regular gas chambers.

I don't know how I would have survived this work if not for my workmate, a hunchbacked criminal named Vanya, who was the kindest soul. Several times a day, for ten minutes at a time, he would shut me in the closet where they stored the dry, clean linen. On this linen I would rest from my "gas chambers."

Not a single one of the women ironers agreed to do this work. I agreed because I simply dreamed of being alone for a bit. It is hard to imagine how terrible it is to always be around other people. In the barracks, during the day someone was always talking near you, and at night, someone was always snoring; on the way to work, someone was always walking next to you. At work the ironers worked together in one room, with two or three women at one table. The drying area gave me at least the illusion of solitude. Hunchbacked Vanya didn't count, he was a person who was diametrically opposed to me in personality. At the same time, he was very quiet. Sometimes, when there was a great deal of linen, they gave Vanya and me an assistant. Thus, for a short while a young fellow worked with us. He was a Latvian and I don't remember his name. In 1936, when the events in Spain began, he was eighteen and tried to be sent there in the international brigade. They didn't send him to Spain, but for his persistence they put him in prison. Since that time he had wandered from camp to camp. By the way, he wasn't the only one; I met other such unlucky "Spaniards."

In general, unlike the saying of Kozma Prutkov, they cut everything which grew. What didn't they put people in prison for. In the GKO theater group, in the jazz band, one of the players was the quietest old man, from a longstanding musical family. His father had worked his entire life as a choirmaster. At the first interrogation, the investigator said to him, "We know everything about you — your father was a police chief (polizeimeister)." He answered, "Not a police chief, but a choirmaster (kappelmeister)." "And what's the difference?!" Thus they sentenced him as the son of a police chief. There was one other who was accused of espionage. For a long time he refused to agree that he was a spy. But after a few days of beatings, he agreed, "Yes, I am a spy." They asked him whom he spied for. Either he still retained a sense of humor or perhaps he simply didn't care anymore, but he said, "I spied for the Indian Princess of Beguma."

He went to trial as an Indian spy.

Such tragic "jokes" could be told in large numbers.

Two months before I finished my sentence, I asked Verka the work-dispatcher to send me to work in the children's home. I wanted Lera to become used to me at least a little bit before our release. For we both had our release day before us: for me, from the camp; for her, from the children's home. I asked Vera without any hope for success. But she sent me there, and unselfishly, for I had nothing to give her and I had no friends like there had been at the GKO.

Work at the children's center was such that there was almost no time for me to sit with my own child, particularly since I worked in another group. But nonetheless, I saw her several times a day.

Thus, my last camp period was spent in the children's center.

April 10, 1941 finally arrived. At the evening head count, the work-dispatcher called my name, took her hand from the list and said in a very expressive voice, "Tomorrow don't come to roll call."

The next day I signed out as a free person. From the small camp compound I went out into the large Kolyma compound. In this large "compound" I still had to live a few years until the end of the war.

PART 3

1

And so I was free. In the camp it seems that you just need to be set free and nothing else matters. But other things do matter. You need to live somewhere and work somewhere.

For a long time I had worked at the GKO worksite; I had gone from one camp to another and then worked in the laundry where only prisoners worked; the last couple of months I was in the children's home, where the director, physician and nurse were free-hires. In other words, I had no friends at all. As for clothing, I had a camp skirt and a cotton jumper which I had bought before my release for fifteen rubles.

But the most important thing was that I was free. I couldn't let my spirits fall, I had to arrange my affairs. I had to make the arrangements as soon as possible in order to remove Lera from the children's home. Then I would go to the "mainland," and not vegetate in this accursed Kolyma.

I received a document concerning my release, which would serve as the basis for receiving a passport. My document said the following: first name, patronymic, surname, year of birth, nationality — (and the appropriate one); place of birth — Berlin; citizenship — not established; previously sentenced; reason for sentence — unknown. With such a document it was impossible to receive a passport. Up walked someone

163

in a sheepskin coat and it was immediately obvious that he was one of the petty criminals, now perhaps working as a driver or shipping clerk. "They've set you free, young lady? Let us exchange opinions, perhaps we can work things out. I can give full guarantees, have no fear." I answered that I had a husband in Kolyma and that I would be looking for him. The exchange of opinions didn't take place, but I would have to repeat this phrase about my husband much like an incantation, and not just once. In passing, I would like to say: I have known of a few instances when such an "exchange of opinions" ended in a genuine and rather solid marriage.

For the time being I slept in the camp, on the same bunks, next to the same people. "Nadya, bring some sausage, if only a bit." "Nadya, bring some pies, at least a couple. I haven't seen any for a hundred years." How could I refuse? I would walk through the gates weighed down with packages, like a Christmas tree. Only now they didn't search me, I was free.

In general, the first problem to solve was where to live. In the city there was a dormitory similar to a hotel. It had separate rooms and shared ones, for five or ten kopecks. People advised me to go there. I took their advice. The director was clearly a former prisoner, a petty criminal. I explained that I wanted a cot in a shared room, that I'd find a job and put things in order. "Why should such an attractive lady get a cot? I'll give you a separate room and in the evenings I'll be your guest, all right?"

"No, not really. You know, I have a husband in Kolyma, so I'd like a cot." "We don't have any available. Good-bye."

I went to a so-called transit house. This was a barracks on the outskirts of Magadan. The people living there were basically free-hires who had come from the "mainland" and were traveling along the road or who had come from the road and were going to the "mainland." Former prisoners were also living there.

There was a director here, as well. He looked a bit more of an intellectual; he was wearing glasses. "I would like a bed." "But, of course, you can have a bed." I simply couldn't believe my good fortune. "What do I have to fill out? Can I do it now?" "Why are you in such a hurry? Come to see me this evening. We'll drink some tea and exchange opinions." "Well, you know, I have a husband in Kolyma...." "We don't have any beds available."

On the street I met an acquaintance, the former head of the camp-site at Ola. He had a family, a wife and two daughters. The older daughter was fifteen and a great admirer of our amateur theatricals. The poor girl, she had never seen anything better and felt that I was a "real" actress. His wife was ill. They always had a prisoner to help around the house who looked after her.

He congratulated me on being set free. "Where are you living, how are you managing?" I told him that I hadn't been able to find any housing. "You should come to my place. I am now working in Magadan, I have a large apartment, come to my place." "Ah," I think, "the old devil. I won't be home during the daytime and I will ask to sleep with Katiushka. He wouldn't crawl into bed when she's there." "All right," I reply, "I'll come on over." "That's good. I sent my family to the mainland, I live alone and the apartment is big." Well, once again, nothing worked out.

By the gates the camp commandant had already told me that free people couldn't live in the compound, "Even more so, since you are bringing in food and feeding half the barracks. Do you think that I don't see? You have three days to be out of the compound."

I figured that first I had to find work and then at work they would probably help me find a place to live. People strongly advised me to get a job at the factory-kitchen. "There you'll eat your fill, and the pay is enough to buy some clothes." The advice was, of course, quite reasonable. Even more so since I felt that all my arrangements in Kolyma were temporary until I managed to reach the "mainland."

I went to the factory-kitchen. The head was a heavyset, well-fed woman, a living advertisement for their establishment. She was working on contract.

"What's your last name? Joffe? Does that mean that by nationality you're from the Jews?" "Yes, from the Jews. I am and will always be." I must say that in Kolyma anti-Semitism was not noticeable. There, people were divided by another distinction, prisoner or free-hire, and nationality didn't interest anyone very much. But this woman was a "pleasant" exception. "No, I don't have anything appropriate for you.

You can't wait on the tables, only prisoners work there, and this applies even more to the kitchen. And up front, in the office, there are no empty places."

Well, to hell with you! I went into the dining area in order at least to have a bite to eat. When I had been released, I had sent a telegram to my grandmother in Baku. My daughters were there now. Since I had received a wire transfer of 300 rubles, I had some money for the first period. Those waiting on the tables at the factory-kitchen were indeed all prisoners, mostly petty criminals (for 58ers, the work was too good). Among them were many acquaintances.

"Sit down, Nadya, this is a table for the help. We can feed you quickly here and you won't have to wait in line." This was Shura, who had landed a cushy job in the camp and was now working here. I sat down and looked around. The enormous room was buzzing like a beehive. How many people there were, and no one for me to talk with. Difa was in the hospital (for her, freedom meant being transferred from the prison hospital to a hospital for free-hires), and for my camp friends, I was already out of the picture. They were sure that as soon as a person was on the outside, then all was fine. Not long ago I had thought the same thing.

Absorbed by my sad thoughts, I almost didn't notice that some man had walked up to the table and politely asked, "May I?" I nodded and he sat down. I glanced quickly—he was a fat, good-natured fellow who looked like Mister Pickwick.

Just then Shura brought me dinner. He turned to her, "Shura, introduce us." Shura sounded like peas rattling across a table: "Come on, now, Nadechka, introduce yourself. Nadechka, this is Vasilii Konstantinovich Goncharuk, he works as a bookkeeper here. He's such a fine man, Nadechka, you pay attention now, he's a very good man. And this, Vasilii Konstantinovich, is Nadya. She is a woman of culture and well-educated; everyone here respects her."

Right then someone called out to him, and Shura quickly whispered into my ear: "You've caught his eye. Look, don't be a fool, he'll dress you up like you were a doll." I remember how they used to say in the camp that, before she was arrested, Shura had been something of an unofficial madam. It would seem that this was very likely. Shura walked away, and we began to talk. Of course, about the fact that I had just gotten out and I had to put my life in order. Just in case, I mentioned that I had a husband in Kolyma and that I hoped to find him. In actuality, I had given up hoping for anything of the sort. On the first day after I was released, I went to the USVITLag and made a personal inquiry. I received the same answer: ten years without right of correspondence. But I had already learned the truth.

About himself, my partner in conversation said that he was Ukrainian, he had been born and raised in Romania, he had lived a few years in Austria, in Vienna, and he had come to the Soviet Union as a deserter. For some kind of crime at work, he had been sentenced to three years and had served his time in Kolyma. The previous year he had been set free and was staying here, since there was nowhere to go and no one to go to. That was all.

When I finished eating and got up to leave, he said that he was free and that if I didn't object he would go with me. We left. Of course, there was nowhere for him to take me, since I had no place to live. My only home was the camp and there they had denied me entry. My companion offered, "Perhaps we could go to my place, I live right near by."

He had a little room, slightly larger than a railway compartment. It was very clean and on the table was a book, *One-Story America*, by Ilf and Petrov.

We sat for a while and then I got up to leave. "You know what," said Vasilii Konstantinovich, "here is the key to this room. Take it for yourself and please live here until you have made other arrangements." "And you?" "I will live during this period at a friend's. I have many friends who will gladly take me in."

Wonderful. It turned out that this man didn't want to "exchange opinions," but wanted to help in some way. "If you don't object, I can come to visit this evening?" It would have been better, of course, if he had not come, it would be so good to be alone. But you can't tell the master of a room "don't come in."

I remained alone. I allowed myself the great luxury of going nowhere and simply being by myself. At nine in the evening Vasilii Konstantinovich arrived, bringing a cooked duck and some pies. At eleven he got up, kissed my hand and left. I locked the door, for the first time in five years.

That's the way things were for the next ten days. During the day I locked the room, went about my affairs. In the evening I returned. At nine Goncharuk came to visit, bringing something good to eat. At eleven he got up, kissed my hand and left. But once he didn't leave. By that time I had convinced myself that this was a man who was by no means a fool, that he was observant, and despite his surface manners (you could sense that he had lived abroad), his cultural level was very low. He had one profound conviction: all people are scum and if a person does something good, it is only because it is to his advantage. And principles in general simply don't exist, they don't mean a thing.

During these days I met an acquaintance from the GKO. He had been convicted as an SDE (socially dangerous element), which was something between a petty criminal and a 58er, and he was now working as a bookkeeper at the GKO, not at the campsite, but in the actual city communal department. He said that the boss of the planning department of the GKO, Julia Mikhailovna Pokrasova, was a very kind, good-hearted person, and that, although her husband was a big official in the USVITLag, she had a good attitude toward the prisoners, especially 58ers. "Talk to her about getting a job." So I went to see her. It turned out that Julia Mikhailovna was ill, but her deputy, Vera Mikhailovna Khmelinana, said that they needed an economist for the position of planner in the transport section and that, of course, both she and Julia Mikhailovna would be glad to accept a specialist with a diploma. She and I clearly hit it off well and parted after agreeing that I would come back in a few days, by that time Julia Mikhailovna should have returned to work.

After a few days I came back. I was introduced to Julia Mikhailovna, and she turned out to be just as friendly as her deputy. I was hired on the spot as an economist in the transport department and when I said that I had nowhere to live, they gave me a paper with the signatures of the head of the GKO and the commandant of the transit point, with instructions to give me a separate room. The transit dormitory was subordinate to the city housing authority. The commandant was my old "acquaintance," the same one who told me not to hurry and to have some tea with him. Now he was very strict and official and assigned me a thoroughly acceptable room, in which there stood a bed, table, wardrobe and a pair of chairs, with enough room left over for a child's bed.

By this time I had already received my passport. I must say that Goncharuk did one more great favor: for two days he poured vodka into the person who gives out release papers, and they gave me new papers.

Thus the papers which served as the basis of receiving my passport looked completely proper: citizenship — Soviet; prior sentence — none.

Now I had a passport, work in my specialty and my own place to live.

I parted with Goncharuk on good terms. He asked, "Can I come to visit you?" Why not? I never forget if a person has done a good deed for me. But I was sure that this episode in my life had already come to a close.

However, fate decided otherwise. But about that later.

Finally the day came which I had dreamed about for so long: I took Lera out of the children's home. I wanted to do this without being noticed, so as not to traumatize the other children. But nothing came of my plans. The nannies and nurses from the whole children's home gathered together. The little children from Lera's group surrounded us in a tight circle, and fell silent. They didn't look away, but stared as I took off her official overalls and put on a fine household dress. I will never forget six-year-old Lidochka, the oldest of all the children in the home. Her mother had died along the Kolyma highway and she had no relatives. After a year they were supposed to transfer her to an orphanage. It is impossible to forget the expression of profound, unchildish grief on the face of this child....

Lera and I went home. The girls gave us a bed and mattress, explaining to the director that the bed had broken and they had thrown it away.

Lera was three and a half years old. She started going to the kindergarten for the children of the free-hires, and after work I took her home. One such kindergarten was located in the same building as the children's home, only the home was on the second floor, and the school, on the first. The only kitchen was also downstairs, but they cooked different food for the different groups (I wrote about this earlier).

When I had been working in the children's home, I often had to run down to the kitchen. I saw how one of the prisoners, a criminal, Katya, who worked as a nanny in the kindergarten, would hand the children to the free-hire parents and always say with an ingratiating smile: "What a wonderful girl you have," or "What a bright little boy you have." And when the flattered mothers walked away, she would maliciously grumble, "That child is such a nuisance, he's just too much."

Now this same Katya was working in the kindergarten where Lera went. On the first day when she gave me my daughter, she said, "Nadya, what a sweet daughter you have." "Katerina, have you forgotten who you're talking to? For I know very well that this 'child is a nuisance and he's just too much.'" Katya was embarrassed, "What are you saying! I say that to free-hires, but you are one of us."

At the end of June, the waters became navigable, and on the first steamship they sent away the sick and those declared unfit for work. Difa and her Zhannochka left with them. I never saw her again. She died three years later in evacuation. I accompanied them to Nogaevo, and on the next day, I mentioned at work that I should probably begin looking into a way to leave.

I must say that I was on the warmest and friendliest terms with both Julia Mikhailovna and Vera Mikhailovna. They both had lived for many years in Kolyma and understood many things. Of course, an invisible barrier separated me from them; in order to understand this completely, you had to go through it. But they were both kind and, to the extent that they could, they tried to be honest.

Julia Mikhailovna's husband was a senior person at USVITLag, and Vera Mikhailovna's husband was an ethnographer, the organizer and permanent director of the Kolyma local museum.

When I mentioned leaving, they glanced at each another, and then Julia Mikhailovna said: "Nadezhda Adolfovna, I have wanted to say this for a long time, but I couldn't bring myself to do it. You really won't be able to leave, at least, not for the foreseeable future. There is an unwritten directive not to give permission to leave to former KRTDs, so that they remain far away from the central cities. They also want to hold on to people who have a higher education, because there is a shortage of qualified cadres in Kolyma."

For me this was like getting hit in the head—for I fell into both categories.

That evening Goncharuk came to visit (he came rather often). I told him about all this. "Now look, I can leave Kolyma at any time, and if you went as my wife, no one would stop you."

Yes, it was worth thinking about.

Then an incident happened which almost brought me a second sentence.

Tsilia Kogan, whom I already mentioned, ran the laundry at the women's worksite. This was, by camp standards, prestigious work, it relegated her to the group of privileged people in the camps with cushy jobs and gave her the chance to avoid living in the main barracks. The laundry had its own small room for its director.

When Difa wasn't in the hospital, but lived in the camp, she found some respite in Tsilia's room from the barracks noise, the stuffiness and cold. There it was always warm and quiet. Sofia Mikhailovna Antonova was also there. I almost never went there, since I didn't like Tsilia. Like Masevich, I don't like toadies and I don't believe enthusiasts.

A couple of times, when I was returning from work, I went for Difa to the laundry, but I never stayed there long. Those who worked under Tsilia were mainly common criminals. I don't know what happened there, but they wrote a complaint against Tsilia, a full-fledged "denunciation." They accused her of every mortal sin and particularly of the fact that in her room Trotskyists had supposedly gathered and conducted anti-Soviet conversations. It was precisely this point which interested the officials. When they began to ask Tsilia who had been at her place, she named me. Later she explained her action in the following way: "I had to name someone, so I thought—Sofia Mikhailovna is old, Difa is sick, but Nadya will somehow hold up."

So they phoned me at work at the GKO and proposed that I go to the NKVD. I arrived there at ten in the morning and left at eight in the evening. For ten hours they asked me the same questions over and over again: did I go to the laundry at the women's worksite, whom did

I meet with there and what did we talk about? And for ten hours, I monotonously answered the same way—that I never went to the laundry, that I never met anyone there and that I talked with no one there.

The investigators changed, but each asked the same thing. Once someone came who was apparently a high official. He didn't question me himself, but stood there a bit, listened a while, and, when he was leaving, said to me, "Well, good luck! I hope that you will nonetheless confess."

But I didn't confess to anything and at eight in the evening they let me go. I was sure that I was threatened with a second sentence.

At the same time, there was a trial against several women from the women's worksite who were also charged with anti-Soviet agitation. I knew several of them, and one, Katya Rotmistrovskaya, slept next to me on the bunks and worked in the children's home in Lera's group.

They shot Katya.

All these years I had been tortured by the thought that Natasha and Kira would grow up without a father and a mother. But nevertheless they were with grandmother, with Uncle Vitya, with their own people. But what would Lera face if they put me back in prison?! Her whole life she would wander from one children's home to another, never knowing her relatives. No one would ever find her, and who, after all could even look for her.

I remembered Lidochka in the children's home, with her sad, unchildish eyes on a child's face. The same fate awaited Lera! I was in despair.

Goncharuk acted as a savior. He swore to everyone that existed that if something happened to me, he would take Lera and go with her to Baku to Uncle Vitya, where Natasha and Kira were living. I didn't know whether to believe him, but I had no other choice but to believe.

Then, when I calmed down, I understood how stupid and senseless all this was. All I had to do was send a telegram to Vitya, saying that if something happened to me, that he and his wife must look for the child in the Magadan children's home; this was the only possible place in which she would end up if they arrested me.

But, as they say, "good thoughts come late."

None of this was necessary. They didn't summon me anymore.

Probably this was partly because I didn't confess to anything, but mainly because the same group of criminal women who wrote the denunciation of Tsilia categorically denied my participation. When they were told my name at the NKVD, they said: "You mean the one who was the actress in the theater group? No, the actress was never there, that's all there is to it."

That's how this episode ended. Soon all this receded into the background. The war broke out.

Those sentenced under the same article as I was, but who were arrested a couple of months after me, remained in the camp "until special dispensation," that is, until the end of the war. Leaving Kolyma was forbidden even for free-hires. They said that former prisoners of my article would be sent from Magadan somewhere deep into the taiga, along the Kolyma highway.

I wanted to send for my daughters, since I couldn't leave myself. They wouldn't even take my letter. They said that a war was going on, and no one could either leave or come to Kolyma.

Here is what my older daughter told me when I met her after a ten-year separation.

> I remember very well how they took grandma away. They came at night when Kira and I were sleeping. They woke me up and said, "Girl, set aside the things which you and your sister will need tomorrow." Mama, you remember the Japanese outfit that you brought once from Japan? I liked it very much, but grandmother didn't allow me to wear it; she said that it was a fancy costume. But I used the opportunity then and set it aside. That's how foolish I was.
>
> They took grandmother away. After that we lived with various relatives—you know them yourself—with some it was better, with some it was worse. At Uncle Vitya's, for example, things were almost all right; our great-grandmother lived there and she loved us very much. Then she died. I remember her death very well. But Aunt Rosa said that you were bad, that you got involved in politics rather than think about your children, and that they had imprisoned you, and someone had to look after your children.
>
> Even then I thought that grandmother, after all, had never been involved in politics, she had never even worked, and yet

they arrested her too. And, in general, mama, Kira and I never thought badly of you, neither you nor papa.

When the war began, we were living with Uncle Zhenia, and he assigned us to some orphanage which was being evacuated. We didn't know anyone there. When the Germans were approaching this place, all the children who had relatives were taken away. Only ten of us were left, along with our teacher.

I remember well that we had a supply of oats, and every day she cooked us oatmeal porridge. Then the oatmeal ran out, and she said that she couldn't do anything more for us, that any of us who could, should go to Moscow.

Kira and I went to the train station, and there stood a military unit which was leaving for Moscow. Some of the soldiers must have felt sorry for us; they sat us on the third shelf and said that we should sit there quietly. They fed us along the way, and we traveled with them all the way to Moscow. And no matter how much we wanted to get there, at that time private individuals were forbidden to enter the city.

We went to see Uncle Zhenia, on the Petrovsky line. He was very upset when he saw us and said that he simply didn't know what to do with us. The factory at which he worked was being evacuated, and he and his family were also being evacuated.

He told us to sit at home and wait, and when the time came to go to the station, he would send for us. We waited for two days, and on the third day some person from Uncle Zhenia's job came and said that the train had left earlier than expected, and that he had not managed to come to get us. At that time we believed him, but now I think that he never intended to come for us. This same man then gave us a message from Uncle Zhenia that we should sell the things at the apartment or exchange them for bread.

I had only turned twelve (and Kira was nine). I didn't know how to sell or exchange anything. The apartment was a large communal apartment, and the neighbors helped us in these operations, but I think that they tricked us a lot.

But, nonetheless, we somehow managed to keep on living.

On October 17, when the Germans were on the outskirts of Moscow, all of our neighbors in the apartment placed icons in the windows and hung a large cross on the front door as a sign that Orthodox Christians lived there. They then called Kira and me into the kitchen and said that they didn't want to have any difficulties because of us, and that if the Germans came, they wouldn't hide the fact that we were Jews, and that we had better leave the house. But we had nowhere to go and so we remained.

We didn't have anything left to sell and I was hired to stand watch in lines.

Moscow was being heavily bombarded, and when they blew the air-raid siren, the line which was waiting for bread ran off to the bomb shelters. I would remain and watch over the line. Those who did this were given bread in return. But we managed to get very little bread in general.

Then someone stole our bread cards, and not only Kira's and mine, but our neighbor's too, an old woman name Ignatovich. I also bought bread for her, and for this we got something in return.

I simply didn't know how I could go home. Kira would ask, "Talochka, give me some bread," and I didn't have any. I wouldn't have any tomorrow or the next day, because we didn't have any bread cards, and Granny Ignatovich would simply kill me.

I wanted to die, so that all this would come to an end. I decided to throw myself under a vehicle.

I did so, and some woman barely managed to drag me out from under the wheels. She asked what had happened to me, and I told her. She was such a wonderful woman that she felt sorry for me. She took me home and warned Grannie Ignatovich not to dare to lay a finger on me.

When she left, Granny Ignatovich said that she wouldn't touch me, but that I would have to give her the same 700 grams of bread each day that she was supposed to receive according to the ration card. "Find it wherever you like, but find it."

Where was I supposed to find bread? For two days I still managed to sell some more things and get some bread, but after that there was no way I could get any more. Kira and I had nothing left to eat, and Kira was extremely weak.

I went to school, which was located in the metro, below the ground. The classes there were irregular. All the classes were together, and every day some came and some didn't.

It must be that I looked very bad because the teacher asked me what was wrong.

I don't even remember what I told her, I walked away and sat in the corner.

Then she walked up to me and gave me a small bag, which held some sugar, and another bag, slightly larger, which had some bread crusts and biscuits. The teacher and other children had gathered these up among themselves.

I went home with this, and Granny Ignatovich took everything away from me, in exchange for the 700 grams of bread, leaving us a few biscuits.

Kira and I ate these and cried because we wanted very much to eat, but the biscuits were hard and wouldn't go down very easily.

The teacher was a good person, she came to see us on the next day, saw how we lived, and said that the situation was impossible, that we would simply die from hunger. She sent us to the orphanage on Zubovskaya Square.

Well, in the orphanage at least they gave us something to eat, only it didn't always make it to us. Sometimes the older boys would take it from us, and sometimes there weren't enough portions and the teacher there would say, "These are children of enemies of the people, they can go without."

Thus we were also hungry in the orphanage, and Kira couldn't even walk anymore, she just crawled.

Then Uncle Vitya came back and took us to his place. He had plenty of food to eat, but for a long time Kira and I still hid pieces of bread or meat. We wrapped them and buried them somewhere in the ground, so that if there was hunger again, then we would have something in reserve.

This is what my daughter told me, and I wrote it down.

Not because I feared that I would forget—I will never forget this until I die—but so that others, too, would be able to read what she said.

2

The war began on June 22, 1941 and immediately the announcements began to be made: "Our troops have abandoned such and such a city," "Such and such populated area...." The Germans didn't advance, they simply rolled from the west to the east.

Every time we listened in fear to the voice of Levitan, which had already become familiar: "This is Moscow speaking...." Then in July there was the famous speech by Stalin. For a hundred years he hadn't given a public speech. And now he was giving a speech, and what a speech it was! "Brothers and sisters!"

I listened to this speech at work. Around me the sensitive audience sniffled—ah, how touching! This speech simply enraged me—it smelled of the seminary. It must be that in his fright he remembered his childhood. And, apparently, his "best feelings" were offended—who had deceived him? Hitler! Hitler, whom he trusted so much, when he didn't trust his own people, his friends or anyone else. But Hitler he believed; no doubt he sensed a kindred spirit. Then he so "suddenly" attacked! How can anyone talk about "suddenness," when Stalin was warned on all sides about the impending invasion. He was warned by our intelligence agents (they say that Sorge even indicated the day of the invasion), he was warned by Churchill, who was already fighting against the Germans. He was warned by our border guards, who noted how troops were amassing on the western border. These people were simply removed from their posts and a few were shot for "sowing panic."

The war had already begun, and there were people sitting in the camps who had been convicted for predicting the war.

By analogy, I recall how I was imprisoned with a woman who was a ChSIR (family member of a traitor to the motherland). Her husband, who was the reason for her being in prison, worked in a "sharashka," invented something, was set free and even received a Stalin Prize. Apparently, when he was being set free, this character didn't stipulate that his wife should be released, and she remained behind bars. She continued to serve time for her husband, who was already on the outside and even wore the pin of a laureate.

In a similar way, during the war people continued to sit behind bars because they had foreseen the war and warned about it.

None other than the German ambassador, Count Schullenburg, had warned about the war. This was an incident unheard of in the history of diplomacy. The ambassador of a country preparing an invasion warns the ambassador of the country which is going to be attacked. However, it is a fact. Not long before the beginning of the war, Schullenburg gave warning about it to our ambassador in Germany, Dekanozov.

Schullenburg was an experienced diplomat of the Bismarck school and apparently a genuine German patriot. He understood that this war threatened the destruction of Germany.

As the course of history showed, he was right.

Schullenburg was hanged, Dekanozov was shot, but there was still the translator, Pavlov. He survived and it was he who told about all this.

What conclusions did Stalin draw from all these warnings?

He annihilated the highest commanding officers of the Soviet army, almost all the most qualified members of the commanding staff.

After his rehabilitation, General Todorsky received access to the archives and these are the figures he cites:

Rank	Number in Red Army	Number Shot
Marshals	5	3
Army Commanders	15	13
Corps Commanders	85	57
Division Commanders	195	110
Brigade Commanders	406	220

That's what happened to the military cadres. Those who survived were dragged out of the camps after the war began: Rokossovsky, Maretskov and others.

So the war was under way and along with the general concerns and sorrows, I was burdened with personal ones—thoughts about my children.

I was very much alone. All my camp friends were scattered along the Kolyma highway. Although they treated me well, my new friends, Julia Mikhailovna and Vera Mikhailovna, were nonetheless people of a different circle. Thus it turned out that the only person who worried about me and my child and who took my misfortune to heart was Goncharuk.

I agreed to marry him. This was mainly out of loneliness and exhaustion. Later I understood that if I ever wanted to get out of this wretched place, then it could only be with the help of one such as he, who had "never been, never belonged to, never been attracted by." And who also had exceptional penetrating power when it came to questions of everyday life.

We went to the registry office to record our marriage and began to live together.

In place of his "little compartment," he received a large, comfortable room. I was expecting a child.

He said that if I did anything, he would simply kill me. Indeed, he very much wanted the child, and also was counting on that tying me to him. It was not so much that he loved me—he was hardly capable of doing so—it was simply out of "Ukrainian" stubbornness.

My fourth daughter was apparently very anxious to come into the world: she was born in the seventh month, was very weak, and we kept her in the hospital longer than usual. For the first time I came into contact with free-hired doctors as a free-hire myself. Until then I had dealt with them only as a prisoner.

I remember the first doctor in the children's home, a gloomy person who would sit for days on end in his own office. The children were dying like flies, but this obviously didn't concern him. If someone tried to call his attention to a sick child, then he would usually say, "And why did they have such a child?"

Finally they removed him and Rozalia Borisovna appeared. I have already written about her. I am still sure that Lera remained alive mainly due to her efforts. And not only Lera.

Rozalia Borisovna had two daughters. If maternal gratitude and maternal blessings have any bearing on one's fate, then these girls should be very happy.

I fondly remember still one other person, Tatiana Alekseyevna, the senior nurse at the children's ward of the Magadan hospital.

Lera fell ill with inflammation in the lungs three times in her first year, and about the same number of times with dyspepsia. Since there was no special children's ward for prisoners in the hospital, Lera and I would each time end up on Tatiana Alekseyevna's ward.

She treated me very well, and if she made any distinction at all between me and the free-hire mothers, it was only in my favor. She always used me as an example of endurance, cultured (as she used to say) behavior and so forth.

By the way, her husband was some highly-placed official and perhaps this was the reason that she could allow herself such "liberalism."

During one particularly difficult episode of inflammation of the lungs, when Lera was in a bad state even without that, she had an abscess, a large boil behind her ear, which seemed almost as big as her head. Tatiana Alekseyevna called for the surgeon on duty. He said that the abscess must be lanced and that he would do it immediately. He was a chain smoker and rolled his own cigarettes, which were always spilling their tobacco. His fingernails were dirty, and, as far as I could tell, he was not sober.

I clutched my child and began to wail that I would not let her be operated on. I begged them to call the chief surgeon. It seems that I even cried.

The doctor left in disgust, and Tatiana Alekseyevna brought in the chief surgeon. He came in—a big, heavy, red-haired and very angry man. He looked at Lera's abscess, started to swear and then began washing his hands. He washed them for a long time; they were large hands, covered with red hair. The whole time he swore a blue streak, despite the presence of Tatiana Alekseyevna. In general he didn't look me straight in the face. Then, without even looking at me, he told Tatiana Alekseyevna that I should leave the room, "otherwise these mothers always act hysterically." Tatiana said that everything was all right, that there would be no hysterics. He swore again and in a second lanced Lera's abscess. They squeezed out a mass of pus and bandaged the unfortunate and tiny little head.

Then for the first time the surgeon looked at me. "You did well," he said. "Too bad you're not a medic, I'd have you work with me."

When he left, Tatiana Alekseyevna said that he was renowned for being coarse and foul mouthed, but he was a superb surgeon. Moreover (as Tatiana Alekseyevna added), he didn't differentiate between sick free-hires and prisoners. I still regret that I can't remember his last name.

There was one other free-hire doctor, Faina Emmanuilovna, whose last name I also forget. She was a therapist and dealt not with the children of prisoners, but with the prisoners themselves. People said that she did everything for them that she could. She even fed at her own expense several "goners," bringing them food from home as a supplement to the meager hospital fare. She apparently saved more than one prisoner, but she couldn't fight against the camp system. One way or another, she had to release a person for work, knowing very well that he was in no condition to work. She had to participate in the medical commission which determined categories of labor. And these categories were established not according to one's health status, but according to the article a person was convicted under. KRTDs were given heavy physical labor for the few days remaining before they literally died.

Thus it turned out that people like Faina Emmanuilovna saved a few prisoners, and with their involuntary connivance, thousands perished.

When Faina Emmanuilovna had worked in Kolyma the three years stipulated in her contract, she immediately quit and left for Moscow.

But in Moscow she didn't live long. Soon she died, having been hit by a car. Several people who met her in Moscow felt that this was not an accident, but suicide.

Who knows....

At the end of 1942 we moved to Ola, to the same Ola where I had served part of my camp sentence, working first as a painter in the construction brigade and then as a salter in the fish factory.

Now I arrived as the head of the planning department of this same industrial complex.

A statistician working for me was Tatiana Petrovna Sergeenko, the wife of the head of the Ola regional department of the NKVD. I must say that she worked very conscientiously, and treated me with respect, perhaps because my work habits put me on very good terms with the main directors of the fish industry.

Her housekeeper was Ella Yegorova, my longtime camp friend, not only in Magadan, but in Ola and Veselaya. Ella didn't have the letter T—she was simply a KRD (counterrevolutionary activity, not counterrevolutionary Trotskyist activity)—and when she grew tired of common labor, became a housekeeper. Ella was an Estonian (Yegorova was her husband's name). Like the majority of Estonians, she was a tidy, thorough, very conscientious and wonderful head of a household. As a housekeeper, she was simply a treasure. Ella was terribly pleased that I turned out to be the boss for the mistress of her household. "Nadya, don't be easy on her, she's a snake; you lean on her just like you should." It seems that my statistician, such a disciplined and efficient worker, was a real "snake" for poor Ella.

I told Tatiana Petrovna that her housekeeper was my close friend. "You probably know that in the past Ella was a teacher and a very cultured person. If she has had to become a housekeeper, then I am very glad," I said, "that she has ended up with you. For you are an intelligent person, and I am sure that in working for you, Ella will have a chance to rest and read a bit."

Either Tatiana Petrovna (who had a hard time finishing some kind of technical school and who chose books so that their binding would match the wallpaper) was flattered by the fact that I included her in the intelligentsia, or else she didn't want to spoil our relations, but Ella did indeed get a chance "to rest and read a bit."

When I had just begun to work, this same Tatiana Petrovna took me to the fish factory, showing me the production process.

"This is the smoking area," she said, "and this is the separator, this is the washer and this is the salter." In the washer I turned my attention to a girl of about fifteen. Later I got to know her and fed her a bit. They called her Valya and this was her story. She was from one of the villages in the Moscow area and worked, like many teenagers, in one of the Moscow factories.

Her mother fell seriously ill and relatives told her that she had to come immediately if she wanted to see her mother alive. She received permission to be gone for three days.

Her mother was indeed in a bad state, but she died in five or six days rather than three. After the funeral, Valya returned to Moscow and was late to work by three days. They put her on trial and gave her two years.

When they read the sentence, she said loudly, "Well, thank you, Comrade Stalin, for my happy childhood."

The court immediately reclassified her criminal status, changing it to Article 58, and gave her five years. Then they sent her to Kolyma.

I looked at this skinny and awkward girl, with the thin braids of hair; she was just slightly older than my Natasha. About a year had passed since the trial, but you wouldn't think that she was sixteen. On the way to the camps and at the transit points, she was with the criminals. I could very well imagine those "universities."

I also thought—What kind of a heart did the woman have (Valya said that her judge had been a woman) who would condemn an unhappy child who had just lost her mother to five years of Kolyma exile?

These were real, tried and true Stalinist judges!

But I have digressed. When Tatiana Petrovna and I reached my "own" salting area, I slowed down. There stood the same vats. And women were standing inside them. They too had bandaged fingers. I remembered how we always scratched our hands on the fish gills, how the cuts bled and how salt fell into the wounds. My hands had constantly ached and gotten infected.

Tatiana Petrovna apparently noticed my interest in the salting area. "This isn't hard work," she said. I looked at her: you should be so lucky, my dear, to get "easy" work like this.

Other women were standing in the vats. I didn't know them, but they were my people, they were prisoners.

3

I lived with Goncharuk until the end of the war. These were very difficult years; nothing can be worse than to live with a person for whom your black is white, and your white is black.

In the end, he managed to do what he was meant to do — he got us onto the "mainland."

In 1946 we finally arrived in Moscow. My mama was here. She had served five years in the Karaganda camps, as family member of a traitor to the motherland, because of her husband Mikhail Ostrovsky. They shot Ostrovsky in December 1937 in Lefortovo, and mama was set free in 1942. She lived outside Moscow in Taininko with her relatives. That's where we went. And there we parted ways with Goncharuk.

But he said that he wouldn't give the child to me under any circumstances. Mama convinced me that I was obliged to think first of all about the children who had no father. I was comforted by the fact that Vasilii always kept changing his mind, that he would soon grow tired of the child and that Lialka would nonetheless end up with us. We left Moscow as a threesome, Lera, mama and myself.

My Uncle Vitya — mama's brother, the same one who during the war had saved my children by taking them away from the orphanage — lived at that time with his wife Raya and my second daughter Kira in one of the regional centers of Azerbaijan, Kedabek. My grandmother had long since died.

My oldest daughter, Natasha, had finished the seventh class and enrolled in the teachers school in Baku.

She had to graduate as quickly as possible and start working.

In Baku I left mama and Lera at the station and went by myself to look for the dormitory at the teachers school where Natasha was living. I found it. They told me that she had gone out somewhere and probably would be back soon. I sat on a bench near the dormitory and wanted to wait, but my heart was pounding so that I couldn't sit still. I slowly walked along the street. All around there were people. Some walked past me, some were coming my way. One girl in a white beret was heading in my direction. She looked at me indifferently and walked by. I called out to her, "Natasha." She didn't resemble at all that six-year-old girl whom I had left ten years ago, but I knew precisely that this was she. She turned around, looked at me in surprise and asked, "Excuse me, have we met somewhere before?"

That's how it was.

We traveled to Kedabek with mama and Lera, after agreeing that Nata would finish this semester at the teachers school, and then, during the second half of the year, would go to the eighth grade. I still didn't know how I would manage, but I didn't want to even think that my daughter would remain without a genuine education.

Kira was in Kedabek. She was in the sixth grade, a skinny dark-haired girl. She and Lera looked very much alike. And both resembled their father.

We stayed as guests for a while in Kedabek, but we had nothing to do there, and I arranged to get a job in another regional center of Azerbaijan, in Shamkhor. It was twice as large as Kedabek, and therefore presented more possibilities for work. I began to work as a planner in the local artel. The artel was large, with many levels, and by regional standards was the leading producer.

Natasha studied in the eighth grade at the Shamkhor ten-grade school. Kira was in the sixth and Lera in the second. Raya found it very difficult to part with Kira. She never had had any children and simply adored Kira.

This was the postwar period, there was the ration card system, and it was hard getting by. For some reason all these Zakavkaz republics have one particular trait: people there earn very little, but they live well. I never learned how to do this....

I was not wrong in my prognosis about Goncharuk. After a few months he came to Shamkhor. I couldn't refuse to take him in, and Lialka was with him. But I already knew very well that I couldn't live with him. After a week he left for his homeland in the part of the Ukraine near the Carpathians. Larisa remained with me.

All my acquaintances looked at me as if I were mad: "Such difficult times, four children and you reject a husband, such a good bread-winner, you have to think of your children." But I was thinking precisely about the children. And about the fact that "not by bread alone...."

But in Shamkhor I was able to work only a year. After a year the local authorities apparently became familiar with the science of geography. They decided that Shamkhor was too close to the Turkish border and, therefore, people who had served their sentences under Article 58 should not live there. So they sent me away. But first they had a conversation with me. Some kind of major from the local authorities was interested in my biographical data. First of all, he directed his attention at my birthplace, the city of Berlin. In connection with this he wanted to find out my relationship with the fascists. I tried to explain to him that I was born in 1906, when there were no fascists in Berlin, and even the most perceptive person couldn't foresee that one day there would be any there. This didn't sink into his head. But what finally pushed him over the edge was the fact that I had received a higher education by graduating from the Plekhanov Institute of National Economy. "Listen," he said to me indignantly, "why are you telling such an outrageous lie? Plekhanov was a Menshevik and a wrecker, how could there be an institute named after him!"

It was this type of "enlightened" figure who determined the urgent necessity of my departure. Where I had to go was not indicated, they only demanded that I leave Azerbaijan. I fell under Article 38 of passportization, according to which I was not allowed to live in many cities: regional centers, border cities, provincial capitals and so on and so forth. I could only live "on a hummock, in the swamp." But I didn't even have an appropriate swamp to live in.

Then my Aunt Raya remembered that one of the nurses who

worked in Vitya's hospital was from the city of Kropotkin in the Krasnodar region (Kavkazskaya station). Her mother had her own modest house there, at least that might be a place to go to.

This nurse said that the Kavkazskaya station was a major railway junction, with many enterprises and organizations where one might very well find a job. Well, for me and for poor Tanya, "all the lots were the same;" if Kropotkin was our destination, then let's head for Kropotkin.

But what could I do with the children? Raya was overjoyed at the chance of getting her favorite back and proposed that Kira live for a while with them. Mama agreed to remain in Shamkhor with Natasha and Lera until I made all the necessary arrangements, but she categorically refused to have Larisa stay with her. "She has a father, let him worry about her." No matter how much I begged or tried to persuade her, she wouldn't agree. "He wanted to have his own child, well, let him have her." I couldn't take a six-year-old girl with me, since I was traveling into the unknown and wasn't counting very much on Vitya's nurse.

I wrote to Goncharuk that I was forced to send Larisa to stay with him. He replied by telegram that he was very glad and was waiting for her. I sold some of my Kolyma clothes and went with Lialka to the Novoselitsa regional center of the Chernovitsky region, where Goncharuk lived and worked. But it would be better not to recall how I left Lialka there (I left at night while she was asleep) and then how I traveled from Novoselitsa to Kropotkin.

The mother of Vitya's nurse in Kropotkin didn't exactly welcome me with open arms, but nonetheless I had a roof over my head for a while.

I walked around Kropotkin in search of work and lived on kasha and tea in the cafeteria in order to save money, thinking that it would be necessary to send money as soon as I could to mama and the children.

But I was fortunate. After a few days, I landed a job as an economist in the planning department of the construction section of the northern Kavkaz railway line. The planning department consisted of two people, the boss (he was called the senior planning engineer) and an economist. I rented a corner of a room from a friendly old woman and things seemed to be in order. The administration of the railway was considered militarized, and our boss was a major. In order to talk with him, I had to say, "Comrade major, request permission to speak."

They worked, as a rule, both evenings and on Sundays (although on Sundays it was only a half-day). Many of the women who worked there (most of whom had families) tried for one reason or another to get out of working evenings and on Sunday.

I, on the contrary, was glad to have something to do (it was much better than sitting in my corner listening to the old woman complain) and readily worked evenings, which earned the favor of my boss. In my opinion, he usually valued work not so much according to quality, as by the quantity of time expended.

We decided that mama and the children would stay in Shamkhor until spring. Natasha was in the ninth grade and we didn't want to tear her away in the middle of the school year. Spring was not far away, and I sent them the lion's share of my pay, which unexpectedly increased greatly. My immediate superior, the senior planning engineer, was a very strong and experienced worker, but he was a drunkard. Once when the cashier fell ill, and he was traveling to Armavir on business matters, he was entrusted with giving out the wages of our workers on location (we were building a station there). He received a large sum of money and drank up half of it. He was tried, and along the way they established that he had taken bribes from factory clerks and falsified the books. He was given a sentence and our major offered me work as senior engineer.

I liked the work and when I traveled to Rostov on business, the travel allowances increased my pay. But regardless of the pay, the trips to Rostov were interesting. It was a large city and very lively. (It is no accident that they say, "Odessa is the mama and Rostov is the papa.") And for me, who since 1936 had seen only camps and then the camp side of Magadan, or backwaters such as Shamkhor and Kropotkin, Rostov was particularly interesting.

The theater was not bad at all, and there were good concerts. It is true, I rarely had occasion to relax, since the administration also worked evenings, but nonetheless I sometimes managed. Once I attended a readers' conference devoted to Ehrenburg, who had come to Rostov. The discussion was about his novel *The Storm*. There were many speeches, including many critical remarks: pro-French moods, the main hero was insufficiently orthodox and so forth.

In his concluding remarks, Ehrenburg thanked the audience for their interest in his novel and for their criticism. Then he pulled some kind of paper out of his pocket and said, "And now, I would like to acquaint you with the opinion of one more reader." Then he read aloud, "While on vacation, I read Ehrenburg's novel *The Storm* with great interest and pleasure. J. Stalin."

There were no more critical remarks.

In the spring mama came with the children and we rented a room. In September the girls went to school — Natasha in the tenth grade, Kira in the eighth and Lera in the fourth. I was making good money, but our life was hard. It was, after all, a big family.

Around us there were many women who had lost their husbands in the war. Life was not easy for them either. My position, senior engineer, belonged to the nomenklatura of the railway administration. I was listed for the longest time as temporary substitute, and they didn't confirm my position because of biographical considerations. But in the end, they confirmed it. I was very glad, now there was some security. By that time, Natasha had finished high school and enrolled in the Stavropol foreign language school. Kira was on vacation in Kedabek and was due to arrive soon. Lera was in pioneer camp.

On the morning of August 20, 1949, I had just managed to have a brief talk with Natasha on the phone (she was in Stavropol) in order to wish her happy birthday, when a girl from our department walked up to me and said that the boss was asking me to come see him for a minute. I went.

In the personnel department, it was not our boss, but a man in an NKVD uniform who was sitting there. He presented an order for my arrest. Thus started my third period of trials and tribulations.

4

He went home with me. He searched our room, although, in fact, it was a superficial performance.

I said good-bye to mama, and he took me away to the preliminary detention cell, which was located at the station. There I spent a sleepless night in the company of several speculators and bribe-takers, arrested during some kind of police sweep.

Early in the morning, with the first train, they took me under guard to Rostov. I tried to understand why they had arrested me. While I was in Kolyma, I still met with former prisoners who had been my comrades in the camps; during the last three years, however, I hadn't met with anyone or written to anyone. But this was hardly what was involved!

I knew very well that if the order were given to arrest a certain category of people, then they would be arrested even though there was no basis for this at all. By the way, that's what had happened: a new minister, Abakumov, came to power and decided to leave his mark in history. So he created the category of "repeaters," that is, he arrested those who had served their sentence during the thirties and survived.

But I found that out only later. I thought, of course, about my children. In the material sense, I could be calm about two of them — Kira and Larisa. Kira was with Vitya and Raya, and no matter where she was studying, she would not be in need. Lialka was with her father. And no matter what sort of man he was, she would be well-fed and dressed. But if one abstracted away from the material side of things, then it was precisely about these two children that I had to worry. Strange as it may seem, Vitya's wife, my Aunt Raya, who had nothing in common with Goncharuk when it comes to upbringing or education or anything else, had much in common with him concerning a number of basic attitudes towards life. It was precisely those attitudes which were absolutely unacceptable for me. And I would not have liked it at all if my children were raised with these attitudes.

It seemed that I had to worry least of all about Lera; she had remained with her grandmother, with my mama. I knew that mama still had some money left from selling things. In addition, she earned a decent salary by giving music and German lessons. But I knew my mother and was by no means relaxed about Lera's situation. As it turned out later, I was right. Mama put her in an orphanage. Natasha took her from the orphanage, but she was studying in Stavropol and lived for the most part on her stipend, and Lera had to return to Kropotkin. Here she ended up not in a regular orphanage, but in some kind of reception center for orphaned children, where there was no school and life was generally terrible.

But I found out about all this a long time later. Right now, however, I thought most of all about Natasha. With regard to the others, at least, there was little for which I would reproach myself. I had worked hard, had denied myself everything and had done for them everything that I could. And if I had given Lialka to her father, then in doing so I had never thought for a moment that it was for all time. I was sure that after a certain period, he would grow bored with her and would send her back to me.

But here was Natasha, an active Komsomolka—what would she think of my arrest? What would she think of me? Why was it that I, who had lived with her for two and a half years, had never talked to her about anything? Here is where I was to blame—why hadn't I told her what 1937 had been all about? Why hadn't I told her about the political trials, about the camps, about the physical destruction of people both in the party and outside it, about collectivization? I had spoken to her about none of this—why?! I had thought, let her live a bit in peace, let her believe that everything was all right, later on I will have time. And now, I hadn't managed to tell her. What was she now thinking?!

How awful it was that all four of them were separated. Could it possibly be that they would live apart, each on her own?

Of course, I also thought about myself. I knew this system well enough to understand that once they arrested you, it meant that they wouldn't let you go soon, if they let you go at all. When I was arrested the first time, I was twenty-three, and now I was forty-three. How much could I take?

For the first time in my life, I truly did not feel like living. The most comforting thought for me was thinking about death—for I could always die. It was with these thoughts that I spent the night in the preliminary detention cell and the day on the train from Kropotkin to Rostov. In Rostov my guard took me to the administration of the northern Kavkaz railway line. Each month I had traveled here on business and I never even knew that in the basement of the building there was a room with bars on the windows, with the typical prison setup: a cot, side stand, stool and slop bucket in the corner.

I never saw my Kropotkin guard again; some kind person on duty brought me food. I poked around at the food a bit, and the person on duty said to me in a low voice: "You should eat, this food is from the restaurant, and you won't be getting such food again soon." He was right, the food was from a restaurant, there were four courses and I indeed didn't see such food again soon. But I wasn't in the mood for it.

After a couple of hours they summoned me and led me into a room, a normal office. There sat a man in civilian clothes, who was about forty years old. He said that he was my investigator and that his name was Kogan. I asked on what grounds they had arrested me, and he answered that this would become clear in the course of the investigation. He asked me several questions of an informational character, but didn't write anything down. It was not obvious why all this was necessary. It seems to me that he simply was in no hurry to find out who I was.

On the next day they took me to the Rostov city prison. It had been built at the time of Catherine the Great and was shaped like the letter E: it was a long building with a wing at each end and in the middle, a small one, like an appendix.

I was met by a heavyset woman with shoulder straps, who said with the voice of a caring hostess, "We know everything about you."

Once again: fingerprints, photograph, body-search. But it was very different from Butyrki. Everything was done here offhandedly, carelessly and without particular fanfare. But I wasn't the same as I had been in Butyrki either. Then everything had seemed to be humiliating and offensive, now, it was simply irritating.

It became clear immediately that this was a prison without very strict rules. Everywhere it was dirty, noisy and the staff stomped about the corridors. If a prison is clean, quiet and the staff walk about as silently as ghosts, then it is a terrible prison. In the Rostov prison, as I found out, you could both exchange letters and shout to one another.

A prison matron led me to my cell. The cell was small, with eight beds, seven women and one bed for me. I introduced myself.

The first person to catch my eye was a very beautiful young Armenian, Rimma Chernikian. In Rostov there is a large region settled by Armenians, Nakhichevan. But as it turned out, Rimma was not from Nakhichevan, Rimma was from Paris. After her parents emigrated in 1917, she was born and raised in Paris. In 1940, when Stalin issued the call saying that all emigrants could return to their homeland, Rimma's father decided that he had to return, at least to die in his native Nakhichevan. His son, Rimma's older brother, categorically refused to go, but Rimma, then nineteen, naturally went with her parents. Her fiance traveled with them (so that he wouldn't part with her); he was Romanian and a captain of the Romanian Royal Fleet. The captain was immediately executed as soon as they made it to the Soviet Union. As I understood it, he wasn't so much executed as simply shot on the spot, without any trial or investigation. Rimma soon married General Lalayanets, who it seems was deputy commander of the northern Kavkaz military district. In 1945, toward the very end of the war, the general was arrested, and soon after that Rimma was too. By that time she had two children, a three-year-old boy and a four-month-old girl. Rimma said that when she was being questioned, her mother brought her daughter twice a day to the prison, and she nursed her. That toddler's milk must have been very bitter....

Rimma received seven years in the camps, had served four of them and now had been brought to her native Rostov, evidently for a new sentence. They said that many who had once received five to seven years, and even ten years, were now having their sentences reviewed and being given, as a rule, twenty-five years.

The rest of the women in the cell had either worked under the Germans (they were called "under-Fritzes") or were believers belonging to various sects.

There were two "under-Fritzes" in the cell. One of them held herself aloof, and people hardly ever spoke to her. She had taught German language in school and when the Germans came, worked as a translator for the Gestapo. She was present during interrogations, during torture and got drunk with the fascist officers. She herself cynically said that she had lived "in luxury" under the Germans. "Now I sit here and at least I have something to remember. I'm not like you, a bunch of hens."

The second had worked under the Germans as a kindergarten teacher. The children in the kindergarten had, of course, been ours, Russian children, including her own child, for whose sake she went to work there. She was from Taganrog, and the Germans had been there more than a year; she had to find some way to survive.

Both of these women had been charged with the same crime— "collaboration with the occupiers."

Among the religious prisoners, the favorite of the whole cell was a seventeen-year-old girl, Eva (her full name was Evangelina). Her grandparents were Baptists who had emigrated to Canada before the revolution. There were several families who bought a farm and organized something of an agricultural commune. They lived very well, but retained their Russian language, Russian way of life and Russian holidays. When they, too, got the chance in 1940 to go to Russia, then some of them, including Eva's parents, decided to return to the homeland. So they returned.

One evening they summoned Eva, seemingly for an interrogation. She returned very quickly, completely in tears, with her teeth chattering. "Evochka, my dear girl, what's the matter?" It turned out that there was no interrogation. Five men were in one room, together with the investigator; they all were drunk, and on the table were bottles and some food. They sat her down, poured her some wine, tried to convince her to drink and began to paw her over. She naturally began to shout and ran to the door. Evidently someone who was a bit more sober understood that this could end badly for them and sent her back to her cell.

I spent several days in this cell and managed to learn two very important facts. First, during the interrogations they didn't beat us and in general didn't use the "active" methods. Second, they didn't arrest family members, that is, as ChSIR (family member of a traitor to the motherland).

One morning, immediately after rising time, they summoned me for questioning. I was taken in a paddy wagon from the city prison to the NKVD headquarters. Immediately I ended up in a "box." I had gotten to know boxes in Butyrki prison. They were something like a standing wardrobe. There were various kinds of boxes: some could only hold one person standing up, in others there was a stool, and you could sit; there were still others which had a table and a stool. My box was of medium comfort, since it had a stool. I sat on this stool for about three hours. They had taken me from the prison immediately after wake-up, that is, after six, and the interrogation began exactly at nine. Kogan had a large watch on his wrist, and I glanced at the time.

This time he was in uniform, with insignia of a senior lieutenant, looking very official. He warned me that everything I said would be noted down in the protocol of the interrogation. Questioning continued from eight in the morning until ten at night. Kogan had a two-hour break for lunch, and I spent these two hours on the same stool, in the same box.

It is true that they brought me lunch, too, although this time it was by no means from a restaurant, it was typical prison soup.

To keep from repeating, I will say that he called me in for questioning sometimes once, sometimes twice a week. They always took me from the prison immediately after rising time, and took me back just before the signal to go to bed, that is, the interrogation, as a whole, lasted fifteen to sixteen hours.

And how everything in the world is relative! When the iron gates of the prison slammed shut behind the paddy wagon bringing me back, what happiness it was—I was home.

But after the first interrogation, they no longer took me back to the cell in which I had been. They took me in the other direction, to the left side of the prison. There I was put in solitary confinement, although there were two cots.

Most of the prisoners in this wing were minors who were crammed in four or five to a one-man cell. They were not put in the large cells so that they couldn't gather together in large numbers.

I remained in solitary until the end of the investigation. Three times during this period, they put a neighbor in on the other cot. Each of them spent a few days with me. I will speak about them later.

It is now hard for me to remember in what sequence things happened at my interrogations: what took place at the first, the third, or the sixth. Therefore I will describe the interrogations without indicating their sequence. I think that this makes little difference.

By the end of the first interrogation I became convinced that Kogan was well prepared. He knew by name all my comrades in the Opposition, he knew the composition of the Moscow Oppositional Komsomol Center, of which I had been a member in 1928-29. (I wrote about this earlier in my notes.) Moreover, they had been supplied with information by one of the former members of this center, since there had been no outsiders, and everything was related with almost stenographic precision.

He named names and asked me about these people. I "remembered" only those whom I knew for certain no longer remained among the living. My testimony could not do them any harm. About the others, I said that I "didn't remember." Kogan muttered angrily, "Why are you always saying, 'I don't remember, I don't remember'?" "In general, I have a bad memory." "Well, you're wasting your time saying this. Everyone who went to school with you says that you had good abilities and a fine memory. Even the professors at the institute remarked about your memory." I answered him by paraphrasing a quotation from Voynich's *The Gadfly*: "It seems that professors perceive and evaluate memory in a different way than investigators."

In the course of the investigation, I began to understand why he had shown such interest in me from the very beginning. My dossier contained a postcard from Rakovsky, which he had written during the period of my first exile, probably in 1929 or 1930. The postcard had the sentence: "I received a letter from L.D., and among other things he writes that according to rumors which have reached him, Nadiusha is somewhere in Siberia. If you have the chance, please send her my sincere greetings."

Kogan was a very limited man and undoubtedly a careerist. He probably thought, "Look at the bird which has come my way, Trotsky himself sends her his sincere greetings." The fool, he didn't realize that for Trotsky I was not a political figure, but simply the daughter of Adolf Abramovich; he even called me by my childhood nickname, "Nadiusha."

I told him, "If you are counting on getting an extra star on your epaulets because of me, then you're wasting your time. Don't count on it." He became enraged, "You know, I have worked for many years with those being investigated, but I have never met a more unpleasant person than you."

I took this as a compliment.

Once, I don't remember what was the cause, he said how important it was to raise children correctly. "I have a daughter," he said, "who is fourteen. From the first grade on, she studied together with one girl, became close friends with her and was often at her home. They liked her there and always welcomed her. Once, when they were having tea, the mother of this girl said that people were wrong in extolling Stalin so highly. 'You shouldn't honor a man as you do a god.' And what do you think my daughter did?" Kogan asked proudly. "Without my advice and on her own initiative, she wrote a letter and sent it where she should have. The woman was arrested. That's a Komsomolka for you."

I became physically nauseous just thinking about this "dear" fourteen-year-old girl. Apparently, from the expression on my face he understood my reaction. "Now your Natasha is also a Komsomolka. I had a talk with her when she was sitting right there where you are now."

I imagined Natasha, sitting in this room, on this stool which was chained down.... And then I heard Kogan's gloating voice. "Perhaps you would like some water?" I knew that he was lying, that Natasha had never been here. And in fact, she never had been. Sometime in the middle of October, mama came to see me. She brought me a small parcel and deposited twenty-five rubles in my prison account. They allowed me to meet with her. Mama said that all the girls were healthy and in school; she didn't say a word about Lera being in the orphanage.

According to the rules existing then, the investigation should not have lasted more than two months. If the investigator couldn't manage within that time frame, and needed an extension, then he had to receive permission from the procurator. Kogan precisely met the deadline—they arrested me on August 20 and on October 20 I signed under Article 206. Article 206 of the trial code signified the end of the investigation. And a person was obliged to familiarize himself with his case. If a person was being tried alone, he would read it himself; if several were being tried together, then the investigator would read it aloud.

After signing the 206th, they put me in a common cell. What happiness this was!

And now about the three women who spent a few days each with me in my one-man cell.

The first was a kind young woman, Zhenya Plotnikova. She finished the German department at the Institute of Foreign Languages, and when the Germans were in Taganrog, she went to work as a translator in some trading company. She didn't work there long, since the trading firm apparently wasn't able to manage and returned to Germany. They proposed that she go with them, but she didn't want to abandon her elderly parents. Now she had been given twenty-five years for "collaboration with the occupiers."

The second was Anya. Anya was German. In the Rostov area there were several German farms. The Germans had lived there since time immemorial, from generation to generation. They were completely Soviet, these Germans, but they maintained their language and customs. Anya was born right here in the Rostov area and finished Soviet school, but at home they spoke German.

When the fascists came, they hired Anya, as one of their own Volksdeutsche, to work in the officers' dining room. She managed to link up with a partisan detachment, the head of which was the former chief of their regional police department. She handed over food to the detachment which she had taken from the dining room, and since the Germans were not shy about saying whatever they felt like in her presence, she also passed on even more valuable information to the partisans.

The head of the partisan detachment soon began to fight in the regular army and went all the way to Berlin. After victory over the Germans he married some woman from Minsk, then settled down to live and work in Minsk.

When he learned that Anya was on trial for "aiding and abetting the enemy," he made a special trip to Rostov and testified at the trial. He said that if it had not been for Anya, then the partisans would have died from hunger. Risking her life, she had taken food from the officers' dining room; moreover, she had passed on valuable information to the detachment. He said that she should be given a medal.

During this period, everyone convicted of these charges was given twenty-five years. Taking into account what the former head of the partisan detachment said, the court gave Anya ten.

The third who was put in my cell shared my name, Nadya. Nadezhda Dobrynina. About herself she said that she had worked the whole war deciphering code for the general staff; she was in prison for divulging military secrets. In general she spoke about herself readily and at length. She was married for the second time, and from her first husband she had a son who was living with his grandmother. "And just imagine," she said, "I was married twice, and both husbands were named Fyodor; I had two lovers, and both were named Boris." She quickly began to treat me to very good and expensive pastries (I had never bought such things on the outside) and good sausage. All the while she would rattle away, "Just imagine, my investigator fought on the same part of the front with my Fyodor, my husband, and now, during interrogations, the investigator gives me things from Fyodor; as you can see, it's the very best."

In the evening, after the bedtime signal, when we had already lain down, she said, "I see that you are such a good woman. Perhaps you would like to send a letter to some of your friends on the outside—I can arrange it."

I said that I didn't have any friends on the outside, not because I suspected her of anything, but because this actually was the case.

The next day, after our walk, since it was a warm day during the Indian summer, we asked the guard not to close the window (during walks the cells are aired out). I walked up to the window, but Nadya lay down on the cot and immediately fell asleep. In general, she instantly fell asleep, simply in the middle of a sentence, and she slept for a long time, whether night or day. I envied her greatly, since insomnia in prison is agonizing. In the exercise yard beneath our window, one of the women's cells was walking about; they were evidently common criminals. Seeing me in the window, they somehow crowded around, and began to wave their arms at me. Some even shouted, "Ko-ko-ko, ko-ko-ko." They obviously were imitating a chicken. In prison jargon, a hen means an informer—everything was clear.

I looked at Nadya. She was sleeping. Her face was thin, exhausted and somehow defenseless. I began to think, "Perhaps it's not true, prison rumors will dream up whatever you like. On the other hand, it was a strange investigator who gave her parcels, and then there was her offer to send a letter out of the prison." I decided to be cautious. Just in case.

The next day they summoned Nadya to an interrogation. When the guard opened the door, I glanced into the corridor—some women were mopping the floors. They took Nadya away, and after a few minutes, someone quietly knocked on my door. I went up to it. A woman's voice said in muffled tones, "Hey, friend! The girl in the cell with you is a hen, watch out." Then the same voice, loudly and joyfully, "We're finishing up, guardie, we're finishing up. We're mopping the last corner."

"Oh, the stinker," I thought, "what made her do it? Could it have been for a piece of sausage? Probably they conned her with 'party' duty and so forth. I have seen such types in the camps."

Nadya returned after about two hours, in tears, but once again with good sausage, smoked fish and other tasty things. "Help yourself," she said to me. My first reaction was to refuse. Then I reconsidered, "And why should I? She received this sausage because of me, why shouldn't I take advantage of it?" I had been in prison for a month and a half without parcels, living solely off bland prison soup.

Nadya looked at me in surprise—I had been so overscrupulous, I had barely agreed to take a couple of little cookies for tea, and suddenly I was heaping things on. Then she announced that the investigator had promised to transfer her to another cell. "Probably you are destined to remain in solitary until the end of the investigation, that's what I think," she said. "So it's too bad that you don't want to send a letter through me to the outside, another chance might not arise. You should at least write your mother. You should write how the investigation is going, and tell her what you are saying or not saying; she's your mother, after all, and she would be interested in all this. And I have reliable channels." "You can say that again," I thought to myself, "reliable channels straight to Kogan."

The next morning, immediately after latrine call, the door opened, "Dobrynina, get your things together. I'll be coming for you soon." Nadya hurriedly shoved her things into her backpack, then reached for the bag with food. I put my hand on it, "This you can leave here...." "What do you mean, leave? Why?" "Just that. Leave it for me." Nadya muttered, "All right, I don't care, take it, please." "No, I don't need any 'please,'" I said. "You sold me out for this piece of sausage, so you can leave it here for me." "What are you talking about, God only knows what you're saying," she muttered.

Just then the guard opened the door. "Dobrynina, ready?" Nadya grabbed her backpack and shot like a bullet into the corridor. For three more days I ate the sausage and smoked fish.

Thus, after signing the 206th, they took me to a common cell, to the same one where I spent several days before the investigation began. How happy I was! Even prison has its little moments of joy. I was once again with other people, my interrogations were over and I never would see Kogan again. By the way, I had to see Kogan one more time. But about that later.

The composition of the cell had changed significantly. Rimma Chernikian wasn't there, nor was the Baptist Evochka, nor was the "fascist" (that's what they called the woman who had worked as a translator for the Gestapo). The two religious prisoners weren't there. But then there was Muza Fedorovna Guzenko, a former KRTD who had been in Kolyma at the same time as I had. I hadn't known her there, but she said that she had heard a lot about me. There was another friendly old woman, whose name I can't remember. She was sixty years old. As a young girl she had lived for two years in Paris. How a Jewish girl from the Pale of Settlement had ended up in Paris I never understood. But she had been there, working as a skilled seamstress in some fashion house. Then she returned to Russia and lived there for forty years in Rostov (not counting the war years, when she was in evacuation). She had a son, who was a colonel, a daughter-in-law and two grandchildren. But she still worked as a cutter in a sewing workshop. To the extent that she could, she fought against all abuses. There they sewed some things on the side made from officially purchased material; from the material someone ordered, they would cut off something for themselves. She spoke about this at some meetings and threatened that if this didn't stop, she would report to where she should. They wrote a letter denouncing her, saying that she had lived in Paris and praised the way of life there and was nothing but a spy. We simply died from laughter when she returned from an interrogation and told about her discussions with the investigator. He asked her whom she had met with when she was in Paris, and what they had talked about. "If I had known forty years ago that I would be talking to you, then I would have remembered. But I didn't know that I would be talking to you forty years later, and so I don't remember anything."

When we were taking out the slop bucket after latrine call, and the guard was walking behind hurrying us along, she said to him, "Hey, komashka. (This was her favorite term of abuse; it meant a small mosquito that buzzes around one's ear.) Komashka, idiot (she had absolutely no fear of anyone or anything), what will you do if they take this miserable slop bucket away from you?"

She simply worshipped her grandson. "Levochka is a marvelous child. He has already joined the Komsomol and soon will come to protect his grandmother." Her son, the colonel, got her out of prison. She was set free, and we were all sincerely glad that this happened.

One more religious prisoner, a Ukrainian, appeared in our cell. She didn't belong to any sect, but was a solitary old maid. She lived together with a friend who was also an old maid. They both fervently believed in God, but never went to church and didn't like priests. They thought that priests were self-seeking and that you could pray at home, God would hear one's prayer anywhere. A neighbor who wanted their room wrote a denunciation, saying that they held prayer services in the communal apartment. So they were put in prison. During the investigation they were in different cells, missed each other very much and were overjoyed at seeing one another when they signed the 206th. They were barely literate, and the investigator read their "case" to them aloud. The second was somewhat younger and was quite active in interrupting the investigator, "No, that never happened." But our Vasilisa stopped her, "Let him read, look at me." She then said benevolently, "Read on, read on, that's your job." Then once again to her friend, "Look at me and let him read." This "let him read" then became a saying among us.

In our cell there were two more religious prisoners, both involved in the same case. This was a violation of prison rules, but so many people were involved in this case that apparently there were not enough cells.

This case was called the case of "the sect of John the Baptist," and in prison they referred to it as the "case of blessed* Ivanushka," because the head of this sect was a certain blessed Ivanushka, who was considered to be a virtual saint.

In our cell was Frosya, a barely literate village woman who cared for this "blessed" person, that is, she was his nanny. Ivanushka himself was in the NKVD's internal prison, and Frosya was very worried about him, "He is so holy, he's like a little child. If you don't feed him, he won't eat, if you don't put him to bed, he won't sleep." Because of what I heard, I got the impression that this Ivanushka was simply a lunatic, who obviously had the gift of inspiring people.

A second woman in our cell from this sect was Marya Vasilievna, a teacher who had finished the pedagogical institute and worked for

---

* The word blazhennyi in Russian means both blessed and somewhat of a simpleton.

many years as a teacher of Russian language and literature in the upper grades of the ten-year school in one large Cossack village. She didn't actually consider herself a member of the sect, it was just that this Ivanushka had lived in her home for a certain while.

I spoke with Marya Vasilievna. "How can it be? I can understand Frosya, who believes that God sits in the clouds and runs the whole show from there. But you are an intellectual and a teacher; how could you fit into all this? For this Ivanushka, judging from everything I've heard, is either mentally defective or an adventurer." "You know," she replied, "now that I don't see him before me, it seems strange to me, too, but when you're with him, then, believe me, you simply can't resist him." According to her own words, she absolutely didn't want him to live in her home, but he pointed a finger at her and said, "Ivanushka will live with you," and she couldn't say no. She said that he was thin, hunchbacked, with a kind of fixed stare. And he was indeed simple, Frosya was right: if you didn't give him anything, he wouldn't ask for it, if you didn't put him to bed, he would remain sitting on a stool even if it meant staying there all night long.

Marya Vasilievna was a witness to several of the minor "miracles" performed by this Ivanushka. Once Frosya told him to eat, "Eat, father, you haven't eaten since morning." He said, "Ivanushka will eat (he always referred to himself in the third person), Ivanushka wants some eggs." The woman in charge of the household where this happened said that she didn't have any eggs. But he insisted, "Some eggs for Ivanushka," and then he ordered Frosya to open some cupboard, and there sat two eggs. The other woman was astounded.

I suggested that he was probably very observant and had noticed where the eggs were. But Marya Vasilievna said, "What are you saying? He was indeed blessed and never saw what was going on around him."

The climax of the "blessed Ivanushka" story I learned from the same Marya Vasilievna, when I met with her a few months later at the Kuibyshev transfer point. Marya Vasilievna described how everyone connected with the case met, as stipulated, to sign the 206th. There were around one hundred people, and rows of benches were placed in a large room, where everyone sat down. The investigator read the case material. "Blessed Ivanushka" sat in the first row. Marya Vasilievna had a hard time recognizing him—where had the hunchbacked lunatic gone to? This was a smart-looking man with a lively expression and deep voice who was well versed on all questions. He often interrupted the reading of the case: "If you please, citizen investigator, such and such a point of the criminal-trial codex says the following. What grounds do you have?" and so forth. Or even: "If you please! Such and such a chapter of the constitution stipulates the following civil rights," and so forth. The investigators took turns, one would read for two hours, then another, and Ivanushka was literally outdoing them all.

In the course of the affair, it emerged that there had been no religious sect whatsoever, and that this was a genuine, anti-Soviet, profascist organization. "Ivanushka" had been an officer in the Soviet Army, then he went over to the Germans and fought against his own people. When the war ended he came to the Rostov area and under the guise of "blessed Ivanushka" created this organization. Around him was a core of people who knew the actual state of affairs, whereas those like Frosya or Marya Vasilievna were simply there for camouflage purposes. Ivanushka received the death penalty. Marya Vasilievna got three years.

On October 20 I signed the 206th, and then sat waiting for the sentence. After our one meeting, mama didn't come to visit me anymore. In the cell I fattened myself a bit off others' food parcels. I earned this extra food by telling stories. Almost every evening I told some story which I, of course, hadn't thought up, but was out of a book I had read. Rostand's *Cyrano de Bergerac* and *The Little Eagle (L'Aiglon)* were particularly popular, perhaps because I recited whole pages of the text in verse from memory. For this they fed me, and I felt that I had earned my bread honestly. Which brings to mind Kogan. By the way, while I am on the topic of Kogan, in the Rostov prison, he was considered to be the most vicious investigator.

The women said that while I was away, one of their cellmates was a young girl named Lida, whom the Germans in 1942 had sent off to Germany. It was very hard for her there. She worked as a maid, then in a factory, she went hungry, became totally exhausted and didn't expect to live. But the area where Lida lived was liberated by the Americans. The Americans were very helpful, they put her in a hospital, fattened her up and sent her home. When she returned to Rostov, she spoke about everything which had happened. They put her in prison. Her investigator was Kogan. He screamed at her, calling her a slut, fascist whore and even worse things that are simply unprintable. When she came back to the cell, she was crying, and the women advised her to demand a medical examination. She did so. The examination established that she was a virgin. Kogan then said, "That's all right, Lida, don't be offended. Our work is nerve-racking."

I was destined to meet this same Kogan one more time. Sometime in January—when exactly, I don't remember, but it was Sunday, late at night, after the signal to go to sleep—they summoned me without my things. They led me to some office, and there stood Kogan. For some reason he greeted me very loudly: "Hello, hello, I've brought you your belongings," and offered me the belt to my dress, which had been taken away when they brought me to the prison. I was shocked. On Sunday, late in the evening, to come to give me my cheap cloth belt! I looked at Kogan and saw that he was drunk, dead drunk. "What are you looking at me for? Do you want to read a newspaper? Probably you haven't seen a paper for ages?" And he handed me a folded copy of *Pravda*. "Here there's a governmental decree about introducing the death penalty. Yes, yes, about introducing the death penalty for particularly dangerous criminals. Here, read it, and I'll be back soon." He placed the paper on the table and walked toward the door.

He wobbled from side to side. I remained alone in the office, which was against prison rules. I sat down and began to read the newspaper. Indeed, it contained a governmental decree about the introduction of the death penalty. Kogan was gone for quite a while, and I managed to read not only this decree, but the entire paper. Finally, he came back. Perhaps he had vomited, and this made him feel better, or perhaps he had just had a bit of fresh air, but he was doing better, or at least, he wasn't staggering when he walked. But nevertheless it was clear that he was extremely drunk. "Did you read it? Death penalty for particularly dangerous criminals." He pointed upwards with his index finger. "And that's what you are—a particularly dangerous criminal." His index finger was pointing at me. Then he suddenly shouted, "Get up." I have to say that, given all his repulsive interrogation methods, he never had yelled at me in this way. In general, no one ever yelled at me. Once more he screamed, "Get up, I'm talking to you!" and pulled out his revolver. I got up. "Go into the corridor." He was no longer shouting, but he held his revolver in his hand. I went out, and he followed after me. The office was at the very end of the corridor, and the corridor was very long, running the entire length of the prison building. Since it was late Sunday evening, it was absolutely empty, without even a guard in sight. I stopped. "Forward." I walked ahead very slowly. I glanced around. He was following me, about two or three steps back, holding onto his revolver. "Don't look back! Forward!"

I walked very slowly and tried to collect my thoughts. "Well, this isn't 1937, and they are at least pretending to obey the law. Even if there is the death penalty, then they have to declare such a sentence. He couldn't possibly just shoot me like this. But then, why not? He is drunk, mad and has a revolver in his hand. He could shoot me in the back of the head and then say, 'She was trying to escape.' Then what would happen to him? Nothing. The worst he would get is fifteen days detention."

I remember how back in Kolyma, at the city housing authority campsite, one of the guards killed a prisoner from the watchtower. He had called out, but the prisoner didn't answer, perhaps he hadn't heard the guard. According to the rules, the guard was supposed to shout two more times, then shoot into the air and only then shoot at the prisoner. But he immediately fired straight at the prisoner. Well, what happened? He got fifteen days in detention, but a man was dead.

No matter how slowly I walked and no matter how long the corridor was, it finally came to an end. I cautiously looked back. He was still following me with revolver in hand. At the end of the corridor, to the right, was an open door, and beyond it a staircase. Just before the staircase stood a guard.

Kogan told him, "Take the prisoner to her cell." He then turned around and went back along the corridor. I sat on the bottom stair—my legs simply wouldn't hold me. The guard looked at me. "Hey, old lady (babonka)! Well, get up, let's go. What's your cell number?" Lord, what a good guard! How well he said the word "babonka." He led me to my cell. What wonderful women in the cell. Could this be the woman I had gotten angry at today over something? Could this other one possibly be someone who often irritated me? How wonderful they all were!

They poured me some tea which was still warm. From the kindness of their hearts they put in so much sugar that it was syrup, not tea, but I drank it with great pleasure. I lay down on the cot, and they covered me with all the blankets. I was shaking. After this I stayed in prison another six months or so, and no one ever summoned me for anything.

No matter how many years have passed, no, not even years, but decades, to this day I cannot walk alone along an empty street if someone is walking behind me. I feel that he will suddenly shoot me in the back of the head. I always stop and let the person go by me.

This is how, first hand, I got to know about the reintroduction of the death penalty.

Many years later, I became interested in the history of capital punishment in Russia.

Until 1905, capital punishment as such was a rare phenomenon. Russia remained longer than any other country without the death penalty under Elizabeth Petrovna.

Here are some figures:

For thirty years, from 1876 to 1905, 486 people were executed, that is, about seventeen people per year (on the average, one or two people per month). It must be taken into account that this was a time of intense activity by the supporters of Narodnaya Volya, a time of terrorist acts, etc.

From 1905 to 1908, 2,200 people were executed, or about 45 per month. For those times, this was "an epidemic of executions."

From July 1918 through October 1919, more than 16,000 people were shot. That is, more than one thousand per month. In comparison, during the eighty years when the Inquisition was at its peak (1420-98), about ten thousand people were condemned to be burned at the stake, i.e., about ten people per month.

In 1937-38, according to unverified data (apparently no verified data exists) about 28,000 people a month were annihilated under Article 58.

By January 1939, according to other sources, 1,700,000 people had been shot.

In May 1947 the death penalty was rescinded.

In January 1950 it was reinstated. It exists to this very day.

I greeted the New Year of 1950 in jail. We put together a collective dinner and put everything we had on the table. A little bottle was found with cranberry extract. We diluted it with water and poured it into mugs. We clinked our cups filled with cranberry extract and wished each other.... What can you wish for in prison? Why, freedom, of course.

At midnight it was rather warm and the window was open — the whole prison could hear a low, well-trained male voice: "Happy New Year, comrades!" We knew who this was. The entire prison knew his story. This was a pilot who had fought from the opening days of the war. The Germans shot him down, he was wounded and captured. He tried to escape from a concentration camp twice, but they caught him and sent him back. He was sent from camp to camp, and everywhere he organized underground groups. In the end, he wound up in France. There he also tried to escape, but this time was successful. He joined the partisans and took part in the French resistance.

After victory over the Nazis, he returned to his native Rostov. They arrested him. He was tried by the regional court and tried by a revolutionary tribunal, but neither one of these organized show trials was able to convict him. But as they said, "You can't try somebody for nothing, but where there is no trial, there is the special board." So he appeared before the special board. I don't know his subsequent fate, but probably he received his twenty-five years.

On April 9 they summoned me with my things. They took me to some office. Behind the table sat a man in uniform. He said, "Sit down and familiarize yourself with the decree of the special board concerning your case." I placed the piece of paper with a typewritten text before me.

I found out what is meant by the expression, "Everything went dark before my eyes." Instead of a white piece of paper, all I saw before me was a dark spot. But gradually the darkness receded, and I read "free exile*... Krasnoyarsk region ... duration—pending special orders."

We were shipped out on the same day. In a couple of hours, I stood in the convoy formation. There were many people, but no one I knew. We were surrounded by guards and dogs.."Step to the right, step to the left...."

We were taken to the station and put in Stolypin cars. The compartment was filled to overflowing, and there were bars on the doors. Just as in 1936. Only then I had shared the compartment with Difa and Olga. And on the other side of the wall, in the neighboring compartment, there had been Pavel. He was with Sasha and Zyama. Now, not one of them was still alive. The men had perished in Kolyma. Olga had returned to Moscow, received a second sentence and died in prison. Difa had died in evacuation. I alone remained. I remembered the *Story About the Seven Who Were Hanged* by Leonid Andreev. There the girl Tanya says, "I alone remained, boys, I alone remained...."

In the Kuibyshev transit prison, they held us for quite a long time. I was in an enormous women's cell, which had about 400 prisoners and double bunks. You would generally know those who were lying not far away. The regime was not harsh. We could go out for walks when we wished. If we wanted to, we could work in the prison kitchen. There you could eat as many potatoes as you wanted, and if you asked to be on distribution, then you could go from cell to cell and see who was where. It was already clear that there were very many repeaters like myself.

Next to me on the bunks lay Alla Sobol, a Muscovite. She had served four years in the camps and was going into exile instead of being set free. In the spring of 1941 she had finished school and was taken to prison straight from the graduation party—in white stockings and with white bows. The whole class was arrested, headed by the secretary of the Komsomol cell. Their favorite teacher, a history teacher, had been arrested as an enemy of the people. When their new teacher showed up, they organized a protest—they banged their desk-

---

* Forced settlement in a given region without a set term. "Free exiles" were usually not deprived of their civil rights.

tops and shouted that they didn't want anyone else, they wanted their old history teacher back. They were allowed to finish the tenth grade, and then after the graduation party were taken to prison. But they weren't held for long, soon they were set free. Only Kolya Miroshnikov remained in prison—his father, the former office manager for the sovnarkom, had been shot in 1937.

Soon the war began. Alla managed to enroll in the medical institute, and when the institute was evacuated to Omsk, she went with it. There she lived and studied until the end of the war. All the boys in her class were at the front and few came back. But in 1945, they all, including those who had fought and those who hadn't, were arrested, convicted and given three or four years. Alla was taken out of the fourth year at the medical institute. In the camp she worked as a medical orderly and was worried most of all about whether she would be able to finish the institute and become a doctor. She was very excitable and nervous. At night she would wake up, cry out and sit there. With my insomnia, I heard all this happening. An older nun, Aunt Masha, slept next to her and watched out over her. I heard how Alla would cry out at night, "Auntie Masha, where am I? Auntie Masha?" Then I heard how Auntie Masha would say reassuringly in a sleepy voice, "You're in prison, my dear, everything's all right, you're in prison, go to sleep, you're in prison, everything is fine."

Lidia Ruslanova spent a few days in our cell. They had brought us there, but she was being sent back. Either to be reinvestigated or to be set free.

From the Kuibyshev transfer point, they sent us in a group which consisted of repeaters who were headed for free exile. And this could be felt. At the stations the guard bought food for those who had money, the iron doors of the compartment were often left unlocked, and along the corridor walked the head of the guards, "Sergeant Seriozha," who would sing his favorite song, "You're the same as you've always been...." He gladly struck up a conversation with us and was very surprised: "You're all a bunch of learned devils—Trotskyists, Bukharinists, no wonder they don't set you free."

Our next stopping place was the Krasnoyarsk transfer point. Here the cell was smaller, and I was put in with Alla Sobol and Lena Royek, who was also from Moscow. Her husband was the brother of the famous actress Konstantsiia Royek. He was still free and came to be with her in exile.

In the cell I came into contact with a new category of prisoners — relatives. In 1937 there had been ChSIRs, family members of a traitor to the motherland. These were mainly wives, but sometimes children. Now, it turned out, they were arresting all relatives, even the most distant ones. Next to me was a young girl, the grandniece of Krestinsky. She had never laid eyes on him. When he was shot in 1936, she was eight years old. There were many such distant relatives in prison.

5

They released us from the transit center on Victory Day — May 9. The city was decorated with flags, music was playing somewhere. In the prison courtyard, they set up a roll call. Each was called by his last name and then handed a piece of salted fish and half a loaf of black bread. This was the final gift from the party and the government. In the future we were on our own. As the saying goes "the drowning must save themselves." I stood there with the fish and bread in my hands. The girls, Alla and Lena, were lost somewhere in the crowd. Then a man walked up to me. He was tall and thin and asked, "Are you Joffe?" I was in no mood to strike up an acquaintance and replied in a rather angry voice, "Well, what if my name is Joffe? In the Moscow telephone book, the Joffes take up two and a half pages."

Boris Arkadievich Livshits, my close friend for the next some twenty odd years, often recalled how I snubbed him when we first met.

That evening they sent us by train to Kansk. All night long Boris and I talked. It turned out that when he had asked if I was Joffe, he had in mind precisely me, and not anyone else from the two and a half pages in the telephone book. He and I had been acquainted since our student days, to be sure, not very closely, but we met in the same company. It turned out we had many common acquaintances and a host of

214

mutually admired books and poems. He finished the economic department at FON, and then at RONION, the latter being a department at the Institute of Red Professors, where he defended his dissertation. In 1936 he passed his defense, and in March 1937 they arrested him. His ties were mainly with the rightists — Astrov, the editor of the journal *Under the Banner of Marxism*, and the Bukharin school at the Institute of Red Professors. Thus we approached the Opposition from opposite directions — he, from the right, and I, from the left.

He was born in September 1901 and had been in the party since July 1917, when he had not yet turned sixteen. By this time he had made the transition from being a religious boy in a Jewish school to being a Bolshevik. When they arrested him, there was no evidence against him and maybe for this reason they gave him only five years, having first knocked out all his teeth during the interrogations. He never signed anything.

Perhaps the unusual circumstances in which we met played a role, but it didn't take much time to know that we should face our future fate together.

In Kansk they put us in a car and drove us to the regional center of Taseevo, 150 kilometers from Kansk. They placed us all in the assembly hall of the local school. Our convoy (of course, it wasn't a convoy, since we were no longer prisoners — I am simply using the vocabulary I had grown used to), our convoy was very large. In the building to which they led us, there was not a single chair, nor a single bench, we could only sit on the floor.

It grew dark and there was no electricity, not a single kerosene lamp, no candles and not even a mangalka. In complete darkness everyone threw down on the floor their coats, suitcases, sacks and bags. People managed as best they could. About every half hour, the door would open, a man would stand on the threshold with a lantern in his hand and call out a few names. Those he named got up, and trying as much as possible not to step on arms, legs or heads, went to the door. Upon returning, they said that people were being divided up for work.

They called me earlier than Boris. In a room lighted by two kerosene lanterns (I even frowned from so much light), several men sat around a table. In the center was a captain of the NKVD and to the sides, as I later learned, were the director of the timber industry, the director of the sovkhoz and other economic planners for the entire region.

Later we called this night "Uncle Tom's Cabin," for this was essentially a genuine slave auction. Only these "buyers" were out of luck, for this was a bad batch of slaves.

Each of those called sat at the table and was asked the same basic question: "Specialty?" There were engineers, economists, scientific personnel, physicians, a few actors and a pair of academicians, one from the Byelorussian and one from the Armenian Academy of Sciences. What an intellectual elite!

Before me a tall, strapping man who was not very young strode up to the table, and in reply to the question "Specialty?," said firmly "Lumberjack." The KGB officer even whistled in delight. "Well, here's a strong one." This man wasn't, of course, a lumberjack, he was a biologist with a university degree, but he had calculated correctly as to who would need him in that capacity. If he signed up as a lumberjack, then he could at least count on a privileged position as a brigade leader.

The biggest wholesale buyer of human commodities was the director of the timber industry. He needed people and if he couldn't have quality, then he at least received quantity.

I ended up at Murma, and when Boris was called, he said that he wanted to go there too, to this timber-rafting town.

Murma is a tiny village and a real backwater. About thirty little houses are scattered along the river, there is a sawmill, post office and one store. Piles of logs lie on both sides of the river. The local inhabitants are aborigines. They each live in their own little house, have jobs on the side, in the summer are occupied with rafting and in the winter, work at the sawmill.

From our group of exiles, about twenty people ended up there, including seven women. The women were put in one of the houses and the men, in the sawmill which didn't work in the summer. Neither the house, nor even more so the sawmill had any beds, trestle-beds or even double bunks of blessed memory.

Our work was to cut off the branches, prepare the logs for floating down the river (they mainly floated down separately, not bound together), pile them up, saw off the tops and clear the ground. All forms of work had fixed norms, and our contingent couldn't possibly meet the norm, or even reach fifty percent. Each piece of bread bought in the store had to be paid for in cash.

All the former prisoners began to think back on the camps—there at least there had been a roof over our heads, and each day they gave a ration of bread and fish soup. Thus it turned out that maybe it was better to somehow live in the camps than to die from starvation in such a state of freedom. Everyone ran down to the post office and sent telegrams to relatives and friends: "Help! Send things! Rescue me!"

I had no one to turn to. Mama and the children were waiting for help from me. I don't know what would have happened to me if not for Boris. After his arrest, a significant sum of money remained in his savings account, and he transferred the money here. I was an object of envy for the rest of the women. First of all, the man clearly had money, second, he undoubtedly treated me very well, and finally, as Murochka, the wife of my late Uncle Vitya used to say, "Tall, clean-shaven and dark-haired—what more does anyone need from a man?" People also envied Boris—here, as in Kolyma, "demand outstripped supply."

One who didn't lose his head was the brigade leader. He was sixty years old and a shipbuilding engineer of prerevolutionary vintage. He had finished two institutes, knew three European languages and had been in the camps for "sabotage." He was a very energetic man. He declared that one of the women was his cousin and that they wanted to live together as relatives. His example was followed not only in Murma, but in other places. Unlike in the camps, here all types of relations, whether marital or kindred, were actively encouraged. People had been sent here, for the most part permanently, and it was desirable that they put down roots. Our brigadier deserved the sobriquet: "progenitor of a glorious pleiade of cousins."

The chief engineer of the timber industry, also an exile, came to Murma. He had fought throughout the war, had a virtual iconostasis of medals and commendations, but towards the end of the war had been wounded and was captured. He was in captivity for just a short while, but this canceled all his meritorious behavior. He received a camp sentence, which was then changed to exile "pending special dispensation." He was a wonderful fellow who understood exactly what had to be done. He advised us to apply for a transfer to the regional center of Taseevo, referring to the fact I wanted to have my schoolgirl daughter sent there, whereas there was no place to study in Murma. He promised to help us with this. I don't know whether he actually did help, or whether our application was all that was needed, but they soon transferred us to Taseevo.

Everything is relative. After Murma, Taseevo was simply a capital city. It had a school with ten grades, a hospital, theater, cafeteria and a few stores. We rented half a house. This sounds very luxurious, but it consisted of two tiny rooms and a heated entranceway. A small garden was included.

Taseevo was a regional center, but the possibilities for work here were only slightly greater than in Murma. Boris and I worked at the brick factory. Once when still in Kolyma, I had to work for a while at a brick factory. There was no mechanization there, and a horse kneaded the clay which would be used to form the bricks. This was called a "one horse-power mechanism." At the Taseevo brick factory, we didn't even have one horse-power. The clay was kneaded with human feet. They then molded the bricks and baked them in the most primitive oven, burning themselves in the process. I managed this to a certain degree, but Boris couldn't at all. He had a wonderful mind, but he couldn't do anything with his hands.

The composition of the exiles in Taseevo was completely mixed, and by no means resembled the makeup of my first exile in Krasnoyarsk. There the exile colony had been a group of political cothinkers. People might differ in their views concerning various inner-party questions, but it was, for the most part, "one big football team."

Here the degree of the fluctuation was immeasurably great. It ranged from Old Bolsheviks with prerevolutionary party membership to semibandit Banderovites.* One very interesting person was Nikolai

---

* Supporters of Stepan Bandera, a Ukrainian nationalist who fought against both Hitler and Stalin for an independent Ukraine in the 1940s. They were crushed by the Red Army after the war and thousands were arrested.

Nikolaevich Reske, who in the past had been a major theater administrator and had been married to a daughter of the famous playwright and director of the Maly Theater, Yuzhin. He had often been abroad and would tell how, on Sobinov's request, he had managed to take a diamond ring to the ballerina Vera Korali, who lived in emigration, could no longer dance and was very much in need.

When they arrested him, his wife renounced him and quickly remarried. She wouldn't even give him his clothes. With bitter humor Nikolai Nikolaevich would say, "That's all right, her present husband is now wearing my things, they fit him perfectly, he didn't get married in vain." Here he lived with his wife, who was also an exile, a very kind woman named Zoya Sergeevna.

Natasha Bernak also worked with us at the brick factory. She had been the wife of the former chairman of the board of the gosbank, Maryasin, who had been shot in 1937. Here she became friends with Anatoly Darman, my old comrade in the Komsomol. We hadn't seen each other for more than twenty years. Back then he had an unusual head of hair, a thick shock of very curly hair. Now when he took off his cap, my hair stood on end. Now his head was like a chicken's egg, not a single hair. Anatoly was here with his mother. His mother, Dalnaya, had joined the party the year I was born, in 1906. She accidentally survived the annihilation of the Old Bolsheviks and had now ended up here.

There was a large "recruitment" in 1945, the majority of whom were like the chief engineer of the timber industry—they were people who had fought in the war. Their grateful fatherland rewarded them with exile.

If I had encountered in the Krasnoyarsk prison a new category of prisoners, relatives, then here I met one more category of exiles. They had been sent into exile not as individuals, like us, or even as families; they had been sent according to nationality: Daghestanis, Chechens, Ingushis.... This included old people and infants. Since they were southern people who were used to sunshine and a warm climate, they had a hard time dealing with the Siberian cold. The mortality rate among them was horrifying.

During this time I received some letters from home. Natasha was studying at the institute, and there was nothing for her to do here. Lera, however, had to be sent for. As for mama, I mailed her a description of the conditions here, and let her decide for herself.

Meanwhile, the work situation became worse. In the fall, the brick factory would cease to function, there were very limited choices otherwise, and many would be sent to various backwaters from Taseevo. They didn't touch us because I had informed the authorities that I was waiting for my schoolage daughter, and the only school around was in Taseevo.

Then in August mama came with Lera. We discussed the situation and decided that we needed to go somewhere else. Some had managed to do this. We sent a letter to the regional administration of the NKVD with a request to be transferred to a place where we would both be guaranteed to find normal work. We had an elderly mother, a twelve-year-old daughter, and under the conditions of Taseevo, we simply wouldn't be able to feed ourselves. Mama traveled with this letter to Krasnoyarsk.

They transferred us to the city of Uyar, which was located on the railway line, near the Kliukvino station. Uyar had a railway station, with a cafeteria, and people were needed everywhere. There was a regional industrial complex, an artel (similar to the one where I had worked in Shamkhor) and a mica factory. The town also had a hospital, a clinic, two schools, two movie theaters and a library.

Since Uyar was located on a railway line, exiled repeaters were as a rule not sent here. Besides us, there was only one repeater there. He had also been a KRTD in the past and also had been in Kolyma. He was here with his wife, who was not, however, an exile. She belonged to the dying breed of "Decembrist wives," and had simply followed her husband into exile. This of course is to her credit, since today's Moscow wives for the most part fear nothing more than losing their Moscow residency permits. Of course, the wives of the Decembrists didn't have to worry about that.

Abram Mikhailovich worked as a bookkeeper in the artel; Nina Grigorievna, who had not managed to finish the medical institute, but who had a diploma as a doctor's assistant, headed the medical station at the mica factory.

The mica factory was the largest enterprise here. The manufacturing process consisted of cutting pieces of mica into thin layers, which could be used in industry, aviation and everyday life.

Boris got a job in the regional industrial complex, first as an accountant, and then he was made a planner.

For a while I worked as a planner in the cafeteria of the railway station. Everyone felt that I had been very fortunate. There nobody spent any money on food, everyone was full and they even took food home. But I didn't fit in there. Everyone drank, morning, noon and night, even the women, and if you didn't drink with them, that meant, "you don't respect me." I said good-bye to all the advantages that went with this job and went to work as an accountant in the mica factory.

Uyar had many exiled Germans from the German republic of Povolzhya. They had been sent here as an entire people, including party members. At first they went to register with their party cards. Then someone came to his senses and took away their party cards. They worked mainly at the mica factory, but since the productive capacity of this remarkable enterprise couldn't give everyone the chance to work, many of them worked at home; whole families worked together, including the children.

These German children were in a terrible situation. When they reached sixteen, they were not given a passport, but the same type of paper which we were given, that is, they became exiles who didn't have the right to go anywhere else. The way was barred for them to study anywhere or to receive any qualified work. They had only the mica factory, and this was for the rest of their lives.

Lera turned sixteen in Uyar, and we were very worried—would they really give her such papers? But no, even our category had certain advantages—they gave her a normal passport.

Nineteen fifty-two came to an end, and 1953 began to unfold. Once they called us into the regional department of the NKVD and made us sign a paper that we had read a new governmental decree. According to this decree, all exiles who traveled more than ten kilometers outside their designated place of exile without special permission would be given twenty-five years in the camps. This document was signed by Molotov.

Nina Grigorievna, who was not an exile, traveled on vacation to Moscow. When she returned, she described how the situation there was terrible: the anti-Semitism bordered on an atmosphere of pogroms. Rumors persistently circulated (supposedly from very reliable sources) that all Jews would be sent from Moscow to Birobidzhan, regardless of sex, age, social position or party membership, and that barracks with double bunks had already been prepared in Birobidzhan. Soon the doctors' trial began. In Siberia, just like in Kolyma, anti-Semitism was not a factor. But now it had become state policy. The newspapers used the terminology of prerevolutionary Black Hundreds' leaflets. In the popular journal, *Krokodil*, an article appeared by the famous journalist Vasily Ardamatsky entitled "Pinya from Zhmerinka."

Lera was the only Jewish girl in her class and earlier this had never been an issue. Now someone placed a drawing on her desk where very crudely, but very unabashedly, someone had sketched a man with an enormous hooked nose and crooked fingers dripping with blood (done with a red pencil no less).

At home we had a radio, the most primitive black dish. We didn't often turn it on, just sometimes to listen to music if they were broadcasting a good concert or good songs.

But one day the black dish relayed to us some wonderful news: Joseph Vissarionovich Stalin was in a very bad state of health. Now we began to listen to the radio constantly, waiting for the news. We both hoped and were afraid to hope—we hoped to God that he wouldn't wriggle out of this one. But no, he didn't, and the happy day arrived when our black dish announced, "He has died."

Funeral meetings were held everywhere. People wept, sobbed and asked one another: "What will happen now?" We knew one thing for sure—it couldn't get any worse.

Our friends, Abram Mikhailovich and Nina Grigorievna, came to see us. We drank a bottle of wine in memory of those who had not survived.

In the summer of 1953, Natasha came to visit us. She had finished the institute, received an assignment in the city of Yoshkar-Ola and had come to see us and rest before her job began. I don't have to say how happy we were. She was pale, thin, and I gave her fresh milk since the woman in charge of our apartment had a cow. Natasha had been seriously involved with a fellow called Apollon Filimonov from her group at the institute, and had written to me about this. I never had been a sanctimonious person, and I understood that romances at that age were entirely normal. The only thing wrong was that the father of this boy was an NKVD colonel and the deputy director of the regional directorate.

The boy was in love and wanted to marry, and my girl didn't understand anything about the situation which had developed. But I knew very well what to expect from this breed. I knew that his parents would sooner die than allow this marriage: a Jewish girl, the daughter of parents who had been arrested, whose father had perished in Kolyma and whose mother was in exile. With such a relative the colonel would risk both his own position and his epaulets, and what would he be able to do without them, a former policeman without any education. As my Rostov cellmate had said: "What would you do if they took away from you this miserable slop bucket?..."

I knew that if the boy wouldn't back off, then they would persecute her. But what could I do two thousand kilometers away, knowing that letters were opened and I couldn't write about any of this.

So, of course, they began to torment her. They tried to have her expelled from the institute, but she was a very good student, and there weren't the slightest grounds to do so. They organized her expulsion from the Komsomol, but the expulsion wasn't endorsed by the regional committee; it seems that some decent people had been found there. Naturally, she could have avoided all these unpleasantries. She simply had to publicly and in writing renounce her mother. But she didn't do this. She never renounced me.

In passing, I would like to speak about Larisa. We became separated when she was only six years old. From her father, with whom she lived, she heard only bad things about me. I sent her letters, but she rarely answered, and then only formally: I'm alive, healthy and in school. When she was thirteen (we were then living in Uyar), I received a letter from some woman in Novoselitsa. She wrote that the girl was living very badly, that she had already left home once to run away from her father and stepmother, but that she had been sent back.

I wanted to take her to stay with us, and Boris supported me very much in this plan. But I knew that Goncharuk would be opposed. Therefore I wrote not only to him, but also to the director of the school where she was enrolled. I knew that in this regional center, where everyone knew everyone else, Goncharuk had a poor reputation, and I hoped that the school would help me out. They summoned Larisa to the teacher's room, and there sat the school director, the director of studies and the entire teachers' council. They asked her whether she remembered her mama. She said that she hadn't seen me since she was six and barely remembered me. They reminded her of Lermontov, who had lost his mother at approximately the same age and yet remembered her. But Larisa hadn't made it to Lermontov. Then they told her that they had received a letter from her mama, and that her mama was obviously well-educated, since the letter had been very correctly written. Even the teacher of Russian language and literature had not been able to find a single spelling mistake in it. After this they told her that, nevertheless, her mother was bad, that she had been in prison and was now in exile. Why did she need such a mother, it would be better if she renounced her altogether.

Then my thirteen-year-old Larisa, who unlike Lermontov couldn't remember her mother, said that she had just finished reading *The Young Guard*, and that she was sure that her mother was just like the Young Guardists—she was for the truth.

In the end, Goncharuk's bad reputation turned out to be better than mine—they didn't let Larisa come to be with me. She came only in Moscow, after my rehabilitation.

Now once again about Natasha. When she came to see us, I understood that the romance with Filimonov was over. They had assigned her to Yoshkar-Ola, and he had been sent somewhere to the Far East. "Well, thank God," I thought. But "thank God even more" (as the Narodnaya Volya terrorist Solovyov said when he assassinated Alexander II). Nothing was over after all. Filimonov came to see Natasha in Yoshkar-Ola, they got married and went to work together in the Urals.

As I had foreseen, nothing good ever came of this marriage. They had no kind of life together, and Natasha left him when their child was not yet one. By the way, I wasn't right when I said that nothing good came of their marriage—something very good happened—Pavlik. They named him Pavel, just like his grandfather, and he even looks like him.

6

After Stalin's death we lived in the expectation of changes. But the changes didn't come immediately. Of course, they immediately put a halt to the doctors' case. Those doctors who survived the "active interrogations" were set free. Common folklore immediately had its say about this:

Dear Comrade Vovsy,
I am truly glad,
That at last it turned out
You're by no means bad.
You worked and slaved and labored
And never closed your eyes,
A stinking police informer
Just wrote a bunch of lies.

And, of course, all talk about resettling Jews in Birobidzhan came to a halt. But the first amnesty concerned only common criminals. Thieves, bandits and recidivists were amnestied. They were sent in whole waves toward the center of the country. Along the way they destroyed stations and cafeterias, they settled in cities and terrorized the local inhabitants and local police.

The next amnesty concerned political prisoners as well, but it was very limited. This amnesty applied only to prisoners who had a sentence of no more than five years, and these were very rare. I had five years because I had been arrested in 1936, when the special board wasn't giving out more than five years. Boris got five years in 1937, but this was a rare exception. What was more important—we didn't know how they would evaluate our exile, as another sentence, or if it would generally be ignored. Boris's situation was even more complicated by the fact that his exile was not "pending special dispensation," but of specific duration, for ten years. And it was unclear which they would count, five years in the camps received in 1937, or ten years in exile received in 1950.

We decided to send fifteen-year-old Lera to Krasnoyarsk. We knew the name of the NKVD captain who was in charge of our cases. So Lera went to see him at his office. Probably there was no small number of people in our situation, because the line was enormous. The captain walked out of his office, glanced at all those waiting and then looked at Lera with her braids and asked, "Are you here to see me?" He called her first. He was interested in knowing how old she was, what grade she was in and what was her business there. She said that she lived in Uyar with her mama and Uncle Borya. Mama had five years in the camps and indeterminate exile, and Uncle Borya had five years in the camps followed by ten years exile. He said, "Tell your mama that she falls under the amnesty and if she wants then she can leave Uyar, and the Krasnoyarsk region in general." Lera asked, "And Uncle Borya?" He smiled, "With regard to Uncle Borya, we'll see."

In actual fact, soon the regional department received a directive that we both were amnestied and that we no longer were exiles. We had to think how we would now live. Mama wasn't with us, since she had gone to Kedabek to her brother's. In Moscow Boris had a family and an apartment, the same one where he had been arrested in 1937. I had nothing and nowhere to go. He decided to go to Moscow, and, of course, I didn't try to talk him out of it. Before he left he helped Lera and me move to Krasnoyarsk, paid a year in advance for the room which we rented, arranged a job for me at the regional administration of the local industry. He had worked in this system during all our years in Uyar. They knew him there and respected him.

Then he left. He said that I too would soon leave, and that he would do everything to create some kind of base for me in Moscow. But it didn't turn out to be so easy. He couldn't find a job for himself for quite a while and went to Milenki, which was a city in the Moscow area where he had worked after getting out of the camps, when he was forbidden to live in Moscow. It was from here that they sent him into exile in 1950. There they once again offered him work and an apartment, and he wrote to me that perhaps it was worth it for me and Lera to agree to come there. But I didn't agree to do so. If I was going to return, then it would be to Moscow. In addition, I had to think about Lera. She was finishing the tenth grade, and Krasnoyarsk had every type of institute, but what would she do in a place like Milenki.

All in all, we lived in Krasnoyarsk for another two years. I worked in the regional industrial administration, first as an economist, then as the deputy director of the planning department. Lera studied in the ninth and tenth grades. My wages weren't bad, and I sent money to mama in Kedabek, but soon she came to Krasnoyarsk, since things weren't working out in Kedabek.

Boris wrote often, but his letters were not very cheerful. He couldn't find any work, they were hesitant to hire those who had been amnestied, and he was making ends meet with temporary jobs. He sent Lera and me food parcels, but I naturally returned any money he sent. In Krasnoyarsk there were rather many like me, former exiles who had nowhere to go. There was Ruth Iosifovna Kozintseva and Alya Efron, Marina Tsvetaeva's daughter. There was a young couple, Nikolai Demchenko and Roza Fisher. Nikolai had been arrested in 1937 because of his father, the former chairman of the All-Ukrainian Central Executive Committee; he wasn't yet eighteen. In the camps in Karaganda he organized a commune: the oldest was seventeen and the youngest was fourteen. They were all children of high officials arrested in 1937. First they took the fathers, then the mothers and then the children. Nikolai and Roza had a four-year-old son, also named Kolya. Then they separated. Nikolai went to Moscow and Roza with her child were among the first to leave for Israel.

Lera, meanwhile, was finishing school, and once again we had to decide what to do. I didn't even want to think about remaining in Krasnoyarsk "seriously and for a long time." Boris kept writing and phoning, insisting that we should come, if not to Moscow, then somewhere not far from Moscow, anything would be better than Krasnoyarsk.

Then we would see, people were increasingly saying that some positive changes for people like us were just around the corner.

Natasha went to Moscow. She had summer holidays and left Pavlik for a while with grandfather and grandmother in Stavropol. By letter I put her in touch with Difa's sister Tamara, and she lived there, becoming very good friends with Difa's daughter Galya. They were born a year apart.

I dreamed of one thing only—to get a job somewhere and bring all my children together. I sent Lera to Moscow, where she was met at the station by Boris and Natasha, and began also to live with Tamara. I still had to stay behind at work.

Then I finally left.

"Farewell, Siberia!" But for the time being, Moscow didn't bode very well. I couldn't get a residency permit or find a job. But I had to live somehow. Lera tried to enroll in the medical institute, but they rejected her for health reasons and didn't even let her take the entrance exams. She had rheumatic heart disease, a legacy of the Magadan children's home. Later she nevertheless finished an institute. Of course it wasn't the medical, but the historical-archival institute.

Meanwhile September arrived and the school year began. Natasha had to return to her place in the Urals, and Lera went with her.

Fima Sadovnikov, from my native Simferopol and a friend since childhood, advised me to go to Kalinin. He had friends there, it was not a bad city and it was not far from Moscow. And so off I went. I had to earn money in some way. I got a job in the same system, the city administration of local industry. I rented a corner in a room. Oh, how bad I felt....

Not long ago we had so many hopes—there was Stalin's death, the Twentieth Congress with Khrushchev's magnificent revelations. And here I was, stuck in the same rut, in the same "hummock in a swamp...." I had neither house nor home, I was renting a small corner from some streetwalker who came home half-drunk every night. Her children were God knows where and were having a bad time. That is how I lived. Then I received information that at my old Krasnoyarsk address, some papers had arrived about my rehabilitation. On October 6 I was already back in Moscow.

In the Moscow city court, I received a paper about rehabilitation, "The decision of the special board of the NKVD of the USSR has been annulled due to lack of evidence concerning the crime with which you were charged."

I received a similar paper for Pavel. Regarding him I received one more paper from the Magadan regional court: "The decision of the NKVD troika for Dalstroy has been annulled and the case closed due to lack of evidence concerning the charges."

This decree was issued eighteen years after this person had been shot "on a groundless charge."

I wrote a letter to the party control commission about restoring his membership in the party. I wrote that it no longer made any difference to him, but "his children remain, and I want the children to know that their father lived as a Communist and died as a Communist."

Yes, "how easily we forgave our debts, forgetting that a movement to the right begins from the left leg."

They reinstated Pavel, posthumously. They summoned me to the Bauman party regional committee, announced the decision of the party control commission, and told me his party card number.

A governmental decree was issued concerning the rights of rehabilitated people. What luxurious rights! They were supposed to give me back the same job I had when I was arrested, give me a residency permit at any address, regardless of whether there was spare living space there or not. They were supposed to place me at the head of the line for receiving an apartment, for myself and for all the members of my family. And if I wanted, then they would give me a paid stay at a sanitorium. I didn't need any such stay, to hell with it! I needed to gather my children. Soon Natasha and Lera arrived. And after a few days we met Larisa. She walked out onto the square near the Kiev station, looked at the tall building and said, "What large huts you have here!" This didn't prevent her from finishing the philology department at the university in a few years, from working with foreigners and being considered a well-qualified translator.

Kira was the only one left, but she was studying at the medical institute in Baku and had married a native of Baku.

We were all registered as living with Beniamina Yulievna Germanovich, a kind-hearted soul, and I took my place in line at the Bauman regional housing department. They warned me that there were many people who had been rehabilitated, and that the line would take no less than a year. We rented one room and then another, and then lived wherever we could until Boris arranged for us to stay at his niece's. She was going away for six months and, at his request, left us her apartment.

They brought Pavlik. I worked in the gosbank, the same system in which I was working in 1936. I could have probably found a higher-paying job, but I was very tired and decided to take the path of least resistance. They were obliged to give me work in this system, well, let them do it. All the more so, since the entire twenty years from 1936 to 1956 were counted as continuous work, and I received a twenty-five percent raise in pay. Natasha also worked as a translator at a design office. But I had one more thing which I had to do. I had to restore my father's grave.

I had already gone to the Novodevichy Cemetery earlier. Of course, many years had passed, but I could picture where the grave should be. But it wasn't there. In fact, it wasn't anywhere. I had been living from hand to mouth at that time in Moscow, what could I do then? Now I had full rights. At that time rehabilitated people were on top of the world. Since we had innocently suffered, we were accepted everywhere and treated well.

At the cemetery I found the person in charge. He was very old, at that time he was probably around eighty. But he was robust. As I learned from our conversation, he was one of the few surviving Old Bolsheviks, and apparently out of respect for his services, he had been given this cemetery sinecure. It turned out that he had known my father and took an active interest in my cause.

We walked to the spot where, according to my calculations, my father's grave should have been. I remembered that immediately after the funeral, the students who listened to father's lectures had planted a small tree at the head of his grave. Now there was a large, branchy tree, and beneath it, in the space between two other graves, was a free plot of earth. The old man scratched his head, "Of course, it's most likely that the grave was here. But the grave is missing. And in order to restore it, we need permission from the public utilities and services department, under the Moscow city executive committee. Let's do the following," he said. "Tomorrow at ten in the morning, come to that department, go to the office of the director, and I will be there. But don't let on that you know me. Then you tell this director that you have just returned from rehabilitation and that you want to restore your father's grave. And that you know precisely that the grave was in the Communist sector, along the avenue, near the monastery wall, about twenty paces from the monastery gates, with a tree at the head of the grave. Just like that. Agreed?" The old man was very pleased with himself. I said, "Of course, I agree, thank you very much." "Just don't give me away." "What are you saying, I wouldn't do that for anything." He stretched out his hand. "A Communist's word?" Once, in the days of my youth, this was the most sacred thing for me — "a Communist's word." Since then I had lived for so many years among "enemies of the people." And here I was once again hearing "a Communist's word."

I had never cried at a single interrogation (and there were certainly specialists there at making people cry), but here I felt that I had a lump in my throat and tears in my eyes....

The next morning I went to the appropriate department. There in the office of the director sat my old man, he didn't even glance at me. I repeated everything as we had rehearsed it. The director then said, "Yes, everything you say is quite exact, but to what extent it corresponds to reality we will now have to determine. Here is a comrade sitting before us who just happens to be the head of the Novodevichy Cemetery." The old man looked at me as if he were seeing me for the first time in his life. "Don't think that he's too old, he has an excellent memory. Now he'll tell us whether your father's grave could have been where you say." The old man looked faithfully at the director and spread his hands in a gesture of helplessness, "Everything she says is correct, what can I say?" Ah, what an actor! The needed directive was issued right on the spot.

That's how I restored my father's grave. Since then I regularly visit the cemetery, and I remember how I was there soon after Khrushchev's death. Of course, in Stalin's times, Khrushchev was one of his cohorts. And of course, his cultural level was very low. Hence his monstrous behavior during the last period with regard to the intelligentsia. Nevertheless, if not for him, then our bones would be rotting somewhere in Siberia. And he alone said what the "adored leader," and "genius of all times and peoples" really was. He said this from the tribune of the Twentieth Party Congress and from the tribune of the Twenty-Second Congress. And no matter why he did this, he still did it. If he didn't go all the way, if he didn't reveal the whole story of Kirov's assassination, and didn't reveal a lot more, then he is not so much to blame for this. No one supported him, on the contrary, all the members of the Politburo were opposed.

It was he who got housing construction moving so that everyone began to get good apartments, it was he who raised pensions high enough so that people could live on them. Thus, despite all his minuses, and there were many, let the earth be his pillow. Now, over his grave, there stands a beautiful symbolic monument sculpted by Ernst Neizvestny. But at first it was a bare mound, decorated with his photograph (in which he looked very relaxed, in a white shirt with the collar unbuttoned). But this mound was always covered with inexpensive bouquets of flowers. One old woman from some village, wearing a dark kerchief, placed a large apple on his grave. "Hey, granny," someone said, "people put flowers on his grave, and here you are putting an apple." "Yes, that's right, my dear," the old woman replied. "The apple will sit there, birds will fly up, they'll peck at the apple, begin to chirp above the grave. Wait and see, it'll be more cheerful for him to lie here."

A year had already passed since I had been placed in line. Suddenly I received a notice to come for an order giving me an apartment. But we celebrated too soon. The order was for a twelve-meter room, and for me alone. And the children?

I went to see the director of regional housing. As I have already said, in the majority of instances, close attention was being paid to rehabilitated people. This person, however, was undoubtedly an exception: he had a fat, rude-looking face and acted in the corresponding manner. As for the rights that my children had to living quarters, he immediately was forced to agree to Larisa, she was a minor and was registered on my passport. He was even inclined to agree with regard to Lera. From her passport it was clear that she had been born in Kolyma, from her diploma it was clear that she had finished school in Krasnoyarsk, that is, it was obvious that she had been with me the whole while. He won back what he had lost when it came to Natasha. She had a higher education, was married, was an independent person, why should she have to live with her mama? What rights did she then have? I tried to ram it into his head that her right consisted precisely in the fact that from the time she was six, she hadn't been allowed to live "with her mama." But it was no use talking to this type.

Running ahead, I will say that soon afterwards, he was removed from his job "for abusing his service position," i.e., he simply took bribes.

Boris took Natasha and Lera, and went with them to see the first secretary of the Bauman regional party committee. This was Yegorychev. Later he became secretary of the Moscow committee and member of the Central Committee, but then one fine day he lost all his positions and titles. At a plenum of the CC after the Six Days War with Israel, he expressed his doubts whether it was worth it to break off diplomatic relations with Israel, that in the end it was their business whom they fought against. At the same time, he questioned whether it was worth it to support Egypt so unconditionally, since it might later turn out bad for us if we did. With regard to Egypt, he was quite perceptive. But for now it went badly for him. They removed him from the Moscow committee, threw him out of the Central Committee and sent him as an ambassador to some African country.

I can't vouch for the accuracy of all this, but such were the stories making their rounds in Moscow. At the time I am writing about, he enjoyed great authority, particularly in the Bauman region.

Boris said that the father of these girls was his friend who had been posthumously reinstated in the party and who was registered in the Bauman region. He explained how things stood with our living quarters. Yegorychev immediately, in their presence, picked up the phone and called the director of the regional housing authority. As was evident from his rejoinders, the director was once again referring to the fact that Natasha was no longer of an age when she had to be living "with her mama." Yegorychev replied with almost the identical words which I had used, "When she was of that age when she should have been living 'with her mama,' she didn't have the chance, so let her live with her now." Apparently, the director said something else, but Yegorychev said categorically, "In short, you offer living quarters to all the family members which she has designated in her letter, and make it a good place to boot. I'll be following this personally."

That was what Yegorychev was like!

After a few days I received an order for an apartment on Aptekarsky Way—two large rooms with a large kitchen.

We had a bundle of books and a folding bed which someone had given us. We bought some needed furniture at a second-hand store, but our apartment still looked like a stage set for one of Gordon Craig's plays, with screens and bags. We didn't have a real set of furniture for a long time, but we gradually began to feel at home.

And then my daughters started to get married. First Lera left to live in her husband's apartment, then Larisa, her husband's parents and Goncharuk went halves in buying them a cooperative apartment. Natasha brought her husband to stay with us on Aptekarsky Way. And this was a very pleasant addition to our family.

Then I left the apartment on Aptekarsky. Lera and her husband had a three-room apartment, and I got my own room.

The years passed. In 1971 Boris died.

And so my memoirs have reached the end. If you look back, you begin to see what a long life you have lived.

Almost no one is left from the people I have written about, almost no one remains from those whom fate brought my way during my difficult life's journey.

But there is my family—children, grandchildren and great-grand-children.

And I am still alive.

MOSCOW
1971-72

AFTERWORD

I returned to Moscow after rehabilitation in the fall of 1956, and wrote this book in 1971-72, when the euphoria from the "Khrushchev thaw" had still not fully subsided, when we still heard such words as socialism, the revolution, the party....

I was personally acquainted with many participants in the October Revolution. Among them were people who renounced a calm, comfortable or properous life because they fervently believed in a radiant future for all mankind.

Many of those whom Stalin considered to be the Opposition paid with years of exile, prison and camps for fighting him, and for understanding that the socialism which had been built in the Soviet Union was not the same socialism about which the best minds of mankind had dreamed.

I would like my readers to remember this short afterword of mine.

N. JOFFE

NOTES

FOREWORD

1. Leopold Trepper, *The Great Game* (London: Sphere Books, 1979), p. 56.
2. E.H. Carr, *The Bolshevik Revolution 1917-1923*, vol. 3 (New York: W.W. Norton & Company, 1981), pp. 76-77.

PART 1

Chapter 2
1. Leninskii sbornik, XXXVI, M., 1959, p. 55 (memo by Lenin).

Chapter 6
1. Leon Trotsky, *The Stalin School of Falsification* (London: New Park Publications, 1974), p. 38.
2. Leon Trotsky, *My Life* (New York: Pathfinder Press, 1970), p. 1.
3. Leon Trotsky, *Leon Sedov: Son, Friend, Fighter* (Oak Park: Labor Publications, 1977), p. 17.
4. Isaac Deutscher, *The Prophet Outcast: Trotsky 1929-1940* (New York: Vintage Books, 1963), p. 362.
5. Ibid., p. 413.
6. Trotsky, *My Life*, p. 582.

Chapter 7
1. Leon Trotsky, *My Life* (New York: Pathfinder Press, 1970), pp. 534-37.

Chapter 8
1. *Moscow Trials Anthology* (London: New Park Publications, 1967), pp. 47-48.
2. V.I. Lenin, *Collected Works*, vol. 15, 1918 edition—now a bibliographic rarity.
3. V.I. Lenin, *What Is To Be Done?* (New York: International Publishers, 1972), p. 11.

INDEX